Business Result

Upper-intermediate | Student's Book

Michael Duckworth & Rebecca Turner

Interactive Workbook material
by Alastair Lane

OXFORD
UNIVERSITY PRESS

Contents

Contents

Introduction

Welcome to *Business Result Upper-intermediate*.
In this book you'll find:
| 16 units | *Practice file* | *Information files* | *Audio scripts* |
| *Useful phrases* | *Interactive Workbook* on CD-ROM |

We hope you find this introduction useful, and that you enjoy using the course.

What's in a unit?

Starting point

- an introduction to the unit topic
- discussion questions

Working with words

- reading and listening based on themes from business and the world of work
- important new words and phrases that you can use immediately in your work
- practise the new vocabulary in a realistic final activity

Business communication skills

- presents key expressions for exchanging information, attending meetings, presenting information, and socializing
- helps you express yourself more clearly in real work situations
- lets you choose which phrases to use from the *Key expressions* list in every unit

Practically speaking

- teaches really useful everyday phrases for small talk, telephoning and short conversations
- helps you sound more natural when you speak English

Language at work

- reviews key grammar from *Business communication skills*
- helps you communicate more accurately in real work situations
- lets you check your knowledge of grammar and practise it in the classroom
- if you need more explanation, refer to the language reference section in the *Practice file*

Case study

- each unit ends with an authentic case study
- find out about situations related to the unit topic that affect real companies and organizations
- take part in a longer work-related activity with lots of opportunities to practise the language from the unit

Fast-track option

If time on your course is limited, *Business Result* has a unique fast-track option to use in class. For each unit, combine the *Business communication skills* section and the *Case study*. This creates a practical, highly communicative shorter course, enabling you to get the maximum benefit from your Business English studies – fast.

What's in the Practice file?

The *Practice file* is like a mini-workbook in the back of the *Student's Book*. It allows you to think about and practise important words, phrases and grammar. It has written exercises on the key language from each unit, plus a language reference section with more detailed grammar explanations.

Use the *Practice file*

- in class to check your understanding
- after class for extra practice.

Follow the links to the *Practice file* in each unit

» For more information and exercises, go to **Practice file 3** on page 107.

What's the *Interactive Workbook* on CD-ROM?

Everyone's needs are different when it comes to using English at work. The *Interactive Workbook* gives you practical tools to use immediately in your work by helping you to practise the language and skills from the *Student's Book*, and make them personal to you and your own work situation. It also helps you review and test your own progress.

Exercises and tests

- review and practise key language with interactive exercises
- check your progress with unit tests

Glossary

- check the meaning of around 600 words and phrases
- personalize the vocabulary to your needs

Phrasebank

- listen to all the key expressions from the *Student's Book*
- learn phrases for exchanging information, meetings, presenting, socializing, telephoning, and travel
- create your own personal phrasebook to match your needs at work

Email

- learn useful phrases for writing the most common work-related emails
- copy model emails to your outbox, or create your own

Listen again

- listen again to the *Student's Book* audio recordings, or download to your MP3 player

Wherever you see this link, it means you can access extra material on the *Interactive Workbook*.

ⓘ » Interactive Workbook »

Case studies with the Expert View from Cranfield School of Management

Each of the case studies in *Business Result Upper-intermediate* is accompanied by an Expert View from Cranfield School of Management, one of Europe's leading management schools. It is part of Cranfield University, renowned for its high-quality postgraduate teaching and research and its strong links to industry and business. The School of Management was established in 1967, and offers a range of MBA, Executive MBA, Executive Education, and Doctoral programmes.

For more information, visit: **www.som.cranfield.ac.uk/som/**

Your panel of experts is made up of faculty members from Cranfield School of Management.

Cranfield UNIVERSITY
School of Management

1 Dr Pauline Weight, Chairman of the Cranfield Management Association (see page 11)

2 Richard Kwiatkowski, Senior Lecturer in Organizational Psychology (see page 17)

3 Dr Harvey Maylor, Senior Lecturer in Programme & Project Management (see page 23)

4 Dr Stephanie Hussels, Lecturer in Entrepreneurship (see page 29)

5 Stephen Regan, Lecturer in Management Economics (see page 35)

6 David Grayson, Professor of Corporate Responsibility (see page 41)

7 Roger Delves, Programme Director, Centre for Customized Executive Development (see pages 47 and 95)

8 Dr Ashley Braganza, Director, Centre for Organizational Transformation (see page 53)

9 Dr Michael Dickmann, Senior Lecturer in Organization Studies (see page 59)

10 David Molian, Bettany Centre for Entrepreneurial Performance & Economics (see page 65)

11 Dr Hilary Harris, Programme Director, Centre for Customized Executive Development (see page 71)

12 Dr Rob Lambert, Senior Lecturer in Management Information Systems (see page 77)

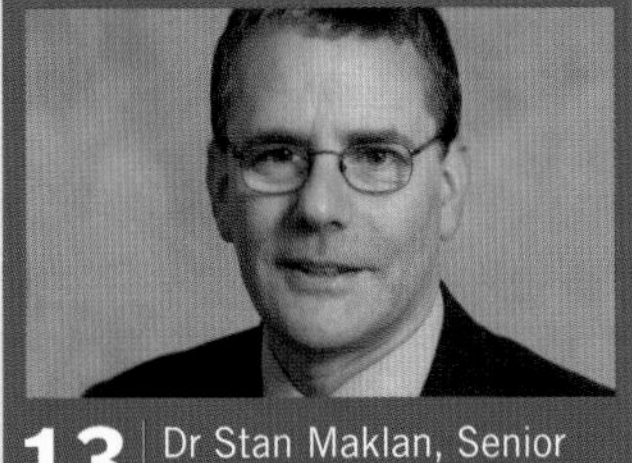
13 Dr Stan Maklan, Senior Lecturer in Strategic Marketing (see page 83)

14 David Simmons, International Development Director (see page 89)

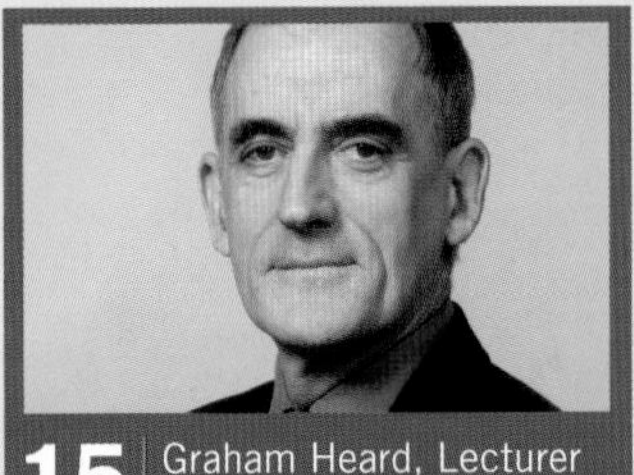
15 Graham Heard, Lecturer in Languages (see page 89)

16 Peter Fennah, Director of Career Development (see page 101)

1 First impressions

Learning objectives in this unit

- Talking about first impressions
- Introducing yourself by email
- Making a follow-up call
- Arranging to meet
- Exchanging contact details
- Talking about your work and company using present simple or continuous

Case study

- Making business connections

Starting point

1 **What are your first impressions of the business in the picture? What kind of business could it be? What impression could it want to give?**

2 **What first impressions do you think people have of you and your company?**

Working with words | Talking about first impressions

1 **Read this text and answer questions 1–2.**

1 Is any one factor more important than others for a company's image?
2 What else does a company operating internationally need to think about?

Impressions

A company's image is like an orchestra. No single instrument is responsible for an orchestra's success or failure. Likewise, the image that a company projects is not based on a single business card, glossy brochure or fashionable display, but on the total impression created by all of these things and more. There are many intangibles that can be critical, like the **reputation** you have, your **principles** and **professionalism**, your **creativity**, and even the warmth of an initial welcome.

For a company to come across well internationally, it also needs to consider the culture of its client or customer. A Finn might take an instant dislike to **extravagance**, a Ghanaian might prefer **innovation** to **tradition**, a Qatari might put personal **rapport** before anything else.

Images can create a negative impression or a positive feeling in a few seconds. If you get it right, that favourable first impression will help in building a successful business relationship.

2 **Read the text again and answer questions 1–4.**

1 What are the 'instruments' that the text mentions? What others could you add?
2 What is the meaning of 'intangibles' in a business context? What others could you add to those in the text?
3 How important do *you* think it is to consider the culture of your client / customer? Can you think of any examples?
4 Discuss an experience you have had of a positive or negative first impression of a company. What factors contributed to this?

3 **Match the words in bold in the text in 1 to these definitions.**

1 something that is expensive or wasteful: __________
2 the ability to produce something using imagination or artistic skills: __________
3 a high standard of skill and behaviour: __________
4 friendly understanding: __________
5 new ideas or methods: __________
6 the views generally held about somebody or something: __________
7 strong beliefs that influence actions: __________
8 a way of doing something that's existed for a long time: __________

4 Choose the correct answer from the words in *italics*.

1 What kind of image would your company like to *project / show*?
2 What sort of reputation do you or your company *hold / have*?
3 Is there anything about your company that always *forms / creates* a good impression for new customers?
4 In your line of work, how important is it for you to *build / assemble* a relationship with customers or clients?
5 Have you ever *experienced / taken* an instant dislike to anyone you met in the course of your work? What were the reasons for this?
6 How do you think you *come / go* across to people you meet for the first time?

5 Work with a partner. Ask and answer the questions in 4.

6 01▷ Listen to Zhifu Li, a website designer in Hong Kong, talking about adapting websites to local needs. Answer questions 1–2.

1 In what way is website localization like other forms of advertising?
2 What differences between websites for Western and Asian consumers does Zhifu mention?

7 Match each of these adjectives from audio 01▷ to an adjective with a similar meaning from 1–12.

expensive ineffective arrogant trustworthy suspicious complex functional modest ostentatious successful wary favourable

1 reliable: ________	5 costly: ________	9 simple: ________
2 unsuccessful: ________	6 mistrustful: ________	10 effective: ________
3 showy: ________	7 practical: ________	11 over confident: ________
4 positive: ________	8 complicated: ________	12 cautious: ________

8 Work with a partner.

1 Which of the adjectives in **7** are positive and which are negative? Explain your choices.
2 Using as many of the adjectives as possible, discuss what makes an effective website in your culture.
3 What aspects of a website would give a negative first impression?

»» For more exercises, go to **Practice file 1** on page 102.

9 Work with a partner. Look at these things which can create a good or bad first impression of a company.

- uniform
- office / business premises
- telephone answering system
- reception area
- meeting / conference rooms
- quality of product / service
- warm greeting
- dress code
- website
- advertisements in the media
- brochures / printed materials
- price
- speaking customer's language
- reputation

1 Which four are the most important and why?
2 Choose two of the factors that create a good impression of your company. Explain how.
3 Choose two of the factors that are less successful at creating a good impression of your company. How could they be improved?

ⓘ »» Interactive Workbook »» **Glossary**

Exchanging information | Introducing yourself by email | Making a follow-up call | Arranging to meet

1 Read this email from Ivan Formanek, owner of a translation agency in Prague.

1 How did he find out about Sean McFee?
2 Why is he contacting him?
3 What does he ask Sean to do?

To: sean.mcfee@sfdesign.com
From: ivanformanek@sspeaking.cz
Subject: Designer for new website needed

Dear Mr McFee

My name's Ivan Formanek and I have my own translation agency – Simply Speaking. I was given your details by one of your former colleagues, Ursula Vladikova. She recommended you to me as we are planning to renew our website.

If you are interested in discussing this further, could you either call us or send an email in reply and we will arrange a meeting with you?

Best regards
Ivan Formanek

2 02▷ Sean sends an email in reply to Ivan and then calls him. Listen to their conversation and answer questions 1–3.

1 What is the purpose of the call?
2 What is the outcome?
3 Why is there a delay before the meeting can take place?

3 Match 1–7 to a–f to make phrases.

1 I'm calling about … ___
2 Yes, I … ___
3 Thanks for … ___
4 I wondered if you'd had time … ___
5 I suggest we meet … ___
6 Fine, whatever's … ___
7 Let's say, provisionally, … ___

a the email I sent you regarding …
b to look through the portfolio I sent.
c remember.
d best for you.
e responding so quickly.
f to discuss things further.
g Tuesday the 13th at 11.00.

4 02▷ Listen again and check your answers.

Tip | *actually* and *currently*

Don't confuse *actually* with *currently*. Use *actually* as an alternative to *in fact* or *as a matter of fact*.

*I'm **actually** going to be in Prague already.*

Use *currently* to express something you are doing at the moment.

*We're **currently** updating our corporate image.*

5 **Put the phrases in 3 into these categories.**

a Making a follow-up call: ______

b Responding to a follow-up call: ______

c Arranging to meet: ______

6 **03▷ Listen to a call Sean receives and answer questions 1–3.**

1 Who is calling Sean and why?

2 How will Sean know how to find Simply Speaking?

3 What transport is he going to use?

7 **03▷ Listen again.**

1 What phrase does Sean use to

a enquire about transport?

b refer to the time of the train?

c discuss the possibility of catching the train?

2 What phrase does Catherine use to offer help with

a directions?

b a taxi?

» For more exercises, go to **Practice file 1** on page 102.

8 **Think of a situation in your own job where you have to introduce yourself to a company or client. Draft an introductory email. Give the email to your partner.**

9 **Work with your partner. Take turns to make a follow-up call to your email in 8. Say who you are and why you are calling. Arrange to meet and discuss travel arrangements and directions.**

ⓘ » Interactive Workbook » **Email**

Practically speaking | Exchanging contact details

1 **04▷ Listen to three conversations and answer questions 1–2 for each one.**

1 How does speaker 2 give contact details?

2 What means of communication is speaker 1 likely to use to contact speaker 2 again?

2 **04▷ Listen again. Put these phrases into categories a–d.**

1 I have an email address for you but I'm not sure if it's current.

2 Here's my email address.

3 Let me take your name and number.

4 I'll send you her contact details by text.

5 Can I have Suzy's number and email address?

6 The one above is my business email. I check it regularly so please use that one.

7 Here's my card.

a Asking for details: ______

b Giving details: ______

c Checking details: ______

d Promising details: ______

3 **Work in groups of four. Exchange your details with each other. Do this in as many different ways as possible. Refer to the *Useful phrases* on page 134.**

Key expressions

Introducing self (email)

My name's … and I (have / work for / represent) …

I was given your details by …

(She) recommended you to me as …

Making a follow-up call

Hello … This is …

I'm calling about the email I sent you regarding …

I wondered if you'd had time to …?

I wanted to see if you are still interested in …

Responding to a follow-up call

Yes, I remember.

Thanks for responding so quickly.

Thanks. I wanted to speak to you about …

Arranging to meet

I suggest we meet to discuss things further.

When would you like to meet?

We can meet …

Fine, whatever's best for you.

Let's say, provisionally, Tuesday the 13th at 11.00.

I'll get my assistant to call you later today to confirm.

See you (in a couple of weeks).

Discussing travel arrangements

You'll be travelling in from …, won't you?

Can you tell me how I get to …?

Is it best by taxi or public transport?

Let me know where you're staying and I'll email you a map and directions from your hotel.

There's a train that leaves at … Will I have time to catch that one?

It only takes … to get to …

Let me know if you need a taxi and I'll book one for you.

ⓘ » Interactive Workbook » **Phrasebank**

Language at work | Present simple and continuous

1 **Read these extracts from audio 02▷ and 03▷.**

a I'm **calling** about the email I sent you …
b Yes, I **remember**.
c We'**re** currently **updating** our corporate image.
d I **go** to Berlin once a month …
e It only **takes** 20 minutes to get to the station.
f I'**m leaving** the day after tomorrow.
g There's a train that **leaves** at 3.00.
h We can meet when I **get** back.
i I'**m covering** for a colleague who's on maternity leave.

In which extract is the present simple used to refer to

1 a routine? ___
2 something always or permanently true? ___
3 a thought / feeling / reaction rather than an action? ___
4 an item on a timetable? ___
5 the future after a time word? ___

In which extract is the present continuous used to refer to

6 an action in progress at the moment of speaking? ___
7 a current (unfinished) project? ___
8 an arrangement in the future? ___
9 a temporary situation? ___

›› For more information and exercises, go to **Practice file 1** on page 103.

2 **You want to find out this information from someone you meet for the first time. What questions would you ask?**

- who they work for
- their responsibilities at work
- their daily routine
- how their English studies are going
- the department or area they work in
- a current project they are involved in
- what their schedule is next week
- how regularly they need English at work

3 **Work with a partner. Ask and answer the questions in 2.**

4 **Which of these phrases would you normally use with the present simple and which with the present continuous?**

for the moment *at the moment* *generally speaking* *for the time being*
on the whole *tomorrow afternoon* *once a week* *most of the time*
every winter *right now* *once in a while* *as a rule* *currently*

5 **Work with a partner. Use the phrases in 4 to make true statements about your activities in or out of work.**

6 **Give a short presentation about your company using these points.**

1 The industry as a whole
- how important it is and whether it employs a lot of people
- any changes taking place at the moment
- future developments

2 Your company
- where it is based and what it does
- current projects and future plans
- what customers like about the company

ⓘ ›› Interactive Workbook ›› **Exercises and Tests**

Making business connections

Background

Business networking with BNI

BNI is a business referral network, which works as a word-of-mouth promotion tool. When companies join BNI, their representatives attend a local / regional group which holds regular breakfast meetings. At the meeting, members are required to give a '60-second speech' – telling the other participants what type of business they are in, what type of business connections they are looking for and any other information that is helpful for generating more business. The meeting agenda is standardized throughout the world. There is time for members to present their company, hear about success stories within the BNI network, and pass on their contact details. The benefits of this type of 'cross-promotion' are clear. Business people who attend the meeting can refer their business associates to someone they meet at the meeting. Or two members may forge a business relationship – a supplier / client relationship or a synergy.

Example of networking success: A printer joined BNI and got to know a real estate company. This company was dissatisfied with its current printer and decided to switch to the printer it met through the BNI group. As a result, $100,000-worth of business was handed over to him!

The Expert View

Networking is defined here as a two-way relationship-building process – promoting what we have to offer, and seeking opportunities through what others have to offer us. In an increasingly fast-moving and competitive global environment, we all need to communicate clearly and create opportunities to develop a network of contacts. Information is available from all corners of the world, but in business nothing can replace the value of building personal relationships. This process often takes time, particularly in some cultures. But when it is done well, networking can deliver a real competitive advantage.

Pauline Weight, Chairman of the Cranfield Management Association

Cranfield School of Management

Discussion

1 **Why might a company join a network like BNI? What are the main advantages of the network?**

2 **What would you say about your company in a 60-second speech?**

Task

Work in groups of four. You are going to attend a meeting of a similar networking organization. Each person chooses one of the four companies from File 01 on page 136.

1 Read your information. Prepare a 60-second speech to give at the meeting. Make sure you
   - give some general facts about your company
   - speak briefly about current activities
   - say what you hope to gain from being a member of the networking organization.
2 Have a networking meeting. Listen to each other's speeches and decide which company it would be useful to forge a business relationship with.
3 It is a week after the networking meeting. Call the business acquaintance you chose and arrange to meet.
4 Meet with your business acquaintance. Discuss and decide how your two companies can help each other and / or promote each other's business.

Case study

2 Motivation

Learning objectives in this unit
- Talking about motivation at work
- Making small talk
- Exiting a conversation
- Using question forms

Case study
- Solving staffing problems

Starting point

1 Which of these things motivate you in your job?
- colleagues
- interesting work
- gifts for achieving targets
- promotion
- training
- flexible hours
- money
- job security

2 What else would you add to the list in 1?

Working with words | Motivation at work

1 Discuss these questions.
1 What is the difference between 'a reward' and 'an incentive'?
2 What different rewards and incentives does your company offer?

2 Read this text. Is it negative or positive about incentive schemes?

Incentive schemes or cash?

Employers often don't know whether to offer **incentive schemes** (such as travel, trips, excursions, social events, merchandise) or cash to help their company achieve its goals. When you ask employees what they want, they generally say 'more money' – but salary increases or **annual bonuses** are not always the best way to **motivate staff**. **Non-cash rewards** such as merchandise and travel can be a far more effective way to **improve performance**, **boost staff morale** and **foster company loyalty**.

Why do non-cash incentive schemes work better?

- They provide a lasting reminder of the **achievement** and the positive feelings that go with it.
- They offer rewards that can be shown to others or talked about – and it is socially acceptable to 'boast' about the achievement. The same certainly cannot be said for cash.
- They provide a guilt-free form of reward, often something employees would not otherwise do or buy, whereas they may feel guilty for not spending cash on necessities.
- They have a higher perceived value. The actual cash value is secondary to the **recognition**.
- The employee's family is often involved in the reward selection and the reward chosen may **benefit** the whole family.
- Extra cash in the monthly pay packet disappears into the bank account or wallet. In fact, 72% of people receiving cash rewards use it to pay bills, can't remember what they spent it on, or don't even know they received it!

3 Read the text again and answer questions 1–4.

1 What are the advantages of incentive schemes for employers?
2 What are the advantages of non-cash incentives for employees?
3 What are the disadvantages of cash rewards?
4 Do *you* think incentive schemes are better than cash rewards? Why or why not?

4 Match the phrases in bold in the text to these definitions.

1 encourage employees to want to work harder: ________
2 something done well by your own effort or skill: ________
3 make employees feel better about themselves and their work: ________
4 praise and reward for something you have done: ________
5 make people work more efficiently: ________
6 programmes that provide extra rewards for good work: ________
7 be useful to someone or improve their life in some way: ________
8 bonuses that do not involve money: ________
9 encourage commitment to the company: ________
10 extra money for good work – added to salary once a year: ________

5 05▷ Listen to three people talking about their jobs and answer questions 1–3.

Claudia

Peter

Macie

1 What job do they do?
2 What benefits, rewards and incentives does their company provide?
3 What other factors give them job satisfaction?

6 Which of these words and phrases from audio 05▷ are

1 material benefits? *profit-sharing scheme*
2 non-material benefits? *fulfilment*

~~profit-sharing scheme~~ ~~fulfilment~~ company car autonomy feel valued be acknowledged commission staff discount attendance reward appreciation on-time bonus compensation plan positive feedback (personal) development praise satisfaction private medical insurance non-contributory pension plan

7 Work with a partner and discuss questions 1–3.

1 Which of the material benefits in **6** are standard in an employment contract in your country? Which are additional benefits?
2 How does this vary according to profession?
3 How important to you are the non-material benefits? How do they compare to the material benefits?

» For more exercises, go to **Practice file 2** on page 104.

8 Work in small groups. You are partners setting up your own company.

1 Decide on the type of company (service or product oriented) and how many employees you will need.
2 What benefits, rewards and incentives will you offer to your employees?
3 What effects will these have for both the employee and the company?
4 How will you make sure your employees receive some of the non-material benefits in **6**?

ⓘ » Interactive Workbook » **Glossary**

Context

A global media company has organized its annual incentive event to reward its most successful members of staff – a one-week cruise. Employees from all over the world have arrived on board and are now meeting on the first evening.

Socializing | Making small talk

1 Work in small groups. Read these tips and decide which five are the most useful.

The art of small talk

1 Introduce yourself and use a 'tag line', e.g. *Hi, I'm Jules from Munich.* This can get the conversation started as your colleague can ask a question about your home town or your trip.

2 When your colleague introduces himself / herself, try to repeat his / her name when you reply, or use their name later in the conversation.

3 Break the ice with a comment about a current news story or a remark about the event you're at, its location and the weather.

4 Avoid these topics of conversation: your health, your private life, gossip. The best conversation topics are sports, books, theatre, movies, food, museums and travel. Try and find a shared experience or something else you have in common.

5 Keep the conversation flowing by not monopolizing the conversation. Ask a question and really listen to your colleague's reply. Then respond with comments from your own personal experience and ask another question.

6 Ask open questions which require more than a one-word answer. If your colleague asks a *Yes / No* question, give some extra information.

7 Sounds like *hmm* and phrases like *Really* can be used to indicate that you are listening and interested, and will encourage your colleague to tell you more.

8 Share information about yourself but keep it positive. People don't like colleagues who are negative, depressed or who complain a lot.

9 Remember your exit strategy. Have some phrases ready for excusing yourself politely and moving to another group of people, e.g. *It was nice talking to you. I'll see you later.* A transition word like *Well …* can also communicate that it's time to stop.

10 If you've enjoyed talking with your colleague, tell them so, e.g. *I've really enjoyed talking with you. I hope we have the chance to talk again soon.* Leave a positive final impression with a smile and strong handshake.

2 06▷ Read the *Context* above. Listen to four conversations from the first evening of the cruise. Work with a partner and answer questions 1–2 for each conversation.

1 Which of the tips in **1** are used or not used?

2 Is the conversation successful or unsuccessful? Why?

Tip | *well* and *so*

Use *well* to introduce a comment or a piece of information in a conversation.

Use *so* to indicate you're changing the direction of the conversation.

A *Are you here with colleagues?*

B *No.*

A ***Well****, you'll soon get to know people.* ***So****, would you like another drink?*

3 **06▷ Listen again and answer questions 1–8.**

Conversation 1

1 What does Harry say to start the conversation?
2 What phrases does he use to end the conversation?

Conversation 2

3 What does Paolo say to start the conversation?
4 How does Sonia respond?

Conversation 3

5 What two phrases show that the speakers are interested in what the other person has said?

Conversation 4

6 What phrases do Adriana and Adam use to greet each other?
7 How does Adriana show that she is listening?
8 What does she say to end the conversation?

4 **07▷ Listen to a second conversation Adriana has later in the evening. This time the conversation is successful. Number these phrases 1–12 in the order you hear them. How do the phrases help the conversation flow?**

___ **a** Don't you …
___ **b** … by the way?
___ **c** Well …
___ **d** What a coincidence!
___ **e** So …
___ **f** Really?
___ **g** In fact …
___ **h** So …
___ **i** I see.
___ **j** That sounds interesting.
___ **k** Well …
___ **l** Apparently …

›› For more exercises, go to **Practice file 2** on page 104.

5 **Work with a partner.**

1 Read conversations 1 and 4 in audio script **06▷** on page 151.
2 Discuss what each speaker could say to make the conversation more successful.
3 Use your ideas in **2** to have the two conversations.

6 **Work with a partner and have a conversation. Keep the conversation going as long as possible. Discuss as many of these topics as you can.**

- hobbies
- education
- sport
- an interesting fact
- TV / cinema
- vacation
- other people
- food
- work
- news
- family
- an enjoyable excursion nearby

ⓘ ›› Interactive Workbook ›› **Email**

Key expressions

Starting a conversation

Hi, I don't think we've met.
Hello. It's (Adriana), isn't it?
Hello, I saw you … but I didn't have a chance to speak to you. I'm …
Hello / Hi, I'm … (from / based in …).
Is this your first (company event)?
I thought I might see you (here).
How lovely to see you here.
How are things?

Showing interest

Really?
I see.
What a coincidence!
That's amazing!
That sounds interesting.
Oh dear …
Oh, I'm so sorry to hear that.

Keeping a conversation going

By the way …
Well, …
Apparently …
I've heard … – is that true?
In fact …
So …
Don't you …?

Ending a conversation

See you later.
It's been nice talking to you.
Look, I have to go. Catch you later.
You don't mind if I go and get myself (a coffee)?

ⓘ ›› Interactive Workbook ›› **Phrasebank**

Practically speaking | Exiting a conversation

1 **08▷ Phrases 1–5 below might seem a little rude if used on their own to exit a conversation. Listen and make a note of the follow-up phrases used to make them more acceptable.**

1 Is that the time?
2 I promised to meet someone else.
3 I'm going to get some food.
4 Is that James over there?
5 Look, I really don't have time to chat at the moment.

2 **Work with a partner. Turn to File 02 on page 136 and choose two of the situations each. Have one or two minutes of small talk, then exit the conversation appropriately. Refer to the *Useful phrases* on page 134.**

Language at work | Question form review

1 **Read these questions from audio 06▷ and 07▷. Match them to categories 1–4. (Some questions match more than one category.)**

a Where do they come from?
b ... is that true?
c Who did you come with?
d Don't you live in Italy?
e Have you spent much time in India?
f You're from Calcutta?
g Who told you?
h It's Adriana, isn't it?
i Dinner was fantastic, wasn't it?

1 Starting a conversation: ________
2 Finding out information: ________
3 Checking or confirming information: ________
4 Showing surprise: ________

2 **Look at the questions in 1 again. Answer these questions.**

1 What is the usual word order for *Wh-* and *Yes / No* questions?
2 In which question, c or g, is *who*
- the subject of the question?
- the object of the question?

3 How can a statement be made into a question without changing the word order?
4 What answer is expected to questions h and i?

» For more information and exercises, go to **Practice file 2** on page 105.

3 **Work with a partner. Think of questions to ask in these situations.**

1 Your company is sending you to work in Hong Kong. You want to know about travel plans and accommodation.
2 You are about to order a product and want to check these details are correct:
Price: €200 / Delivery: 5 days / Delivery charge: €8 / Guarantee: 1 year
3 You're at a conference and meet someone who went to the same college as you.
4 You're waiting for an interview and make conversation with the person next to you.

4 **Question tags are often used to start a conversation or keep it going. Work with a partner. Add a question tag to these conversation openers and statements. Reply with a suitable comment (not just *yes* or *no*).**

Example: *A* *Everyone enjoyed themselves,* ***didn't they****?*
B *Yes, it was a great party.*

1 That wasn't a very interesting presentation.
2 The negotiations have been going pretty well.
3 The manager was in a good mood today.
4 The meeting won't finish late.
5 Emily's looking tired these days.
6 You're going to Alpbach tomorrow.
7 Ken can't speak Japanese.
8 Nobody got here on time today.

5 **Work with a partner. Student A and Student B turn to File 07 on page 137. Take turns to ask and answer questions about a tourist attraction.**

ⓘ » Interactive Workbook » **Exercises and Tests**

Tip | Question use

Use questions to start and develop conversations in social situations
- to find out information about the other person
- to check or confirm information
- to show surprise (or other emotion)
- to encourage a response.

Solving staffing problems

Background

Improving staff morale at Palmate Hellas

Palmate Hellas is the Greek subsidiary (270 employees) of an international company specializing in household products. The company has quite a loose structure, which worked well when it was first introduced. Each department is responsible for its own personnel and has a budget allocated to it each year for new hires and personal development. There is quite a difference between departments' priorities for spending their budget and sometimes personal development is not as promoted as other areas. HR is reported back to on an annual basis and it has an advisory role, enforcing policies and guidelines and only intervening in staffing issues when necessary. The one policy which is enforced company-wide is that of fixed working hours. Over the last five years, Palmate Hellas has had to deal with high staff turnover and absenteeism in particular departments. The company has decided to carry out an employee satisfaction survey (to find out what staff think about the company) with a view to reducing staffing problems.

Discussion

1 What are some reasons for low staff morale and motivation in companies?

2 How important is it for companies to have guidelines in place to ensure their employees are kept motivated? What examples do you know of?

3 What reasons could there be for the staff's lack of motivation at Palmate?

Task

Work in groups of four. Student A, turn to File 05 on page 137. Student B, turn to File 10 on page 138. Student C, turn to File 30 on page 144. Student D, turn to File 41 on page 147.

1 Read the information in your file from Palmate's employee satisfaction survey.
2 Ask and answer questions in your group to complete this table.

Prospects / Training	Communication
Middle management comments	**Working conditions**

3 Discuss what could be done to solve the company's staffing problems.
4 Draft a list of priorities and present these to the class. Choose the five best ideas.
5 Turn to File 46 on page 148 to find out what changes the company actually implemented.

The Expert View

Staff morale and productivity are linked in complicated ways. Employees want to know that they are respected by the organization and are being treated fairly. Increasingly, organizations understand the need to address issues such as quality of working life and work-life balance. This is done through a package of benefits as well as pay – these may include flexible working, training provision and other innovations. Whilst company-wide policies need to be consistently and equitably applied, the key is to treat everyone as an individual, with their own circumstances, needs and desires. This will enhance their self-esteem, improve competence and aid their contribution to the effectiveness of the organization.

Richard Kwiatkowski, Senior Lecturer in Organizational Psychology

Cranfield School of Management

Case study

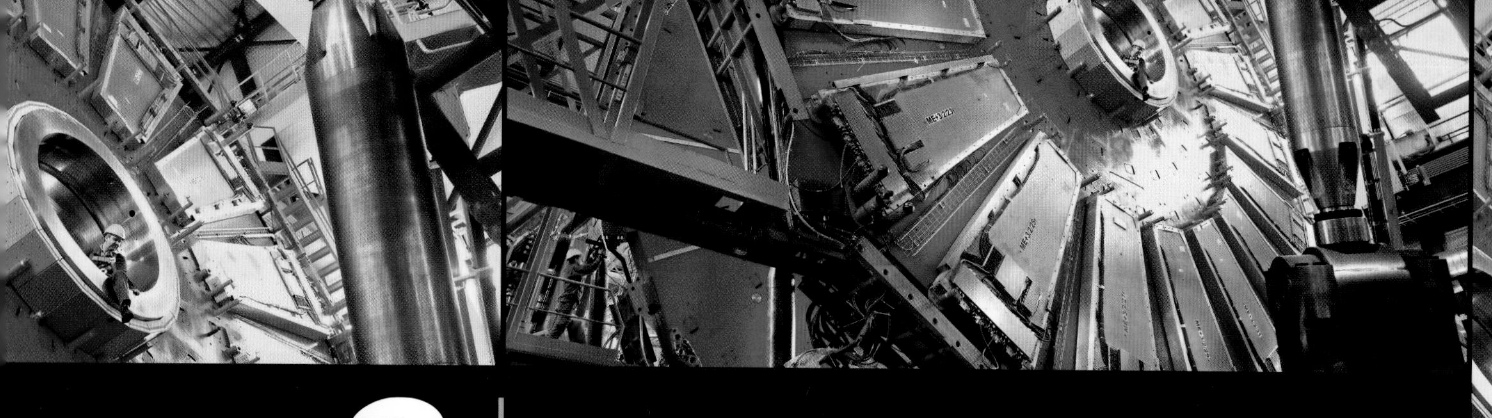

3 On schedule

Learning objectives in this unit
- Talking about managing projects
- Asking for and giving an update
- Making and responding to suggestions
- Catching up with colleagues
- Updating on current projects using the present perfect and past simple

Case study
- Organizing a road show

Starting point

1 In your experience, what are the key factors in managing a project (however big or small)?

2 What can go right with a project? What can go wrong?

3 What projects are you currently working on in or out of work?

4 What progress are you making? What problems have you had?

Working with words | Managing projects

1 What are the five most common problems in managing projects? Read the text and compare your ideas.

2 How do the problems mentioned in the text affect the project? What solution can you think of for each problem?

1 Not enough planning time

The planning stage may not be as exciting as the development stage, but it's just as important, if not more so. Lack of planning will always result in changes later on, eating up money and man-hours.

Solution: ____

2 Communication breakdowns

Anyone who runs a business knows that communication is absolutely vital to the success of any project. Breakdowns can occur between the project team and the end users (i.e. the clients or employers), and there can also be problems between the individual members inside the project team.

Solution: ____

3 Unrealistic budget

If your budget is unrealistic to start with, it will be impossible to stay within budget. As you run out of money, departments fall behind, resources are slow to arrive, and – because of budget constraints – the project, once again, goes out of control.

Solution: ____

4 Not checking progress

As the project goes along, the unexpected happens. Various different people use their own ideas to fix these challenges and – when you're on the point of finishing – you're suddenly faced with a huge list of problems that need to be addressed and you miss the deadline.

Solution: ____

5 Not reviewing existing standards

If most or all of your projects run behind schedule and over budget, ask yourself if you maintain the same standards time after time. Do they work? If you keep doing the same thing, you're likely to get the same results.

Solution: ____

3 Match these suggested solutions to the problems in the text in 1. Do you agree with the solutions? Why or why not?

A Never assume that everyone understands. Make sure that everyone can talk to each other and share information. Resolve any conflicts straight away or you will run into a lot of problems and complications later on.

B Take time to review how projects have gone in the past. Keep a running list of what worked, what didn't, and how to do it better next time.

C Spend longer on research and preparation. Make contingency plans, and don't just concentrate on making it to market before your competition. If you get there first but your product is faulty, you'll get nothing but complaints and a bad reputation.

D Create an accurate forecast. Outline ways to develop better upfront planning of the resources. Make sure you allocate enough funds to each department and keep track of spending.

E Define 'checkpoints' throughout the project so you stay on track. Monitor everyone's performance and prioritize tasks when there is a problem. Addressing problems quickly will save time later. You can still make the launch date you've set or even finish ahead of schedule.

4 Do you associate these phrases from the texts with successful (*S*) or unsuccessful (*U*) projects, or both?

run out of money *within budget* *behind schedule* *upfront planning* *over budget*
miss the deadline *stay on track* *out of control* *budget constraints* *lack of planning*
make the launch date *accurate forecast* *ahead of schedule* *unrealistic budget*

5 Choose the correct answer from the words in *italics*.

1 Good communication will help you to *resolve / address* conflicts quickly.
2 When time is short, you must *promote / prioritize* tasks and do the most important ones first.
3 Try to *hold / keep* track of spending so that you don't go over budget.
4 Make sure you *allow / allocate* sufficient resources to the different departments.
5 Always expect the unexpected and *manufacture / make* contingency plans.
6 It is important to *examine / check* progress at every stage of a project in case there are any problems.

6 Choose a verb from the list that can go with *all three* phrases in each group.

stay *set* *run* *keep* *check*

1 ________ smoothly / out of time / into problems
2 ________ on track / within budget / the course
3 ________ the facts / progress / details
4 ________ a budget / a timescale / a launch date
5 ________ to a budget / track of / costs down

» For more exercises, go to **Practice file 3** on page 106.

7 Work with a partner. Turn to File 06 on page 137. Use the words and phrases in 4–6 to discuss what has gone right and wrong for the project. Suggest how the project could be managed better.

8 Work in small groups. Using the ideas from the texts and your own experience, make notes on how to manage a project successfully. Then give a short presentation to the class.

ⓘ » Interactive Workbook » **Glossary**

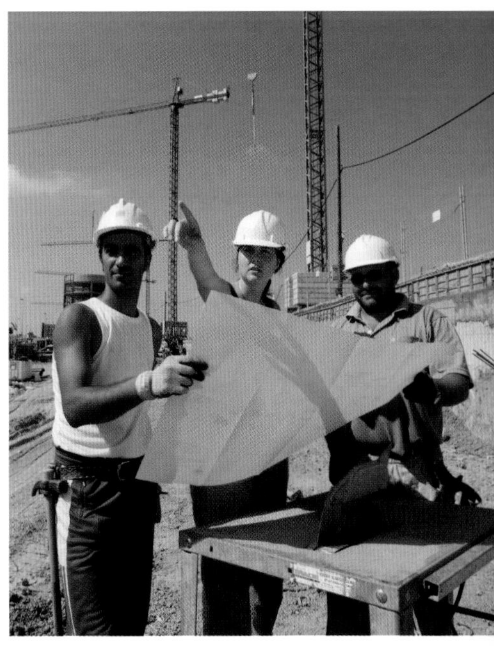

Context

The Tech-Tariff project is a collaboration between MMT-Tec (service provider) and Anvikon (mobile phone manufacturer). The aim is to launch a high-tech phone with new advanced features from Anvikon in combination with MMT-Tec's new tariff which includes free videophoning and multimedia message services. Sarah and Michelle from MMT-Tec and Ian from Anvikon are meeting to discuss the progress of the project.

Meetings | Asking for and giving an update | Making and responding to suggestions

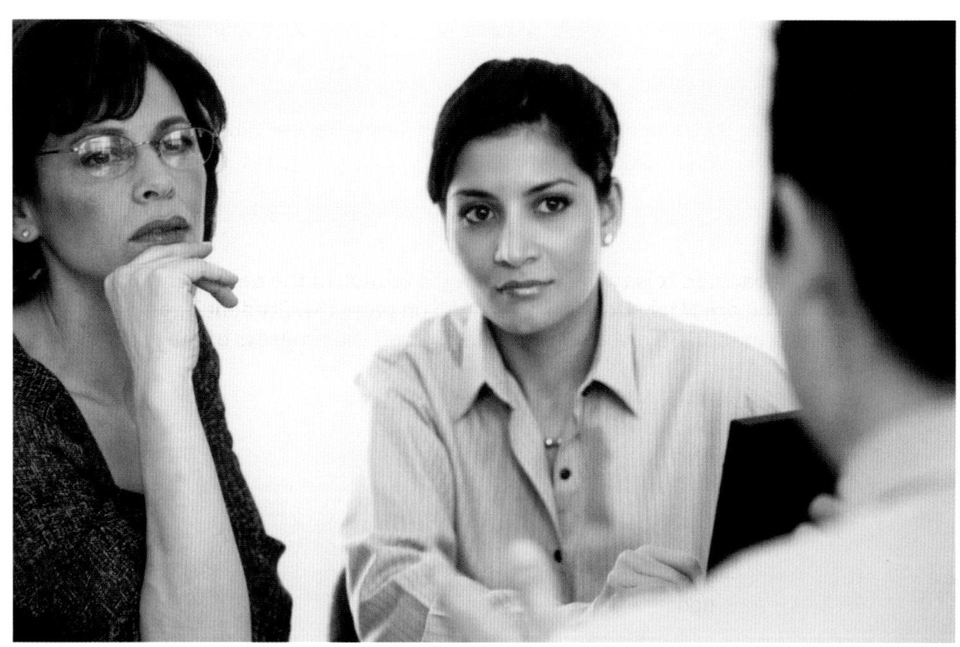

1 **09▷ Read the *Context*. Listen to Part 1 of the meeting and make notes about the items on the agenda.**

Tech-Tariff Update Meeting – 2 Sept

Agenda

1 Update on marketing activities (MMT-Tec):
- Launch date [1] Set for 15th November
- Advertising campaign [2] ____
- Launch party: Venue [3] ____
  Catering [4] ____

2 Update on Anvikon activities:
- Handset [5] ____

3 Project schedule [6] ____

2 **09▷ Listen again and answer questions 1–3.**

1 What four phrases does Sarah use to ask for an update on the project?
2 What three phrases do Sarah and Michelle use to clarify the problem with the battery?
3 Turn to audio script **09▷** on page 152 and underline all the phrases Michelle and Ian use to give an update on the project.

3 **10▷ Listen to Part 2 of the meeting and answer questions 1–3.**

1 Why didn't Ian like the idea of finding another battery supplier?
2 Why didn't Sarah like the idea of not mentioning the battery life?
3 Which proposal did they finally decide on?

Tip | *things*

Use *things* to speak / ask about situations in general.

*How are **things** with you?*
*How does your side of **things** look?*
***Things** aren't running as smoothly as I'd hoped.*

4 10▷ **Listen again.**

1 Complete these suggestions made by the speakers.

a ______________ another battery supplier?

b ______________ keep the same battery but not mention its lifespan.

c ______________ and see what the technicians suggest …?

d Using a different phone for the launch ______________.

e ______________ look at what we can reschedule.

2 What do the speakers say to respond to each of the suggestions in 1?

» For more exercises, go to **Practice file 3** on page 106.

5 Work with a partner. It is two days before the launch of the new Tech-Tariff phone. Student A, you are Michelle. Turn to File 08 on page 137. Student B, you are Ian. Use the information below. Update each other on the progress of the project. Make sure you

- clarify any information you're not sure about
- make and respond to suggestions as necessary.

Student B

1 Read the 'To do' list you received from Michelle and the notes you have written under your tasks (I).

2 Michelle will call you. Answer Michelle's questions about your tasks.

3 Ask Michelle to update you on her tasks (M).

4 Make and respond to suggestions as necessary.

Launch date 'To do' list

Bring Anvikon merchandise to venue (I)

Done! Already sent. Suggestion: bring extras and leave in car?

Finalize timetable of day with sound engineers (M)

Brief Anvikon staff about handset demonstration (I)

Problem – illness in office – rescheduled for tomorrow when all sales staff are present. Suggestion: time – mid-afternoon?

Check replies from the press – who's coming? (M)

Send Anvikon PR manager's speech to MMT-Tec (I)

Not ready! Will contact him again today. Suggestion: PR manager emails it direct to MMT-Tec?

Make sure Sarah's briefed on everything (I / M)

On track! Have logged everything – will send brief to Sarah tomorrow p.m.

ⓘ » Interactive Workbook » **Email**

Key expressions

Asking for an update

How does your side of things look?
How's the … coming along?
How far are you with …?
How are things with …?
What's the current status of …?

Giving an update

Up to now (the launch date) has been (set) …
He (booked the venue) two weeks ago.
I've already …
I haven't … yet.
We're on track.
Things aren't running as smoothly as I'd hoped.
We've hit a problem with …

Clarifying a problem

So what do you mean exactly?
So what you're saying is …?
So the real problem lies with …?

Making a suggestion

How about (+ *-ing*)
We could (+ verb)
Why don't we (+ verb)
… would be my proposal.
If you ask me, we should …

Responding to a suggestion

That's a good idea.
It's worth a try.
I don't think that would …
That's possible (but …).
That's not an ideal solution.
I'm not convinced.
I suppose so.

ⓘ » Interactive Workbook
» **Phrasebank**

Practically speaking | Catching up with colleagues

1 11▷ **Listen to four short conversations. What is being discussed in each conversation?**

2 11▷ **Listen again and answer questions 1–2.**

1 What questions does each person ask?

2 What does each person say about what they are doing (or have done)?

3 Work with a partner.

1 Make a list of three things that you do now, have done recently or used to do. Give this list to your partner.

2 Have conversations with your partner about these activities. Refer to the *Useful phrases* on page 134.

Language at work | Present perfect and past simple

1 Read these extracts from audio 09▷.

a Up to now, the launch date **has been set** for the 15th of November ...
b We'**ve hit** a problem with the handset battery life.
c He **booked** the venue two weeks ago.
d I'**ve already received** offers from various catering companies.
e I **haven't made** a final choice **yet**.
f I **sent** you a proposed agenda yesterday.

Which of the extracts refer to

1 a present situation resulting from a past action – we don't know or say when the action happened? ___
2 a finished past action – we know or say when it happened? ___
3 something that has or hasn't happened during an unfinished period of time? ___

Which word in extract d and which word in extract e means that

4 something has taken place earlier than expected? ___
5 we expect that something will take place? ___

2 Which of these time expressions used when giving an update can we normally use

1 with the past simple?
2 with the present perfect?
3 with either – but under what circumstances? Give examples.

up to now *so far (this week)* *since our last meeting* *in the last month*
today *last week* *a couple of weeks ago* *this morning* *yesterday*
to date *just* *over the last few months*

» For more information and exercises, go to **Practice file 3** on page 107.

3 Work with a partner. Student A, turn to File 03 on page 136. Student B, turn to File 42 on page 147. Update each other on your project.

4 Work with a partner. Student A and Student B, turn to File 37 on page 146. Follow the instructions and ask and answer questions about these 'To do' lists.

1
- Print out and collate six copies of proposal to submit to management.
- Contact office suppliers to check delivery date of latest order.
- Email all staff with agenda for next team meeting.
- Compile mailing list for this year's brochure.

2
- Email colleague and ask for all the details about the conference.
- Confirm acceptance of conference place with conference organizers.
- Book return flights to Madrid – Friday to Monday.
- Find two possible hotels in centre of Madrid.

5 Work with a partner. Think of five personal goals or plans you have had during the last six months. Tell your partner which of these you have achieved and when, and give some details. Which have you not achieved and why?

ⓘ » Interactive Workbook » **Exercises and Tests**

Organizing a road show

Background

Investor relations at Wolters Kluwer

Wolters Kluwer (WK) is a global company, based in Amsterdam, which provides information products and services for professionals in the health, tax, accounting, corporate, financial services, legal and education sectors. It employs approximately 18,400 people worldwide and has operations across Europe, North America and Asia Pacific. WK believes it is important to communicate with current and potential investors to provide up-to-date company information and to build a relationship of trust. It does this by issuing regular press releases, publishing quarterly financial results and organizing 'Divisional days' when investors can learn more about the work of one of WK's five divisions. It also runs a series of investor 'road shows' in cities worldwide. At the road show, WK representatives give presentations to update potential investors on WK's key activities, financial performance and future developments.

Discussion

1 **How does a policy of communicating with investors help big companies to build a relationship of trust?**

2 **What do you think is involved in the organization of an investor road show?**

Task

1 **Work in groups. You are a project team organizing a series of investor road shows in the Far East (Shanghai, Hong Kong, Tokyo, Seoul, Singapore) on behalf of WK.**

1. Read the road show guidelines provided by WK.
2. Brainstorm the tasks for each item in the guidelines.
3. Make a schedule for the project (you have eight weeks before the first road show). Decide on a timescale for each of the tasks.
4. Allocate the tasks to the different members of your project team.

Wolters Kluwer *Guidelines for investor road shows*

- Prepare a timetable (when to visit each city and in what order).
- Prepare a target investor list (including key information on the investor and size of possible investment in company). We recommend 30 investors at each road show.
- Send out invitations to potential investors and keep a record of acceptances and declines.
- Book venues for the presentations and arrange refreshments.
- Arrange travel details for WK representatives – flights, car hire, hotel accommodation.
- Print a copy of the presentation and prepare a handout for each participant.

2 **You are now four weeks away from the first road show.**

1. Decide which of your allocated tasks you have already done (make a note of when you did these) and which you still have to do.
2. Decide on two tasks which have been delayed. Think of reasons for the delay.

3 **Hold a project update meeting to check that the project is on schedule.**

1. Discuss progress of your tasks.
2. Make suggestions for dealing with problems.
3. Make a revised schedule for the final month.

The Expert View

There are two fundamental principles of project planning. Firstly, if you fail to plan, you plan to fail. The creation of a plan that represents your best guess of what will happen with a particular project is a vital part of project management. The plan includes the tasks that need to be completed, their sequence and the resources required for them. The military have a saying: 'A plan never survives first engagement with the enemy'. In other words, things never work out quite how you expect. This is the second fundamental principle – you must be flexible, in order to respond to inevitable changes as you try to execute the plan.

Dr Harvey Maylor, Senior Lecturer in Programme & Project Management
Cranfield School of Management

Case study

4 | New ideas

Learning objectives in this unit
- Talking about ideas and innovations
- Presenting an idea, product or service
- Thanking and responding
- Talking about present, past and future ability

Case study
- Investing in a new idea

Starting point

1. **What is the difference between an 'invention' and an 'innovation'?**
2. **What is your favourite invention, and why?**
3. **What innovation would improve the quality of your life at work? And outside work?**

Working with words | Ideas and innovations

1 **Read the text and answer questions 1–4.**

1. What are the aims of the Ashden Awards?
2. How does the charity achieve its aims?
3. What is 'sustainable energy'? What kinds of sustainable energy can you think of?
4. Do you know of any local schemes in your country or around the world that might qualify for an Ashden Award?

the **Ashden Awards**
for sustainable energy

The Ashden Awards for Sustainable Energy is a charity that rewards and promotes excellent sustainable energy solutions in the UK and the developing world.

Each year, the Ashden Awards holds a competition to find and reward organizations which have carried out practical and innovative programmes that demonstrate sustainable energy in action at a local level. These are based on the use of local, renewable energy sources.

The charity raises international awareness of the potential benefit of local sustainable energy projects to deal with climate change and to improve the quality of people's lives. It also aims to encourage more people and communities across the world to take up the challenge of finding new ways of meeting their energy needs.

The charity helps the development of sustainable energy projects in several ways. It gives cash prizes, to enable winners to take their work forward. It also publicizes the winners and their work through a worldwide media campaign, which aims to inspire others to follow their example. And by bringing together the winners with the main decision-makers and opinion formers, they aim to change thinking and policy among governments and non-governmental organizations (NGOs).

2 **12, 13▷ Listen to details of two projects that have won an Ashden Award.**

1. What is the main purpose of each project?
2. What are the advantages of the technology in each project?

3 **Match the adjectives in A to the nouns in B to make phrases used in the text and audio 12▷ and 13▷. What other combinations are possible?**

A		B	
technological	practical	concept	design
key	potential	feature	proposition
cutting-edge	innovative	benefit	idea
major	commercially-viable	breakthrough	solution
revolutionary	state-of-the-art	technology	advantage

4 **Work with a partner. Create a sentence for each phrase in 3.**

5 **Match these phrasal verbs from the text and audio 12▷ and 13▷ to a verb 1–9 with the same meaning.**

carry out *come up with* *pay off* *take up* *bring down*
bring about *take forward* *get round* *set up*

1 avoid (a problem): ____________
2 cause (something to happen): ____________
3 create (an idea, a solution to a problem): ____________
4 develop (a plan, a project): ____________
5 have a good result: ____________
6 perform (an activity, reseach): ____________
7 reduce (costs): ____________
8 respond to (a challenge): ____________
9 start (a business, a project): ____________

6 **Complete the texts with the correct form of a phrasal verb from 5.**

At the Barefoot College, we've [1] ____________ an idea to [2] ____________ the problem of sustainable energy for lighting in remote mountain villages in India. We've [3] ____________ a project to supply solar power to these villages, and we train local people to install and maintain the systems. Many of our new engineers are women – they've really [4] ____________ the challenge of learning new skills. The main advantage of our training programme is that the new technology we install works properly and has a long life – so it can [5] ____________ real improvements to people's lives, and to the environment.

At KXN we've developed the technology to [6] ____________ a plan for improving the refrigeration of vaccines in northern Nigeria. Standard refrigerators are useless in remote areas because the mains electricity supply is so unreliable or not available at all. After [7] ____________ research and trials, our solution was to buy special refrigerators which use photovoltaic (PV) cells to generate and store electricity from sunlight. The initial investment was high, but it has [8] ____________. This type of refrigerator has excellent insulation, so it needs relatively little electricity to keep the contents cool. This has helped to [9] ____________ the overall cost of vaccination for people in these remote areas.

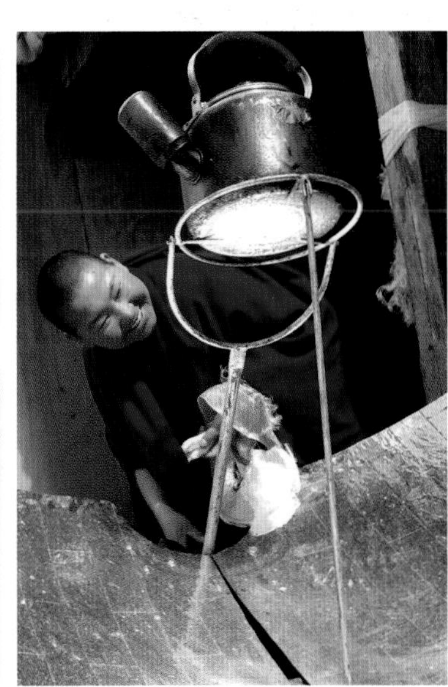

» For more exercises, go to **Practice file 4** on page 108.

7 **Work with a partner. Prepare to talk about an innovative idea for a new invention or new system. This can be connected with the place you work, live or study. Choose at least eight words from 3 and 5 to use in your talk.**

ⓘ » Interactive Workbook » **Glossary**

Context

PharmaLab is a medical research company seeking to increase security in its research centre. Securikey develop and supply hi-tech security systems. Shireen Casey from Securikey has been invited to present her company's solution to PharmaLab's management team.

Presenting | Presenting an idea, product or service

1 How is security managed in your workplace? Is there too much security or not enough?

2 14▷ Read the *Context*. Listen to Part 1 of Shireen's presentation and make notes to complete the slides.

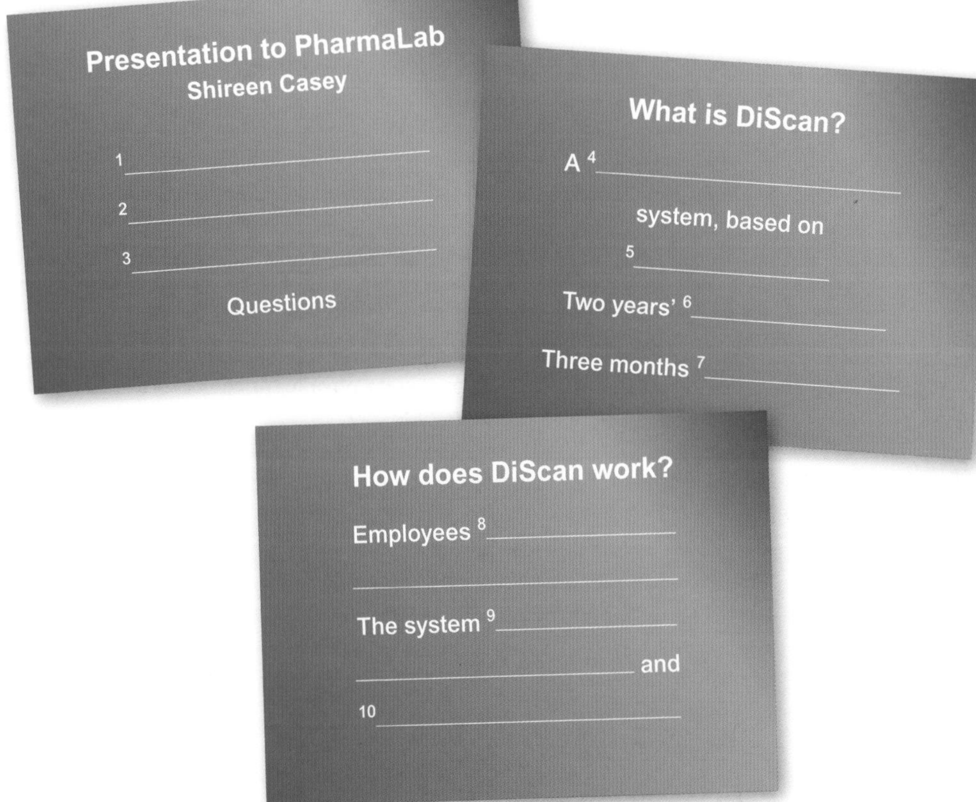

Tip | Linking ideas

Use *although, however, in comparison to* and *whereas* to link contrasting ideas or facts.

__Although__ it may sound radical, it's up to you how far-reaching you want it to be.

It's a very sophisticated system. __However__, it's really easy to use.

This means that DiScan is extremely secure __in comparison to__ systems where a code is needed.

You can learn someone else's code, __whereas__ you can't copy their fingerprints.

3 **14▷ Listen again and complete these phrases.**

1 Good. OK. What I'd like to ________________ three things.
2 First, I'll ________________ of the product.
3 After that I ________________ a short demo film.
4 Does that sound OK? ... OK. We ________________ DiScan.
5 ... based on fingerprint scanning. It's ________________ intensive R&D.
6 How does it work? Well, ________________ – employees are identified by their fingerprints.

4 **15▷ Listen to Part 2. What are the main advantages of DiScan?**

5 **15▷ Listen again and answer questions 1–2.**

1 Make a note of the phrases Shireen uses to
  a explain the advantages of DiScan
  b compare current and future ability.
2 What phrases does Shireen use to
  a check that the audience are following what she is saying?
  b move on to the next point?

» For more exercises, go to **Practice file 4** on page 108.

6 **Use the slides and your notes from 2 to 5 to give a similar short presentation about DiScan.**

7 **Prepare a short presentation about a new idea, a product, a system or a service that you know about, or are interested in. It doesn't have to be connected with work, but it can be. Make sure you**

- preview your talk
- talk about benefits
- discuss current and future ability.

ⓘ » Interactive Workbook » **Email**

Practically speaking | Thanking and responding

1 **16▷ Listen to six short conversations at work. What has happened in each situation?**

2 **16▷ Listen again and make a note of the phrases used to thank someone and respond. Which phrases might be more suitable for a more formal situation, and which for a more informal situation?**

3 **We often add a comment when we thank someone or respond. Turn to audio script 16▷ on page 153 and look at the comments the speakers made.**

4 **Work with a partner. Take turns to thank each other and respond in the following situations. Make sure you choose an appropriate phrase for the situation, and add a comment. Refer to the *Useful phrases* on page 134.**

- A colleague brings you a cup of coffee.
- A taxi takes you to the station after work.
- A friend pays for lunch.
- A stranger holds the door for you.
- Your manager supports you at a difficult meeting.
- Someone on a train lends you their mobile phone.
- A client invites you to present your new project to their team.
- Your team leader helps you with a report – which took until midnight to finish!

Key expressions

Introducing / Previewing a talk
What I'd like to do in this presentation is ...
First, I'll give you a brief overview of the product.
Then I'll talk about ...
After that I'd like to show you ...

Introducing a product or service
We call the system (DiScan).
Basically, (DiScan) is ...
It's the result of ...
It is already being used ...
It's a pretty simple concept.

Explaining benefits
There are two main benefits of using (DiScan).
The biggest potential benefit of (fingerprint scanning) is ...
This means that ...
Another advantage is that ...
The other major advantage of (DiScan) is ...
And this is another great thing about (DiScan) ...

Comparing current and future ability
With your current system ... (they) can / can't ... However, with (DiScan), (they) will / won't be able to ...
At the moment, you can / can't ..., whereas in the future, you'll / won't be able to ... as well.

Moving on
OK, let's look at what (DiScan) has to offer.
OK, now I'd like to move on to ...

Checking
Does that sound OK?
So, is everything clear so far?

ⓘ » Interactive Workbook » **Phrasebank**

Language at work | Present, past and future ability

1 **17▷ Listen to Richard Lake talking about his new business idea to some potential investors and answer questions 1–4.**

1 What is Boatnet?
2 What is the current situation for boat owners who want to use the Internet?
3 What will Boatnet enable them to do in the future?
4 What protection does Boatnet have against competitors?

2 **Read these extracts from the presentation.**

a I **could see** that there was definitely a market.
b Boat owners want to **be able to access** the Internet.
c You still **can't access** the Internet from your boat.
d Our subscribers **will be able to access** the Internet for a basic monthly fee.
e We **were able to test** the system extensively.
f We **can offer** the service for £25 a month.
g We'd like to **be able to increase** this.
h Have you **been able to get** any sort of protection for it?
i We **couldn't get** a patent.
j So other companies **won't be able to compete** with you?

Which extracts refer to

1 present ability? ________
2 past ability? ________
3 future ability? ________

3 **Use the extracts to complete the rules with these words and phrases.**

has / have been able to *can* *couldn't* *was / were able to*
be able to *could* *is / are able to* *wasn't / weren't able to*

1 To talk about general or present ability, we use ________ or ________.
2 To talk about future ability, we use ________ after *will*, *might* and *may*, and verbs like *want to* or *would like to*.
3 We use ________ to talk about past ability with a connection to the present.
4 We use ________ to talk about general ability in the past, and before *hear*, *see*, etc.
5 To talk about a specific situation in the past, if we mean 'tried and succeeded', we use ________. But if the sentence is negative we can use ________ or ________.

» For more information and exercises, go to **Practice file 4** on page 109.

4 **Look at these rapidly-changing technologies and talk about past, present and future ability when using them.**

Example: *In the past, I **wasn't able to** use my mobile phone for taking photos – I **could** only text or make calls. With my current phone, I **can** take photos and video clips, play games and download music files. In the future, I'd like to **be able to** use my phone for international videoconferencing as well.*

5 **Work with a partner and discuss similar changes affecting your own lives, in or out of work. Talk about technology, systems or methods of working, or choose from the list.**

- electronic equipment
- work practices
- vehicles
- education
- travel
- medicine

Ⓘ » Interactive Workbook » **Exercises and Tests**

Tip | *managed to*

Managed to can also be used when talking about a specific action in the past especially when we succeed in doing something difficult after trying hard.
*I **managed to** pass my driving test at the fifth attempt.*

Investing in a new idea

Background

Concrete Canvas – the building in a bag

Will Crawford and Peter Brewin are joint directors of Concrete Canvas, and have developed an innovative product – an inflatable concrete shelter. They came up with the idea in response to a competition to find new uses for cement. They visited refugee camps in Africa to do further research. They believe their product could get round the problem of supplying cheap, easy-to-use shelters in disaster situations such as earthquakes and tsunamis.

The shelter is basically a sealed plastic sack that measures under two metres square. Inside is a fabric that has been soaked in cement and this is attached to the outside of an inflatable plastic liner. To inflate the shelter, the sack is filled with water, the fabric is unfolded and a chemical pack releases gas into the plastic liner. Twelve hours later, the thin concrete fabric has set in the shape of the inflated liner, creating a rigid but lightweight shelter. No training is needed, and the weight and size are similar to those of tents used by aid organizations and the military.

Crawford and Brewin aim to test their idea with an aid organization such as Médecins Sans Frontières or CARE. If the testing goes well, they hope to raise the necessary funding to take the project forward. Initially, they need an investment of $300,000 to build and field-test prototypes.

SOME FIGURES

Useful life of a tent in some conditions: less than 3 weeks

Useful life of Concrete Canvas shelter: minimum 10 years

Time needed to put up shelter: 40 minutes

Time until shelter is ready to use: 12 hours

The Expert View

Two essential factors for the success of a new venture are a unique business opportunity, combined with an excellent understanding of the market and resource requirements.
To convince an investor, the entrepreneur needs to make a business pitch that is well presented and easily understood – and which covers the business idea, the market, resource requirements and future growth potential. As an investor, you need to pick an idea which offers a good return on investment and has a management team with good leadership skills and market understanding. Be aware the greater the risk, the greater the need to gain a higher rate of return!

Dr Stephanie Hussels, Lecturer in Entrepreneurship
Cranfield School of Management

Discussion

1 What advice would you give to Will Crawford and Peter Brewin about obtaining the investment they need?

2 What information would potential investors need before deciding to put their money into this product?

3 Do you think this is a good project to invest in? Why?

Task

In this activity you will be both an entrepreneur and an investor. Your aim is to be *either* the winning entrepreneur *or* the winning investor. The winner is the person or team with the most money at the end.

Entrepreneurs

- Present a new idea to the investors and get them to invest as much money as possible in it. You have three minutes to make your 'pitch'.

Investors

- You have $500,000 to invest. Your aim is to invest as much money as possible in the winning idea.
- You can invest all your money in one idea or divide it between different ideas.
- You can't invest in your own business idea, and you don't have to spend all your money.

Turn to File 09 on page 138 and follow the instructions.

5 | Customer service

Learning objectives in this unit
- Talking about customer service
- Dealing with customers
- Reassuring and sympathizing
- Using direct and indirect questions when dealing with customers

Case study
- Dealing with customer service problems

Starting point

1 Discuss a good and bad experience you have had of customer service when buying a product.

2 Was your impression of the product affected by the service?

Working with words | Customer service

1 **18▷ Listen to a woman talking on a radio show about a customer service encounter and answer questions 1–4.**

1 What was the woman's problem and was it resolved?
2 Does she have a positive or negative view of the shop's customer service?
3 Do you think she will use the shop again?
4 Did the shop assistants make the right decision? Why or why not?

2 **Read some of the comments about the encounter posted on the show's website.**

1 I suppose you could support the assistants' 'go by the rules' attitude. But, as a store owner myself, I think it's wrong to quibble about a couple of minutes; staff are there to be **courteous** and **responsive**, and I wouldn't be happy if that happened in my store. It's so much easier and more cost-effective to keep an **existing** customer than to find a new one. My personal rule of thumb is: a **satisfied** customer might tell a friend, a **dissatisfied** customer will complain to everyone they know.

2 Of course you want to meet the customer's needs and you don't want to lose **loyal** customers by appearing **uncaring**, but the customer must also understand that
a) hours are posted for a reason
b) employees have lives outside the shop, and
c) for security reasons, once the tills are closed, no one is allowed in the shop.

3 I work in a bank where we've introduced an unpublicized rule which really helps to foster customer loyalty. The doors officially close at 5.00, but they let anyone in until 5.10. The feedback we get from the cashiers is very positive; by letting people in, we exceed the expectations of customers who arrive just a little late, and no one really expects to be let in if they arrive after 5.10.

4 This is actually a management failure, though everyone seems to be blaming the shop assistants. If I were the owner, I'd tell the staff that in a situation like this, they should try and find a solution. I'd point out the importance of customer satisfaction and I'd give them the power to make decisions – with examples of what they can and can't do. And I'd make sure they understood the effect of **attentive** and **efficient** service as well as **discourteous** and **sub-standard** service on potential customers – and their regular ones.

5 I agree with the last post. Management need to regularly measure customer satisfaction and make sure service quality is part of everyone's work experience. **High-quality** customer service is all about bringing customers back. And about sending them away satisfied so they give positive feedback about your business to others, who may then try the product or service you offer for themselves and in their turn become **repeat** customers.

3 **Work with a partner and answer questions 1–3.**

1 Say what the main points of each post are and whether you agree or disagree with it.
2 Which post do you agree with most?
3 Can you think of a better solution to the problem?

4 **Match the adjectives in bold in the posts to these definitions.**

1 not sympathetic: ________
2 polite / impolite: ________ / ________
3 helpful: ________
4 not as good as normal: ________
5 well organized: ________
6 reacting quickly and positively: ________
7 happy with something: ________
8 of a very good standard: ________
9 faithful and supportive: ________
10 returning: ________
11 not happy with something: ________
12 present: ________

5 **Which of the adjectives in 4 describe**

1 customer service?
2 customers?

6 **Use some of the adjectives in 4 to write another post for the radio show website.**

7 **Complete the questionnaire by matching 1–7 to a–g.**

Customer service questionnaire

1 What do you do to meet ... ___
2 What new procedure might help you to exceed ... ___
3 In what ways do you measure ... ___
4 Have you introduced ... ___
5 Do you think it is easier to keep ... ___
6 How do you try and get ... ___
7 How do you avoid losing ... ___

a feedback about service from your customers?
b customer satisfaction and service quality?
c existing customers or to win new ones?
d your customers' expectations of the service you provide?
e customers to your competitors?
f your customers' needs and keep them satisfied?
g any unpublicized rules to improve customer service?

8 **Work with a partner. Ask and answer the questions in 7 about your own company or a company you know.**

» For more exercises, go to **Practice file 5** on page 110.

9 **Work in small groups. Decide on the five most important factors in good customer service.**

Example: *Try to meet your customers' needs with efficient and attentive service.*

10 **Write a customer service feedback questionnaire. Think of six questions to find out how customers view your company and whether they are satisfied with the service that is provided.**

Example: *Tick the words that best describe your experience of this company.*

- *uncaring*
- *sub-standard*
- *courteous*
- *efficient*

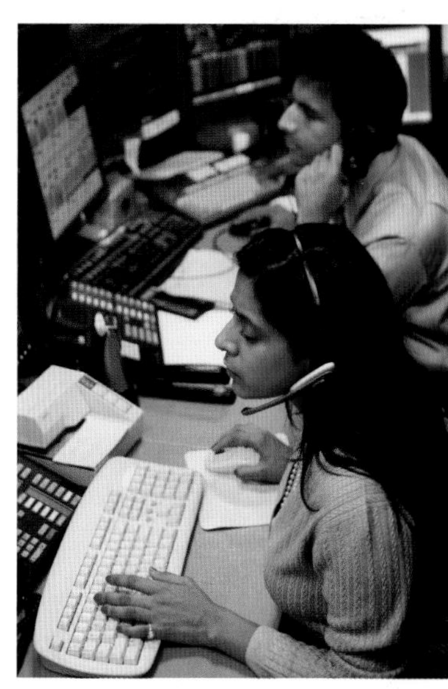

ⓘ » Interactive Workbook » **Glossary**

Context

JC Office Supplies is an international company located throughout Europe. Departments are centralized in certain countries, e.g. Internal Procurement is based in Poland, so employees have to deal with internal customers as well as their external clients.

Exchanging information | Dealing with customers

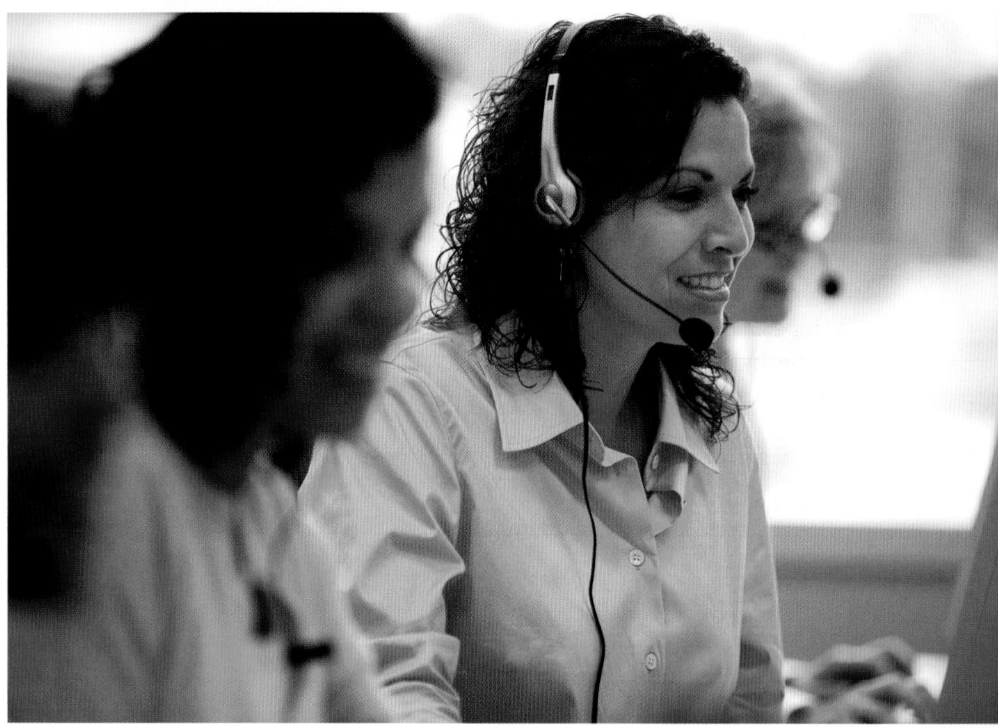

1 **Who are your internal customers? Do you treat them differently to external customers?**

2 **19▷ Read the *Context*. Listen to three phone conversations workers at JC have with both internal and external customers and complete these forms.**

1

PROCUREMENT DEPT.
INTERNAL ORDER FORM

Name: Paola
Dept: 1 ____
Country: Italy
Order for: 2 ____
Order no.: 3 ____
Approval date deadline: 4 ____
Notes: 5 ____

2

IT HELP DESK CALL LOG

Caller: Johann
Country: Denmark
Problem: 6 ____
Action: 7 ____

3

CUSTOMER SERVICES
COMPLAINT FORM

Customer: Donna Fitzpatrick
Company: 8 ____
Order no.: 560H
Complaint: 9 ____
Action: 10 ____

Tip | *by* and *until*

Use *by* to refer to a deadline or the latest date when something must be finished.

I need the report ***by*** *Friday.*

Use *until* to refer to a period of time to do something in.

We have ***until*** *Friday to finish the report.*

3 **19▷ Listen again. For each conversation, make a note of the phrases the speakers use to**

1 make an initial request for information about the problem or situation
2 ask further questions to establish the facts about the problem or situation
3 clarify / check the facts and information
4 promise action
5 refer to time or deadlines.

» For more exercises, go to **Practice file 5** on page 110.

4 **Work with a partner. You are going to deal with a phone call from an internal customer. Student A, turn to File 36 on page 146. Student B, use the information below. Read your information and take turns to make and receive the call. Make sure you**

- request information about the problem or situation and establish the facts
- clarify the information and check that it is correct
- promise action.

Student B

1 You work in the Sales Department and call the Communications Department.
Problem: the dates for your business trip have changed.
Further information: you need the original flight cancelling and a new one booking; this also applies to the hotel.
Deadline: by next week.

2 You work in the Travel and Logistics Department and receive a call from an internal customer.
Action to promise: email new details as soon as you have them.

5 **Work with a partner. Decide what phrases the caller and receiver might use in these situations. Then take turns to make and receive a call.**

1 A team leader from Operations calls Human Resources. The employment contracts for two new workers are needed by the end of the day – there's already been a delay of six weeks.

2 The Communications Officer from a company calls a printing company. The company magazine hasn't arrived and it is due to be sent out to employees tomorrow.

ⓘ » Interactive Workbook » **Email**

Key expressions

Requesting information
What seems to be the problem?
How can I help (you)?
What can I do for you (today)?

Establishing the facts
Can / Could you tell me when …?
Can / Could you explain exactly what the problem is?
Can / Could you give me …?
Talk me through (it / what happened).

Clarifying / Checking facts
Let me get this straight …
What you're saying is …
You mean …?
If I understand you correctly, …
Could I just clarify what you're saying?

Promising action
I'll look into it straightaway.
What I'll do is … and …
I'm going to have to look into this.
I'll get back to you (shortly).
Once I've / As soon as I've …, I'll call you back.

Referring to time / deadlines
by (Friday) at the latest
by tomorrow / lunchtime / the end of the week
in time for the deadline
as soon as
shortly

ⓘ » Interactive Workbook » **Phrasebank**

Practically speaking | Reassuring and sympathizing

1 **20▷ Listen to four short conversations at work. What has happened in each situation?**

2 **20▷ Listen again. How does the first speaker ask about the situation in each conversation?**

3 **Which is the best response to each situation, a or b? Why?**

1 a Forget it. b I know it's hard at first, but you'll soon find your feet.
2 a I'm sure you did the best you could. b It sounds as if you don't care.
3 a You did the right thing. b How awful!
4 a You couldn't have done any more. b Oh no!

4 **21▷ Listen and check your answers.**

5 **Work with a partner. Have similar short conversations using these situations (or ones of your own). Refer to the *Useful phrases* on page 134.**

- a difficult interview
- an argument with a colleague
- a long negotiation about a new company policy
- a tough presentation to a new client
- a call to a customer to say a product has been discontinued

ⓘ » Interactive Workbook » **Glossary**

Language at work | Direct and indirect questions

1 Match the indirect questions (a–e) from audio 19▷ to the equivalent direct questions (1–5).

a Can you tell me when you sent it to us?
b Could you explain exactly what the problem is?
c Do you know why it's doing this?
d Can you tell me if you've got an order number?
e Could you let me know how long it will take?

1 Why is it doing this? ___
2 How long will it take? ___
3 Have you got an order number? ___
4 When did you send it to us? ___
5 What exactly is the problem? ___

2 When might you use an indirect question rather than a direct question? How do you change a direct question into an indirect question?

» For more information and exercises, go to **Practice file 5** on page 111.

3 Work with a partner. Think of two direct and two indirect questions to ask for each of these situations.

Example: You want to see the store manager to make a complaint, but he is out.
When will the manager be back? / Do you know when the manager will be back?

1 A customer is calling about an ongoing complaint. You need to know which of your colleagues the customer spoke to last time.
2 You are arranging a delivery for an important client. You want to know whether morning, afternoon or evening would be the most convenient time for delivery.
3 A customer is very agitated and upset. You can see that something is wrong, but it is difficult to understand what she is trying to say.
4 You are waiting at a station for a train that is over an hour late. You think it may have been cancelled and go to the information desk to find out.
5 A customer is calling about a faulty product. It may still be under guarantee, so you need to find out how long the customer has had it.

4 Work with a partner. Student A, turn to File 11 on page 139. Student B, use the information below. Think about what questions you need to ask to get the information you need. (Use a mix of direct and indirect questions as appropriate.)

Student B

1 You work in a travel agency in Amsterdam. Use this information to answer your partner's questions about flights to / from New York and hotel accommodation.

10.00	Depart Amsterdam (AMS)	Tue 20 Mar	Delta 81	€980 rtn
13.00	Arrive New York (JFK)	Duration: 8 hr	Direct flight	
17.40	Depart New York (JFK)	Fri 23 Mar	Delta 80	
06.45	Arrive Amsterdam (AMS)	Duration: 8 hr 5 min	Direct flight	

Park Central Hotel

Location: across from Carnegie Hall, one block from Broadway, two blocks from Fifth Avenue

Cost: €1,060 for three nights (accommodation only)

2 You are staying at a hotel in Prague. Ask at Reception for suggestions for things to do in the city. Find out about:

- places of interest
- opening hours
- cost of entrance
- how to get there

ⓘ » Interactive Workbook » **Exercises and Tests**

Tip | Using different types of question

Use indirect questions
- to open an enquiry or change to a new topic of enquiry
- to establish a level of politeness
- to ask for sensitive or complex information.

Use direct questions
- to ask follow-up questions
- to be more focused or direct
- to ask for simple factual information.

Dealing with customer service problems

Background

Differing expectations of customer service?

CBE Brasilia supplies companies around the world with first-class coffee beans. One of its clients is Kool Kaffee, a chain of popular coffee shops, originating in Germany, but now doing business in most German-speaking countries as well as a few of its eastern European neighbours. Recently, Kool Kaffee has experienced a problem with one of its Internet orders with CBE Brasilia.

- 1 March – a bulk order of coffee beans was made.
- 2 April – delivery arrived but Premium Selection and Midnight Espresso beans were missing; there was no documentation from CBE concerning the order – only the documents on the package from the shipping company.
- Kool Kaffee called customer services immediately. They were polite and friendly but said there was no record of the order being placed. Further calls were made to customer services on 4, 10, 11 April. An email was sent 16 April.
- Kool Kaffee called again on 18 April and were told there was no record of the order or of their communication with the company since the incomplete delivery.
- CBE Accounts Department was contacted. They found a receipt and details of a delivery with the signature, 'dot.com'. However, this receipt was for the same goods but for Kool Kaffee CH – the Zurich office, which made a purchase on the same day.

Discussion

1 **What's your opinion of the way that CBE Brasilia dealt with the situation? Could it have dealt with the problem more effectively? Could the problem be related to the different expectations each culture has of customer service?**

2 22▷ **Listen to José Buenadir from CBE Brasilia describe the problem and how it was resolved.**

1 Was this a satisfactory resolution to the problem? Why or why not?
2 What lessons should the company learn from this situation?
3 What changes could it make to improve its customer service?

Task

1 **Work with a partner. Student A, turn to File 13 on page 139. Student B, turn to File 33 on page 145. You are going to make two phone calls each: one to an internal customer and one to an external customer. Read each situation and then make and receive the calls.**

2 **Form two groups, Student As and Student Bs.**

1 Consider the two situations where you received the call. Which course of action did you promise your client? Turn to File 48 on page 149 and work out your score.
2 Do you agree with the score and explanation?

The Expert View

Expectations of what constitutes good customer service are always influenced to a degree by cultural values. So a disagreement between two businesses over a customer service issue may be as much about different expectations and attitudes as about the business issue itself. If one party believes they are dealing with the problem in an acceptable way, it may be difficult for them to understand why the other party is not satisfied with their response. When dealing with a customer service enquiry in an international context, it's important always to consider what outcome the other person is looking for. What are they really concerned about, and what do they expect to happen?

Stephen Regan, Lecturer in Management Economics
Cranfield School of Management

Case study

6 Ethical business

Learning objectives in this unit

- Talking about ethical business
- Explaining plans and arrangements
- Inviting and recommending
- Responding to spontaneous invitations
- Talking about the future

Case study

- Promoting ethical business

Starting point

1. **What effect (positive or negative) can companies have on the environment and the local community?**
2. **Do you know of any companies that are well known for their social responsibility? Is this a selling point for the company?**
3. **Do you know of any companies that have an image problem because of their activities?**

Working with words | Ethical business

1. **Work with a partner. What are the characteristics of an 'ethical business'?**
2. **Read the text about a company called Patagonia. In what ways is the company an ethical business? How does this compare to your ideas in 1?**

Our Reason for Being

Patagonia grew out of a small company that made tools for climbers. Mountain climbing is still at the heart of our business, but we also make clothes for skiing, snowboarding, surfing, fly fishing, paddling and trail running. All of these are silent sports. They don't require a motor or the cheers of a crowd – the rewards come from connecting with nature.

Our values reflect a business that was started by a band of climbers and surfers who love wild and beautiful places. This means that we act responsibly and take an active part in the fight to repair the damage that is being done to the health of our planet.

We acknowledge that the wild world we love best is disappearing. That is why we share a strong commitment to protecting natural lands and waters. Caring for the environment is very important to us. We donate our time, services and at least 1% of our sales to hundreds of environmental groups all over the world who are working to protect and restore the environment.

But we also know that our business activity – from lighting our stores to dyeing shirts – creates pollution as a by-product. So we work steadily to reduce the impact we have, and do more than simply comply with the regulations. We use recycled polyester in many of our clothes and only organic, rather than pesticide-intensive, cotton.

Staying true to our principles during thirty-plus years in business has helped us create a company we're proud to run and work for.

3. **Read the text again and answer questions 1–5.**
   1. How have the company's founders influenced what the company does now?
   2. What does the company have a commitment to? How does it show this commitment?
   3. What points are made about the manufacturing process?
   4. Why are the owners proud of the company?
   5. Do you or would you buy products from companies like Patagonia? How important is it for you to buy products from ethical companies?

4 **Choose a word / phrase from A and B to make phrases to complete the questions.**

A		B	
act	comply with	time	an active part in
share	reduce	responsibly	true to its principles
take	donate	the impact	a strong commitment to
stay		regulations	

1 Do most companies in your country always ________________ or do they sometimes bend the rules?
2 Do you know of any companies that ________________, services or money to help local organizations?
3 How can businesses ________________ they have on the environment?
4 Why should a company ________________ and deal with any pollution that is a by-product of its business activity?
5 Does your company ________________ the life of the local community. If so, what does it do?
6 Should a company ________________ and values even if this means a loss of profit?
7 What companies in your country ________________ protecting the environment?

5 **Work with a partner. Ask and answer the questions in 4.**

6 **23▷ Listen to a radio interviewer questioning Shamsul Aziz, a spokesperson for a leading gas and oil exploration company. Answer questions 1–4.**

1 How would you describe the interviewer's style?
2 How does the spokesperson react to the questions?
3 What does the company do for
   a its staff? **b** the environment? **c** the local communities where it operates?
4 Do you think the company is doing enough for the environment and local community?

7 **Which of these nouns from audio 23▷ do you associate with**

1 an ethical company?
2 an unethical company?

bribery ethics deception responsibility fairness generosity values corruption prejudice credibility greed discrimination

8 **Complete the table with the adjectives of these nouns from 7.**

Noun	Adjective	Noun	Adjective
deception		ethics	
responsibility		corruption	
fairness		prejudice	
generosity		greed	
credibility		discrimination	

9 **Work with a partner. Turn to File 14 on page 140. Read about two companies and discuss how ethical you think they are, using some of the nouns and adjectives in 7 and 8.**

» For more exercises, go to **Practice file 6** on page 112.

10 **Work in small groups to prepare a short speech at a press conference. Follow the instructions in File 16 on page 140.**

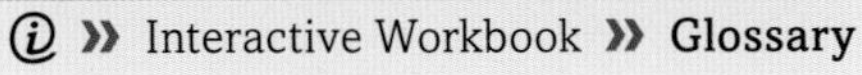

Context

Hummingbird Teas sells speciality teas from China, India and South Africa. The unique selling point of the business is its ethos. It sources teas from small, local farmers and supports fair trade. It has recently brought in Clare, from a PR company, to help raise its profile. Clare has been organizing a trip for reporters from ethical consumer magazines to see Hummingbird's operation. She is meeting with the reporters to give details of the trip.

Presenting | Explaining plans and arrangements | Inviting and recommending

1 24▷ **Read the *Context*. Listen to Part 1 of the meeting and make any necessary changes to these notes.**

- Trip planned to China or South Africa (to be confirmed)
- Five days travelling around different tea plantations
- Opportunities for sightseeing will be provided
- Two possible dates for trip: February and March
- Two internal flights

2 24▷ **Listen again. Complete these phrases for explaining the plans and arrangements for the trip.**

1 We ________ once you've decided what you'd like to see.
2 So, ________ how Hummingbird's operation works in China.
3 The ________ spend four days at one of the sites where the tea is grown.
4 You ________ accompany the workers in their daily work.
5 We've looked at all the options, and ________ two dates.

3 25▷ **Listen to Part 2 of the meeting.**

1 What activities and visits can the reporters take part in?
2 What advice does Clare give about the guide?

4 25▷ **Listen again and complete these phrases.**

1 We ________ watch the tea being prepared.
2 English isn't spoken so ________ with our guide.
3 On the subject of language – ________ a project set up to promote schooling in the Tibetan language.
4 That ________ really interesting.
I ________.
5 … as it ________ travel with our interpreter.
6 A visit to the site ________.
7 I was there for the first time last month … It's ________.
8 Mmm … ________ I'm looking for.
9 Well, alternatively, ________ introduce you to the team who work for Hummingbird in China.
10 That would be great – ________.

Tip | *advise* and *recommend*

Advise and *recommend* are both quite formal ways of making a suggestion. Be careful with the word order.

*We **advise** you to set this up directly (with the locals).*
*We **recommend** (that) you stay with our guide.*

5 **Put the phrases in 4 into these categories.**

a Inviting: ______

b Recommending: ______

c Responding to an invitation or recommendation: ______

» For more exercises, go to **Practice file 6** on page 112.

6 **Read this information about activities organized by Hummingbird Teas. Work with a partner. Choose information A or B and take turns to invite and make recommendations of things to do or points to look out for. Decide for yourself if you want to accept or decline.**

A

Hummingbird Teas

Invitation: Information day – How and why does Hummingbird Teas practise fair trade?

Recommended activities on the day:

- Presentation about the Slow Food movement in Europe and how Hummingbird Teas' activities complement this
- Tea tasting – rare and exotic teas

Advice: Arrive early for tea tasting – only ten people in each group

B

Hummingbird Teas

Invitation: Informal visit day, including presentation – The man behind Rooibos tea

Recommended activities on the day:

- Hummingbird Teas helps to make a difference – Slide show of tree replanting in the Himalayas
- Tea-making workshop – How to make the perfect cuppa

Advice: Taste teas at workshop before buying

7 **Work with a partner. Your company has arranged an open day to give customers an insight into its operation. (If you don't work for a company, use File 15 on page 140.)**

1 Make a list of
- the things you plan to show your guests on the day
- any recommendations of things to do or points to look out for
- things you hope to invite your guests to do.

2 Find another partner (from a different company if possible). Take turns to
- explain your plans for the day
- make any recommendations
- invite your partner to do things
- respond appropriately.

(i) » Interactive Workbook » **Email**

Key expressions

Explaining plans and arrangements

We'll email you the (final) itinerary.
We're planning to …
The idea is to …
We're going to arrange …
You'll get the opportunity to …
The flight leaves on …

Inviting

We'd like to invite you to …
You're welcome to …
Alternatively, we'd be delighted to …

Recommending

We strongly recommend you …
It would be a good idea to …
… is highly recommended.
It's well worth a visit.

Responding

That would be great.
That sounds really interesting.
Good idea.
That makes sense.
I'd like to take you up on that.
It's just the kind of thing I need.
That's not really what I'm looking for.

(i) » Interactive Workbook
» **Phrasebank**

Practically speaking | Responding to spontaneous invitations

1 **26▷ Listen to three invitations and answer questions 1–2.**

1 What are the people being invited to do?

2 Are the invitations accepted (*A*), partly accepted (*P*) or declined (*D*)?

2 **26▷ Listen again. What phrases do the speakers use to**

1 invite?
2 accept?
3 partly accept?
4 decline?

3 **Invite as many people as you can to these activities (or make up your own). When you receive an invitation, decide if you want to accept, partly accept or decline. Refer to the *Useful phrases* on page 134.**

- go to the cinema (to see?)
- watch a football match (which team?)
- go to the theatre (to see?)
- go for dinner (where?)
- go swimming in the lunch break (where?)
- have a coffee (where?)

Language at work | Talking about the future

1 Match these extracts from audio 24▷ and 25▷ to situations 1–5. What tense is used in each situation?

a She'**s coming** in later on this morning to speak with you.
b This **will give** you a real insight into their lives.
c We've looked at all the options, and we'**re going to** arrange two dates.
d The February flight **leaves** on the 15th.
e A ... it would be a good idea to travel with our interpreter.
  B That makes sense. We'**ll speak** to our colleagues and let you know.

1 someone making a decision as they speak ___
2 someone talking about a plan, intention, something they have already decided to do ___
3 someone talking about an appointment or arrangement ___
4 someone making a prediction ___
5 someone talking about a timetable or schedule ___

» For more information and exercises, go to **Practice file 6** on page 113.

2 Work with a partner. Decide which option in *italics* is not possible in each sentence.

1 I can't see you on Friday – I'*ll do* / *'m going to do* / *'m doing* a training course in London.
2 According to the weather forecast, it'*ll be* / *'s going to be* / *'s being* hot tomorrow.
3 The flight from Paris *arrives* / *is going to arrive* in Tokyo at 10.45 each day.
4 A By the way, I'm out of the office tomorrow.
  B OK, I'*ll let* / *'m letting* Christina know.
5 I'm not in the office on Monday – I'*m going* / *'m going to go* / *'ll go* to an exhibition.
6 I *meet* / *'m meeting* / *'m going to meet* with Mrs Brasseler at 3.30 this afternoon.
7 A Could you give me some information about Mr Ward's visit?
  B Of course, I *email* / *'ll email* the details now.
8 I think Greta *is noticing* / *will notice* a lot of changes in the office when she returns from maternity leave.

3 Work with a partner. Ask and answer these questions using *will, going to,* the present continuous or the present simple.

1 Have you got a busy weekend?
2 Are you doing anything tonight?
3 What's the weather forecast for the weekend?
4 What time is the last train?
5 What do you think about the threat of global warming?
6 Are you free tomorrow afternoon?
7 Have you booked your next holiday?
8 What plans have you got for projects at work or home?

4 Write future dates and times that are important for you on a piece of paper. Think of work commitments, career plans or key events for your company. Use words like *in 2012, 7.30 tonight, next Friday, next October, when I am 60,* etc. Compare your dates with a partner. Ask them to explain the importance of each date.

Example: *A Why is 25 May 2019 important?*
B That's when the company ***will*** *be exactly 50 years old. We'**re going to** have a big celebration with all our major clients – it* ***will*** *be a big achievement for us.*

ⓘ » Interactive Workbook » **Exercises and Tests**

Promoting ethical business

Background

A Tribes Travel

Core business: fair trade, ecotourism and responsible travel

- We use a Fairtrade travel mark for all our ecotourism. This involves: paying people a fair wage for the services they provide, making sure these people aren't exploited, and ensuring our tourism (and money generated from this) has a positive effect on local people and the environment.
- We promote learning about each other's cultures through local guides and involve local people in the trips.
- Our tourist groups are small to ensure minimum impact on the wildlife, environment and local communities.
- We have an affiliated charity which supports poverty reduction, education, cultural preservation and conservation projects within areas affected by tourism.

B Ben & Jerry's Ice Cream

Core business: selling ice cream

Company's mission is to inform public about and assist in ethical and environmental matters.

Our projects are

- the Climate Change College (being run in many countries) – to inform about changing climate
- UK: working with the Fairtrade Foundation to buy sugar from Paraguay and vanilla from India for vanilla ice cream
- global warming project: plant in Netherlands uses renewable energy for manufacturing (wind, sun, water, biomass); factories in Vermont have invested in wind energy and plan to reduce CO^2 emissions by 10% in the next three years
- buying 'climate tickets' to fly our businesspeople – to counteract the effect of flying on the environment.

Discussion

1 **Who are the likely target customers for each of the products? What kinds of things matter to these customers?**

2 **How do the companies' activities promote their ethical position?**

Task

1 **Work in two groups. Choose company A or B. You are going to plan an event or a series of events to inform a wider market about the company's operation and activities.**
   1 Decide what events / activities could raise the profile of the company's ethical position.
   2 Make a plan of the event(s).

2 **Prepare a brief, informal presentation.**
   Part 1: Give details about what the company does. Explain its position on ethical matters.
   Part 2: Explain the plans and arrangements for the event(s). Include invitations and recommendations as appropriate.

3 **Each group gives its presentation to the class. While you are listening to the presentations, decide which company seems to be the most ethical. After all the presentations, vote for your favourite in terms of ethical position and ideas for events.**

The Expert View

There are higher expectations of business today from customers, employees, and even investors to minimize negative environmental and social impacts, and to maximize positive ones. This is frequently described as corporate responsibility, or running a business in an ethical and sustainable manner. Leading companies have realized that this is not just about risk-minimization – it can also be a way of maximizing business opportunities. Such businesses recognize that a genuine commitment to operating ethically and sustainably can be a source of competitive advantage. Certainly, corporate responsibility cannot be treated as an 'extra'– it has to be built into business purpose and strategy.

David Grayson, Professor of Corporate Responsibility

Cranfield School of Management

Case study

7 | Making decisions

Learning objectives in this unit

- Talking about personality and decision-making
- Participating in a decision-making meeting
- Talking about social plans
- Talking about countability and quantity

Case study

- Resolving an expansion crisis

Starting point

1. Think of one or two good decisions you have made. How much were you guided by facts and figures? How much did you follow your intuition?
2. Does having more time produce better decisions? Or do you decide faster *and* more wisely when under pressure?

Working with words | Personality and decision-making

1 Read this text about personality and decision-making. Which personality type

1 thinks it's important to be on time?
2 enjoys an argument?
3 finds it hard to concentrate on one thing at once?
4 is more interested in the future than the past?

Are you an extrovert or an introvert?

Extroverts are often **outgoing** and enthusiastic. They are good with people and enjoy a public role. They prefer to do lots of things at once and can be easily distracted. They're talkers rather than listeners and can be **impulsive**.

Introverts are often **self-contained** and reserved. They can be very **focused** when working on tasks and prefer to focus on one thing at a time. They are good listeners, they think before they act and prefer to be behind the scenes.

Are you a sensor or an intuitive?

Sensors are often sensible and **pragmatic**. They are good at understanding details and remembering facts and specifics. They are reliable and **methodical** and work at a steady pace. They trust their own experience and use established skills.

Intuitives are often energetic and **creative**. They like to focus on the big picture and on future possibilities. They like things that are new and different and prefer to learn new skills. They are **thoughtful** when making decisions and trust their instincts.

Are you a thinker or a feeler?

Thinkers usually take a **rational** approach to decision-making and prefer to remain **detached**. They are honest and direct, valuing fairness. They can be ambitious and critical. They take few things personally and like arguing and debating issues for fun.

Feelers are often **instinctive** in their decisions rather than relying on facts or reasons. **Tactful** and diplomatic, they avoid arguments and take many things personally. They appear warm and friendly, like to be appreciated and are good at complimenting others.

Are you a judger or a perceiver?

Judgers often make decisions easily and quickly. They appreciate plans, rules and schedules and are usually punctual. They are **determined**, keep to their deadlines and like to complete projects. They are serious and **conventional**, and like decisiveness in others.

Perceivers are often **indecisive**; they like to be **flexible** and to keep their options open. Being unconventional, they dislike rules and deadlines. They like to start projects and prefer to play now and work later.

2 **Match the adjectives in bold in the text to these statements.**

1 'I am not influenced by other people or my emotions.' *detached*
2 'I always do things in a careful and well-ordered way.' ______
3 'I find it hard to make up my mind about things.' ______
4 'I focus on what I want to do and don't let anyone stop me.' ______
5 'I do things based on my own feelings.' ______
6 'I am happy to change my plans when necessary to suit my friends.' ______
7 'I am confident and friendly.' ______
8 'I like to think about things carefully.' ______
9 'I can produce new things using my imagination.' ______
10 'I do what is normal and acceptable.' ______
11 'I make decisions objectively.' ______
12 'I don't do things that will upset or annoy people.' ______
13 'I depend on myself.' ______
14 'I pay careful attention to what I'm doing.' ______
15 'I do things as I think of them without considering the consequences.' ______
16 'I like to find practical solutions to problems.' ______

3 **Work with a partner. Choose five of the adjectives in 2 and explain what kind of people you like to work with the most and why. Then choose another five adjectives and explain what kind of people you like to work with the least and why.**

4 **Work with a partner.**

1 Find things in the text that the personality types
 a are good at / with **b** like / prefer to do.
2 What are you good at / with? How do you like / prefer to approach decision-making?

5 **Decide which personality type you are most like in each section in the text.**

1 Write down the letter for the type you choose in each section.
 - Extrovert (E) or Introvert (I)? ___
 - Thinker (T) or Feeler (F)? ___
 - Sensor (S) or Intuitive (N)? ___
 - Judger (J) or Perceiver (P)? ___
2 Turn to File 18 on page 141 to find out what your choice reveals about you.
3 Share the information with a partner. Say if you agree or disagree with it and why.

6 **27▷ Listen to four people talking about decision-making. Which personality type best applies to each speaker?**

Speaker 1: Extrovert or Introvert?
Speaker 2: Sensor or Intuitive?
Speaker 3: Thinker or Feeler?
Speaker 4: Judger or Perceiver?

7 **Match the verbs in A to the noun phrases in B to make phrases from audio 27▷.**

A		B	
weigh up	consider	(my) own judgment	different perspectives
delay	have confidence in	my decision	all the options
rely on	get	two things	my instincts
trust	decide between	feelings	information

8 **Work with a partner. Use the phrases in 7 to talk about the way you made one or two recent decisions in or out of work.**

» For more exercises, go to **Practice file 7** on page 114.

9 **Work with a partner. What personality types from the text would be most suitable for these jobs and why?**

- air traffic controller
- human resources manager
- sales manager
- office administrator
- website designer
- accounts controller

ⓘ » Interactive Workbook » **Glossary**

Tip | *good at / good with*

Use *good at (something / doing something)* to talk about a skill or activity.

*Marc is **good at** languages / speaking Italian.*

Use *good with (something / somebody)* to talk about using something or dealing with someone.

*Joel is **good with** people.*

Context

The Scandinavian company KYM has a budget deficit. Each region has been asked to cut costs. Three regional customer service managers (Jens from Denmark, Matt from Finland, Anna from Sweden) are meeting to discuss where savings can be made. The meeting is led by Sinead, a consultant brought in to oversee the measures.

Meetings | Participating in a decision-making meeting

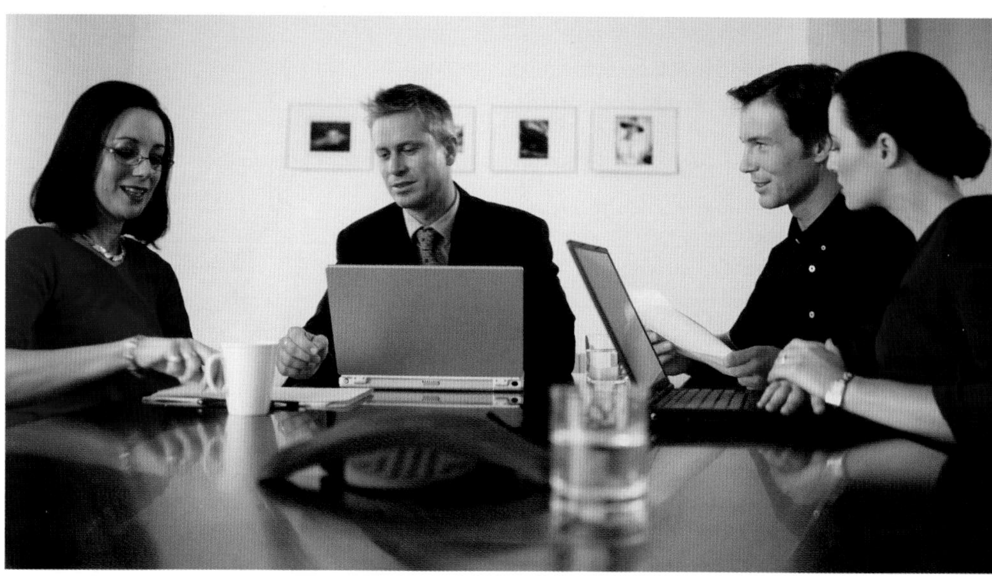

1 **28▷ Read the *Context*. Listen to the meeting and tick (✓) the points discussed.**

1 Freeze on recruitment ___
2 Cut back on overtime ___
3 Reduce office resources ___
4 Change telephone provider ___
5 Reduce client expense accounts ___
6 Cut back on business trips ___

2 **28▷ Listen again and complete the phrases in these sentences.**

1 Yes, well, ______________________ our costs for personnel are very high.
2 … number of employees. ______________________ the overtime figures. They're ______________________, and they're costing us …
3 The ______________________, we need to look at why we have so much overtime.
4 … a lot of waste. ______________________ printing emails out on expensive copy paper.
5 So ______________________ is monitoring the office supplies …
6 I'm ______________________.
7 As ______________________, we'd make hardly any savings …
8 Matt ______________________. But ______________________ cut expense accounts …

3 **Put the phrases in 2 into these categories.**

a Presenting / Supporting an argument: ________
b Giving an opinion: ________
c Responding to an opinion / argument: ________
d Clarifying a point: ________

4 **Sinead is leading the discussion. Turn to audio script 28▷ on page 156 and underline the phrases she uses to**

1 set the agenda for the discussion
2 manage turn-taking
3 invite people to express their opinions
4 move on to a different topic
5 indicate enough time has been spent on a topic
6 monitor action points.

» For more exercises, go to **Practice file 7** on page 114.

Tip | *getting at*

Use *getting at* to talk about what someone means.

*What **are** you **getting at**?*
*So what you**'re getting at** is …*

5 **Work in small groups. You are going to continue the meeting from audio 28▷.**

1 Look at this agenda item and decide on your opinion of each suggestion. Add two extra suggestions to the list.

Reduce staff benefits / activities

- reduce subsidies in staff cafeteria
- cancel annual staff away day
- restrict Christmas event to staff only
- introduce a PIN number for photocopying and limit number of copies per person

2 Choose eight phrases from *Key expressions* that you have never used or are not very familiar with. Write these on separate cards / pieces of paper. (Don't include phrases from *Leading the discussion.*)

3 Continue the meeting from audio **28**▷. As you participate, 'play' your phrase cards by placing them in front of you when you use the phrase correctly. Your colleagues will return the card to you if the phrase is used incorrectly.

4 The winner is the first person to play all their cards.

6 **Work in groups of four. You are at a departmental meeting. You have €50,000 left in your annual budget. As a group, try to decide how to spend the money.**

1 Before the meeting do the following.
- Decide on what type of department you are.
- Make a list of five suggestions for spending the money (the money can be divided between more than one idea).

2 Prepare for the meeting with a partner. Decide which suggestions on the list you agree / disagree with and think of arguments to support your opinions.

3 Hold the meeting, taking turns to lead the discussion.

4 Report back to the class on any decisions you made.

ⓘ » Interactive Workbook » **Email**

Practically speaking | Talking about social plans

1 **29▷ Listen to five short conversations about plans for the evening / weekend / holidays. In which conversation is the second speaker**

a certain about plans? ___

b certain about plans but unhappy with them? ___

c certain about having no plans? ___

d fairly certain about plans? ___

e uncertain about plans? ___

2 **29▷ Listen again. For each conversation, make a note of the phrases used to**

1 ask about plans

2 respond to a question about plans

3 react to someone's plans.

3 **Talk to as many people as possible in the class. Ask and answer questions about your evening / weekend / holiday plans. Refer to the *Useful phrases* on page 134.**

Key expressions

Presenting / Supporting an argument

If we look at the facts, we'll see …
Look at … They're here in black and white …
The fact is … / The thing is …
The advantage / drawback is …
If we …, it'll mean …
A classic example is …

Giving an opinion

I (don't) think (we should) …
If you ask me, we should …
…, that's my view.
In my opinion, …
As far as I'm concerned, …
I think it would be crazy to …

Responding to opinions / arguments

Exactly / Absolutely.
You're right / X is right.
What … says is right.
Yes, but …
I'm not convinced.

Clarifying

Could you give us some detail, please?
What I mean is …
So what you're getting at is …
In other words …

Leading the discussion

Today, I'd like to establish …
(Jens), could you start us off, please?
What's your position on this?
Hang on, let's hear what (Jens) has to say …
I don't want to spend too long on this point.
Can we move on to …?
Let's turn to the next item …
Let's look into it … and discuss it again at our next meeting.
Let's draw up some action points on …

ⓘ » Interactive Workbook » **Phrasebank**

Language at work | Countability | Expressing quantity

1 **Read these extracts from audio 28▷. Match the nouns in bold to 1, 2 or 3.**

a We'll find there's a lot of **waste**.
b It could be a **project** for one of our work experience students.
c We'd make hardly any **savings**.
d We need to look at why we have so much **overtime**.
e We should look carefully at client travel **expenses**.
f I don't want to spend too long on this **point**.

1 a singular countable noun ________
2 a plural countable noun ________
3 an uncountable noun ________

2 **Decide if these nouns are countable (*C*), uncountable (*U*), or both (*C/U*). If the noun can be both, is there a difference in meaning between the two options?**

news product colleague expenditure paper information suggestion business travel experience time fact accommodation journey software correspondence proposal money equipment insurance document advice

3 **Put three more of the nouns in 2 into each box in the diagram (make the nouns plural if necessary).**

a / an / the / one	*product* ________
(too) many, (not) many, (a) few, fewer, very few	*facts* ________
lots of, plenty of, more, most, some, (not) enough, hardly any, (not) any	*facts* ________ / *news* ________
(too) much, (not) much, a little, less, very little	*news* ________

4 **Complete the sentences with these quantifiers.**

too much any enough very little a some too many fewer

1 There's ________ money left in the budget so we can't buy that new software.
2 The meeting went well – there were ________ points of disagreement than expected.
3 The project is late because we spent ________ time on the planning stage.
4 I need ________ information about hotels in the area.
5 They didn't take ________ of my suggestions on board at all.
6 We haven't got ________ chairs for the meeting – could you get a couple more?
7 Currently we're employing ________ people – we have to make some cuts.
8 Would you like ________ drink?

» For more information and exercises, go to **Practice File 7** on page 115.

5 **Work with a partner. Compare these situations, using as many of the phrases in 3 as you can.**

- working for a multinational company vs working for a small family firm
- communicating by email and text vs communicating face to face
- working with an experienced colleague vs working with a trainee

6 **Work in small groups.**

1 Discuss how you could improve the services and facilities in the building / local area / town or city where you work.
2 Present your ideas to the class and give reasons for the improvements.

ⓘ » Interactive Workbook » **Exercises and Tests**

Tip | *most*

Use *most* to refer to something in general.
Most *people have jobs.*
Use *most of the* to refer to a more specific group.
Most *of the people I know have jobs.*
Remember not to say ~~*the most people.*~~

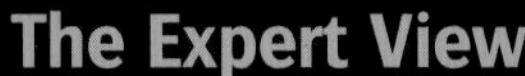

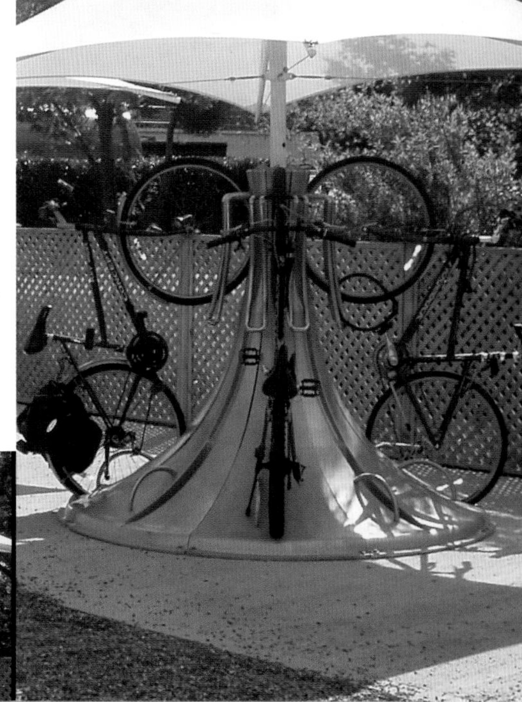

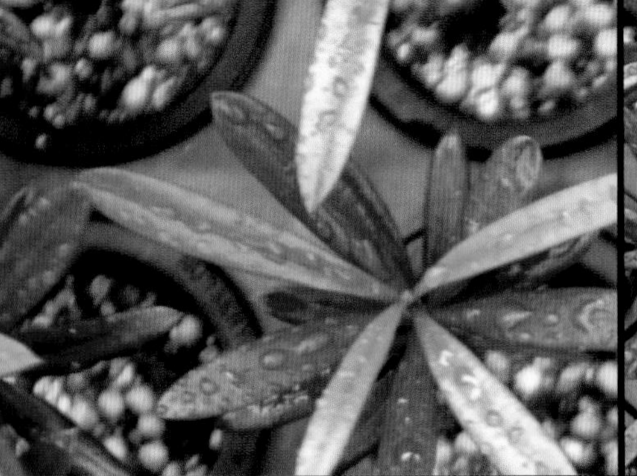
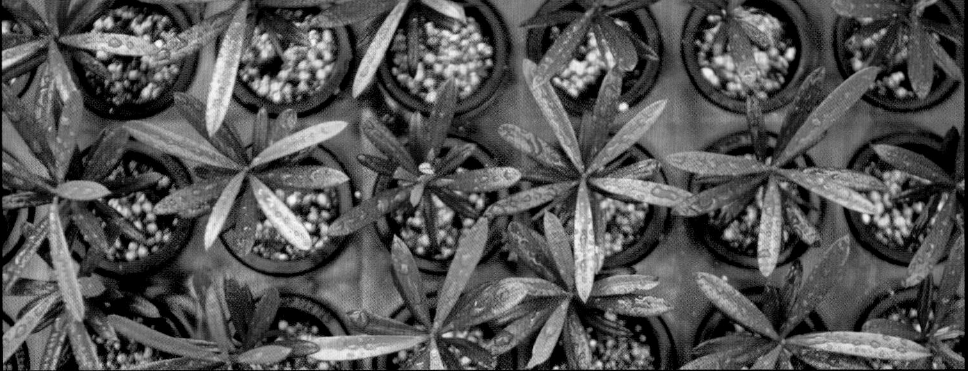

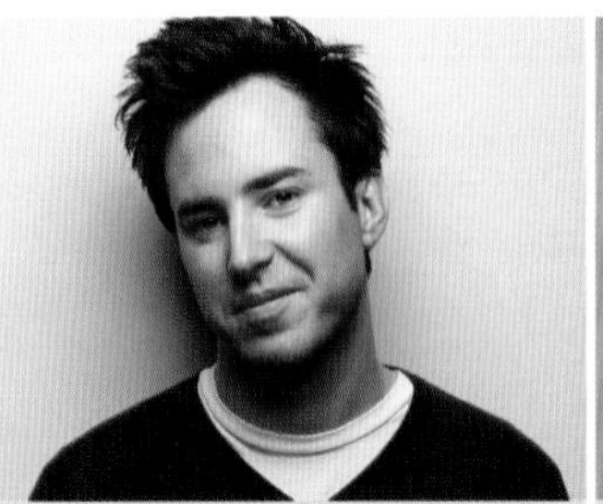
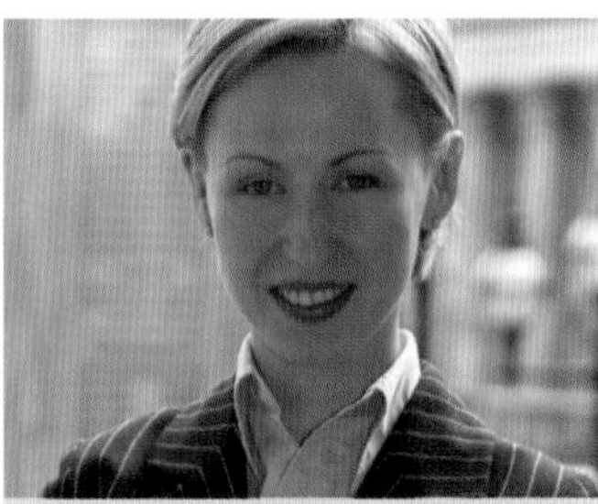

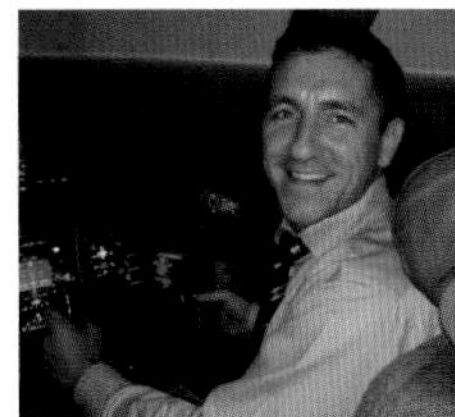

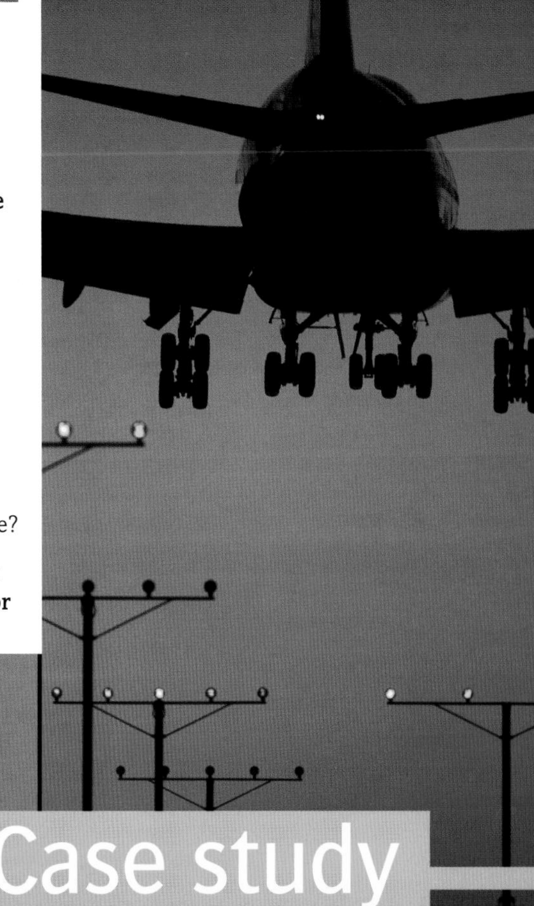

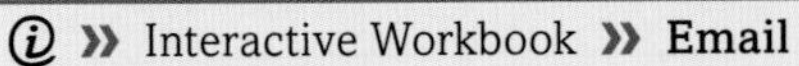
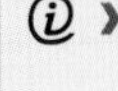

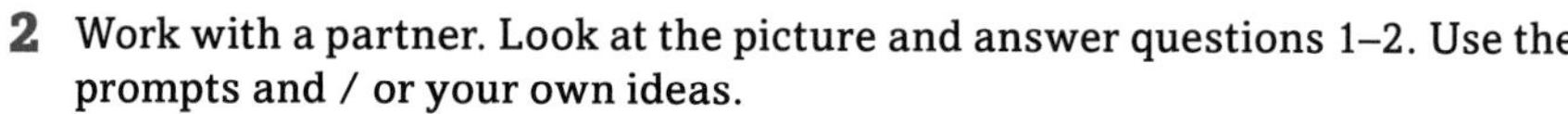

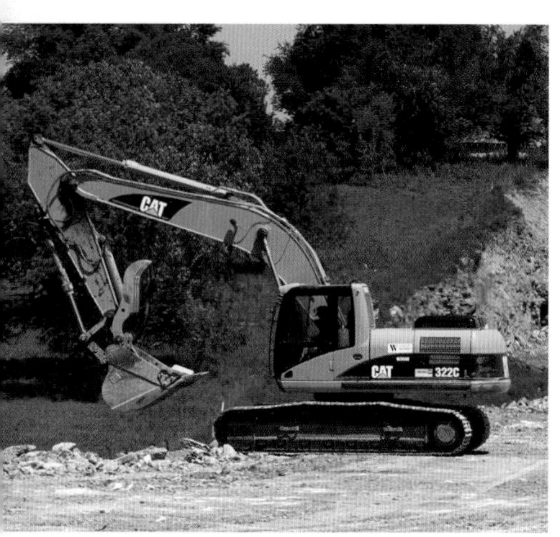

3 **What do these numbers refer to in the text? How do you say them?**

1 10^{18}	6 20th
2 28.8	7 206.2%
3 1910	8 21st
4 2007	9 5,000 nm
5 $^1/_{10}$	10 322,000,000

4 **Match the words / phrases in bold in the text to these words / phrases with a similar meaning.**

1 marginally: ____________________
2 a little more than: ____________________
3 a great deal: ____________________
4 just under: ____________________
5 roughly: ____________________
6 about: ____________________

5 **Work with a partner. Ask and answer questions 1–5. It is unlikely you will know the exact figures so use the words / phrases in 4 to give an estimate.**

1 What's the average price of a car (economy, mid-range, luxury) in your country?
2 How much does your family spend on travel costs each month?
3 What percentage of items in your home contain electronic chips?
4 What Internet connection speeds are currently available?
5 How many emails do you get in a week? What percentage of these are useful?

6 **51▷ Listen to an Irish music producer being interviewed about music downloads on the Internet. What does he say about**

1 downloads of singles in Ireland?
2 sales of singles in music stores in Ireland?
3 sales of albums in music stores in Ireland?
4 the Internet being a threat?
5 the Internet being an opportunity?

7 **Where would you put these phrases from audio 51▷ on the line?**

grow gradually *crash* *rise substantially* *drop slightly*
stay the same *grow rapidly* *a significant drop*

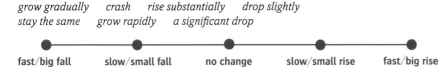

fast/big fall — slow/small fall — no change — slow/small rise — fast/big rise

8 **Where on the line would you put the phrases in *italics* in these sentences?**

1 Oil price *shoots up* by 30% on Middle East worries.
2 Gold *plummets* to all time low.
3 There are worrying signs of *a significant increase* in unemployment.
4 Doctors express concern at *a noticeable rise* in teenage smoking.
5 We'll see *a slight fall* in house prices as mortgages rise.
6 All quiet as FTSE *levels off.*
7 *A substantial drop* in exports predicted as euro rises.
8 Cost of borrowing *rockets* as interest rates double.

›› For more exercises, go to **Practice file 13** on page 126.

9 **Work with a partner. Using as many different phrases from 7 and 8 as you can, talk about changes in the cost of living in your country in the last ten years.**

10 **Work with a partner. Prepare and present a short talk about a company. Turn to File 27 on page 144 for instructions.**

ⓘ ›› Interactive Workbook ›› **Glossary**

Tip | *by* and *from ... to*

Use *by* to refer to a difference.
Car ownership grew ***by*** *approximately 50%.*
Use *from* to refer to an initial figure and *to* to refer to a final figure.
The price has fallen steadily ***from*** *$^1/_{10}$ ...* ***to*** *about one ten-millionth of a cent.*

Working with words

1 Match 1–8 to a–h.

1 Many women feel there is a glass ceiling … ___
2 Some banks have a corporate culture which … ___
3 I could take early retirement which … ___
4 He felt the new job was a sideways move … ___
5 When the factory downsized … ___
6 Setting up a new company involves dealing with official agencies and … ___
7 To save costs, the company made … ___
8 I can't move house because of the children's schools, so … ___

a would mean stopping work at 55 rather than 65.
b relocation is not an option.
c a lot of rules and red tape.
d rather than a promotion.
e a lot of the staff redundant.
f is very masculine and competitive.
g a third of the workers were laid off.
h stopping them from getting top jobs.

2 Complete these sentences. Use the answers to complete the puzzle and find the hidden word.

1 It's a lot cheaper to try and ________ staff than to continually find replacements.
2 Mangement failed to adequately ________ the project with experienced personnel.
3 Management want to ________ several staff to our new store on the outskirts of the city.
4 When they ________ the new Operations Manager, everyone will be informed immediately by email.
5 We believe in job ________ and giving you the opportunity to do different jobs in the company.
6 We intend to ________ a lot of time and money in the new HR department.
7 Two ______ vacancies must be filled as soon as possible.
8 You start at the bottom, and if you do well and work hard, the company will ________ you.

Business communication skills

1 Anton and Carolina from the workers' council are meeting with Bob from HR to negotiate the annual staff trip. Complete this extract from their meeting with the correct answer from 1–10 below.

Anton What we need to [1]________ on today is what to do for the staff trip. Let's look at what our [2]________ are.

Carolina [3]________ about we charter a plane to Morocco for a weekend?

Anton We do have that on our list of options, but [4]________ need to stretch the budget if we did that.

Carolina Yes, you're right. Bob, how does HR view things? What can you [5]________ us?

Bob Well, the workers' council always offers a staff trip – so we can't stop this – but what we [6]________ is it should be educational as well as entertaining.

Anton You mean, [7]________ we include something cultural we can choose any of our suggestions?

Bob Yes. Let's say you take the Morocco option. [8]________ you offer excursions to places of interest as part of the package, HR might veto the whole trip.

Carolina OK. We can [9]________ with that and would organize the trip to comply with HR's wishes.

Anton So, a quick [10]________ – if …

	a	b	c	d
1	a talk	b meet	c decide	d discuss
2	a possibilities	b options	c opinions	d alternatives
3	a What's	b Who	c Why	d How
4	a we'll	b we	c we'd	d we've
5	a lend	b help	c propose	d offer
6	a plan	b propose	c aim	d intend
7	a provided	b would	c were	d supposing
8	a until	b providing	c unless	d if
9	a be	b remain	c stay	d live
10	a review	b recap	c repeat	d outline

2 Put the words in *italics* in the correct order to complete the sentences.

1 *discuss / the / areas / we / to / need /are* ____________ the weekend rota and overtime.
2 *to / one / would / option / be* ____________ cancel the event.
3 *we / don't / on / why / take* ____________ two temporary staff for our busy period?
4 *far / who / so / got / we / so / have?* ____________ Gavin will …
5 *sounds / a / plan / like / that* ____________ – could you let Jan know the details?

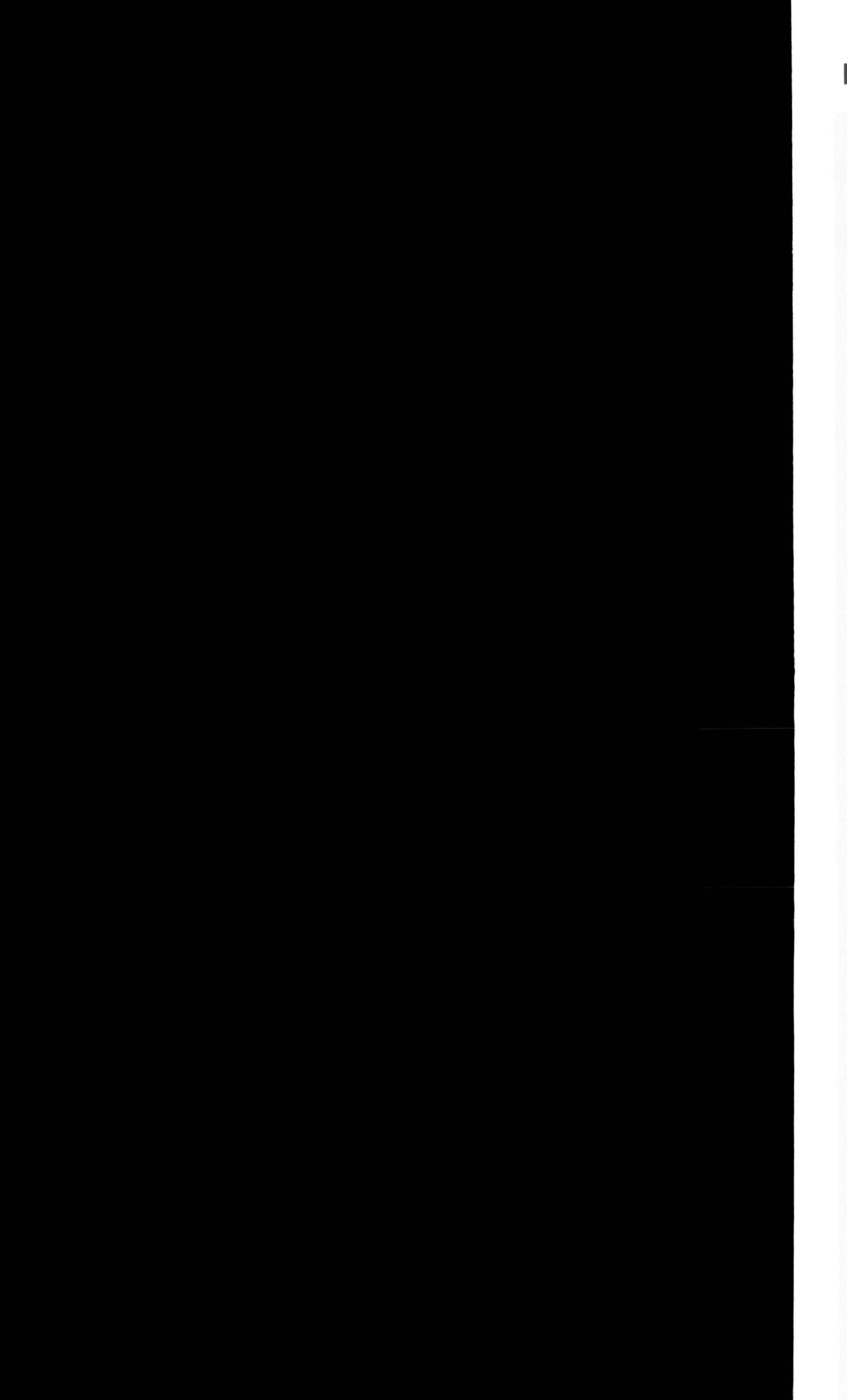

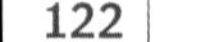

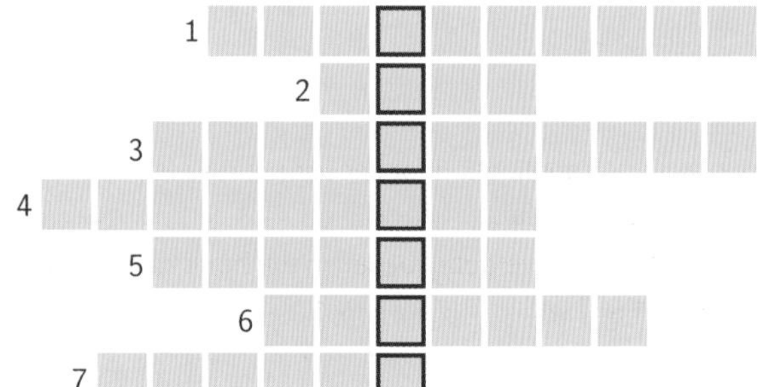

OXFORD
UNIVERSITY PRESS

Great Clarendon Street, Oxford OX2 6DP

Oxford University Press is a department of the University of Oxford. It furthers the University's objective of excellence in research, scholarship, and education by publishing worldwide in

Oxford New York

Auckland Cape Town Dar es Salaam Hong Kong Karachi Kuala Lumpur Madrid Melbourne Mexico City Nairobi New Delhi Shanghai Taipei Toronto

With offices in

Argentina Austria Brazil Chile Czech Republic France Greece Guatemala Hungary Italy Japan Poland Portugal Singapore South Korea Switzerland Thailand Turkey Ukraine Vietnam

OXFORD and OXFORD ENGLISH are registered trade marks of Oxford University Press in the UK and in certain other countries

First published 2008
2012 2011 2010
10 9 8 7 6 5 4

ISBN: 978 0 19 476809 2 (pack)
ISBN: 978 0 19 476810 8 (book)

Printed in China

ACKNOWLEDGEMENTS

The authors and publisher are grateful to those who have given permission to reproduce the following extracts and adaptations of copyright material: p 36 Reproduced by kind permission of Patagonia (www.patagonia.com); p 55 Reproduced by kind permission of Ian Dickson, Tesco Europe; p 60 (James Murray Wells) Interview created by kind permission of Glasses Direct; p 60 (Jurga Zilinskiene) Interview adapted by kind permission of Jurga Zilinskiene, Today Translations Ltd.; p 71 Interview adapted by kind permission of Robert Turner, FWZ; p 90 © Crown copyright 2007. Reproduced under terms of the Click-Use licence

Although every effort has been made to trace and contact copyright holders before publication, this has not been possible in some cases. We apologize for any apparent infringement of copyright and if notified, the publisher will be pleased to rectify any errors or omissions at the earliest opportunity.

Illustrations by: Becky Halls/The Organisation p 87

The publishers would like to thank the following for permission to reproduce photographs: Alamy pp 53 (Russsian Babushka dolls/Carole Hewer), 67 (Africa phone/Alan Gignoux), 76 (Ablestock), 78 (display board/Mehdi Chebil), 78 (engine/Rob Bartee), 90 (sea anenome/David Boag), 95 (fruits/Terrance Klassen), 140 (Rob Walls); Courtesy of the Ashden Awards for Sustainable Energy www.ashdenawards.org, p 24 (*above*: increasing the efficiency of water mills in Nepal by replacing wooden runners with precision-made metal ones), (*below*: biogas plant under construction Kitarama prison, Rwanda); Axiom Photographic Agency p 12 (Luke White); Courtesy of Concrete Canvas Ltd. p 29; Courtesy of Cyclepods Ltd p 47; Corbis pp 13 (Claudia/Artiga Photo), 17 (Stephen Beaudet/zefa), 19 (construction site/Chris Sattlberger), 28 (camera/Randy Faris), 30 (Don Mason), 35 (coffee/Benjamin Lowy), 38 (Ryan Pyle), 42 (Onne van der Wal), 48 (Bangalore/Jon Hicks), 80 (A. Inden/zefa), 101 (children/Rafiqur Rahman); Courtesy of Ian Dickson p 55; Eyevine p 84 (Geert Hofstede/Menno Boermans/HH); Getty Images pp 11 (meeting/Yellow Dog Productions), 13 (Peter/Ron Krisel), (Macie/David Lees), 18 (Peter Ginter), 20 (White Packert), 26 (Terry Vine), 36 (Alan Kearney), 44 (Photolibrary), 48 (shoe factory/Chung Sung-Jun), 49 (Paula Dale/Paul Taylor), (Christian Amiel/Symphonie/Iconica), (Chitra Sampat/Ron Krisel), 54 (Tyler/Chabruken), 56 (William Edward King), 59 (relocation/Yoray Liberman), 68 (Peter Dazeley), 77 (medical equipment/Peter Ginter/Science Faction), 84 (Panoramic Images), 89 (Gavin Hellier/Robert Harding), 92 (Nuts/Iconica), 96 (Roberto/Ghislain & Marie David de Lossy/Iconica), (Jenny/Sami Sarkis/Photographer's Choice), 98 (Kim Heacox); Mercy Ships UK Ltd p 67; Bruce Osborn/Ozone Inc. p 65 (Miho Inagi/Maruichi Bagel); PA Photos p 60 (Taiwanese yew plants, anti-cancer drug production/Wally Santana/AP); Photolibrary.com p 90 (chefs/Anthony Blake); Punchstock pp 7 (Radius Images), 8 (Di[illegible]irou/PhotoAlto), 23 (John Wang/Didital Vision), 28 ([illegible] (laptop/Digital Vision), 31 (call centre/Blend [illegible] 50 (Digital Vision), 54 (escalators/image100), (Fabia/Digital Vision), (Karl/Digital Vision), 62 (Digital Vision), 71 (airport/Corbis), 73 (meeting/Digital Vision), 74 (Digital Vision), 78 (internet/Lawrence Manning), 83 (Stockbyte), 86 (Digital Vision), 96 (rock formations/Eastcott Momatiuk/Digital Vision), (Freya/Photodisc); Reuters p 6 (Victor Fraile); Rex Features pp 25 (Sipa Press), 66 (Mongolia tent/Jeremy Sutton Hibbert), 108; Science Photo Library pp 37 (turtle/Matthew Oldfield, Scubazoo), 72 (Peter Scoones), 78 (transistors/Ton Kinsbergen); Still Pictures p 41 (Antarctic/Mark Shenley); Courtesy of Robert Turner p 71; Courtesy of James Wells p 60; Courtesy of Jurga Zilinskiene p 60

Images sourced by: Pictureresearch.co.uk

Cover photo by: Chris King

Photos on p5 courtesy of Cranfield School of Management

The authors and publisher would also like to thank the following individuals for their advice and assistance in developing the material for this book: Lucy Adam, Peter Anderson, Kate Baade, Hannah Blanning, Jayne Chivers, Jo Cooke, Allison Dupuis, John Ferris, Joanne Fessler, Cindy Hauert, Christopher Holloway, John Hughes, Zsofia Kocsardi, Alastair Lane, David Massey, Penny McLarty, Yvonne O'Connor, Sylvia Renaudon, Margaret Ristagno, Paulina Scheenberg, John Sydes, Susan Tesar, Jonathan Villis.

The publisher would also like to thank the faculty, course participants, and alumni of Cranfield School of Management who contributed so much to the development of the course. Particular thanks are due to David Simmons, Director of International Development, whose enthusiasm, generosity, and persistence really have made all the difference.

Special thanks to Yvonne Harmer.

62

Manager So what you're saying is you want to take an extended holiday?

Lena No, not really … I'd see it as a sabbatical. A journalist friend has invited me to be her photographer on her next assignment. A team is heading out to the Antarctic to document the impact of global warming.

Manager And you'd like several months off to accompany her?

Lena Yes. It's been a long-term goal of mine to do something like this. I did photography before I moved into IT, but I never saw it as a career. The thing is, I've been inspired by the people I studied with who've become professional photographers.

Manager Hmm. So … you take nine months off and we're left without a technical author and no team leader.

Lena I know, but it's a once-in-a-lifetime opportunity.

Manager But how do *we* benefit from this?

Lena Well, I think it's a win-win situation. I'd enjoy developing my creative side … I'd fulfil a lifelong ambition … so I'd come back to my job feeling more contented and satisfied with what I'd achieved in life …

Manager Yes, and …?

Lena And the experience I'd gain would be invaluable for managing the team.

Manager This isn't common practice, as far as I know. I'm not sure if …

Lena I understand your misgivings – what if I don't come back, and so on – but the plus points are that I'd be working in extreme conditions with a team of strangers, and my leadership skills would be put to the test …

Manager Mmm, I'm not convinced – go on.

Lena But there are also other benefits for you. I intend to put on an exhibition of my work after the trip and I'd like to do this with the support of the company. It would mean we'd get a lot of media exposure as well as great advertising opportunities.

Manager Yes, that sounds interesting; it's certainly worth thinking about.

Lena I really feel that this is a chance I can't afford to miss.

Manager Well, this would set a precedent. I'll have to discuss it with HR … It's not going to be easy to persuade them. I'm afraid your arguments aren't very convincing from a business point of view.

Lena That's hardly fair. I've never refused to take on more work or to do overtime when it's been necessary. I've been extremely loyal when lots of employees went to the new competition and … well …

Manager OK. Fair point. I'll see what I can do.

Lena I'd really appreciate it if you could speak to HR and initiate a meeting for all of us.

Manager OK. I think I can manage that, Lena.

63

1

A Hi, Sami. Where were you yesterday? You missed the meeting.

B Didn't anyone tell you? I took the day off. I thought it was about time I used up some of my overtime.

A What did you do?

B Nothing much. I caught up on some DIY jobs I started in the summer!

A Not a very exciting way to spend your day off!

B I know. I didn't really enjoy it, but it needed doing.

2

A Are you back from your holiday already?

B Yes, we just had a long weekend away.

A How was it?

B It poured with rain the whole time!

A Oh, no.

B It didn't really matter. We were on a three-day spa break.

A Nice.

B Yeah, I wasn't particularly keen on going at first – I thought I'd be bored – but I must say it was great for relaxing, switching off.

A Oh, lovely …

3

A Did you have a good weekend?

B Yes, we managed to get away for the day on Saturday.

A Anywhere nice?

B We visited my partner's family. It made a real change. They all love golf, so I was able to get a game in.

64

Interviewer Can you tell us something about your placement with SPARK?

Consultant Of course … what would you like to know?

Interviewer Well, maybe you could start by telling us where you were based and what you did.

Consultant OK. Well, we were based in Manila, in a small office, working with a mixed-nationality team – some locals, but mainly British and Swedish expats. Our task was fundamentally to strengthen the SPARK organization, which involved working through a lot of business process documentation. Something I was already very familiar with.

Interviewer So what did you find most enjoyable during your placement?

Consultant Well, it was a very different experience for me and I liked the fact that there were immediate results. It was great to see real changes taking place in front of me.

Interviewer I can imagine … You can actually see your work benefiting other people. So what did you feel you gained from this experience, personally?

Consultant Well … I feel I've returned with new skills and … I think I'm more confident than when I left … and I know I can achieve things on my own, make good decisions. It was good just to spend some time in a developing country … you get a real sense of how important developing countries are becoming for Western business generally. So I feel that the knowledge and cultural awareness that I've developed during my time with ADP … erm … has not only benefited SPARK and VSO now, but I'm sure they'll benefit Accenture in the future. Overall, it's been a fantastic experience. I'd recommend it to any of my colleagues.

Thomas Well … one success certainly was helping to produce the in-house magazine. I thought it was well produced with interesting content. I really enjoyed doing it, particularly interviewing colleagues from other countries for the staff profile column.
Angelina Yes, and I think you demonstrated great prioritizing skills, especially with the tight deadlines you had to meet.
Thomas How can I improve my chances of working more with international colleagues?
Angelina Well, you ought to sign up to one of our language courses. That'll put you in a better position for being selected when international projects come up. It's a pity we didn't think about this when you joined us. If you'd started a language course then, you'd be quite proficient now.
Thomas OK … Can I identify that as a personal goal for the coming year?
Angelina Of course.
Thomas Erm … What I didn't enjoy was when the magazine budget was cut … we had to lose a couple of staff on the editorial team and I ended up doing most of the work myself.
Angelina Hmm … You shouldn't have been expected to take on so much. I noticed your overtime hours were quite high at that time. Look, if this happens again, you need to let us know.
Thomas OK.
Angelina Are there any areas you feel you need to improve on?
Thomas Er, no … not really.
Angelina Hmm, all right. One area I'd like to mention is training. You turned down an office management course we offered you. Why was that?
Thomas I didn't think I really needed it. Besides, we were short-staffed. If Katy hadn't left, I probably would have done the course.
Angelina Mmm … You really should have done that course. I think it would have helped you deal with your workload better.
Thomas Yes … If I'd known that at the time, I might have done it.
Angelina I think you certainly need to focus on gaining some more qualifications. Let's put this course on your list of goals for the coming year, too. Now … were there any constraints that affected your performance?
Thomas Well, I mentioned that we're short-staffed and despite all this extra work, to be honest I've found it difficult to delegate. How should I do this?
Angelina You need to start by …

So that brings us on to the office environment and resources. You've managed to create a very positive atmosphere in the new office. The move went very smoothly thanks to your team's organization.
Thomas Thanks.
Angelina On a less positive note … You could have thought a bit more about the call centre rota. Feedback from that department has been poor.
Thomas I know. If we'd taken the old system to our new location, the rota would have been easier to organize … but no one likes the new scheduling program. What's the best way to solve this, do you think?
Angelina I'll need to look into it. Let's arrange a meeting to discuss it next week.
Thomas Thanks. We could do with some training on the new program – there are some functions we don't really understand.
Angelina I'll check the budget.
Thomas If there's enough money, I'd also like another software program. I've already spoken to IT about it.
Angelina OK. Put your request in an email and I'll consider it.
Thomas Thank you. Oh … and while we're talking about money, could we discuss …?

60

1

A Hello. Peter Li?
B Yes, that's right.
A Nice to meet you. I'm Jacqueline, Florence Talbot's PA.
B Ah, I think we've spoken on the phone.
A That's right. Please take a seat. Can I get you something to drink? Coffee or tea?
B A cup of tea would be nice.
A Certainly. Florence is just taking a phone call. She'll be out in a few minutes.

2

A Hello, Andrea … welcome to HGP Birgit. Let me take your coat.
B Thank you.
A You can leave your bag over there, if you like.
B Thanks.
A Did you have any trouble finding us?
B No, not at all, but the traffic was terrible.
A Yes, it's always like that on Fridays. I hope you managed to avoid the roadworks.
B Well, I went via the industrial zone …

3

A Hello. You must be our new technical adviser?
B Yes, that's right. Tom Schofield.
A Nice to meet you. Michel is in a meeting at the moment, but he'll be right with you.
B OK, no problem.
A So you've driven over from England today?
B Yes, I had quite a good journey. You have good roads in France.
A What was the weather like when you left? It's been raining all day here.
B Oh, it was much worse than this!
A Really?! … I can't imagine how it could possibly be …

Unit 16

61

Interviewer So you're quite happy with the idea of people in your organization taking a career break?
Employer Yes, although we prefer to use the term 'flexiwork', which is a better description.
Interviewer How did the idea come about? I mean, a lot of employers wouldn't like the idea of their staff disappearing for a year or so …
Employer We introduced flexiwork at a time when our industry was having a bit of a downturn … things were quiet … it meant we could cut the wage bill but also retain staff for when the situation improved again.
Interviewer So it was basically just a cost-cutting measure?
Employer No, it was more of an experiment … one that wouldn't be too expensive … and it's been very successful … in fact, it's now official company policy.
Interviewer Do you think this is something that other companies will take up?
Employer I'm not sure – I think we're lucky because we specialize in consultancy. A lot of our work is project-based, and our consultants do three months here, six months there … so it's quite easy for us to fit this kind of thing in.
Interviewer I think most people would see the advantages for the employee, but are there any other benefits for the company?
Employer Well, yes, apart from the cost savings that I mentioned before, it does a lot for our retention rate, so we don't get nearly so many resignations. If someone wants to broaden their horizons by having a long career break, they can have one, no problem. The other advantage is when we're recruiting, when we're looking for new talent. If we say we don't just allow career breaks, we actively encourage them – as part of your career development – that's very attractive to prospective employees.
Interviewer Presumably there are some people who go off for a few months and don't come back?
Employer For some people, yes, it acts as a catalyst for them to head off in a new direction … but for most people, it gives them a chance to recharge their batteries and they return with renewed enthusiasm. From the point of view of motivation, it's great, it's a win-win situation. And in terms of personal development, people come back having learned something new – maybe a new language – or they've developed a soft skill like leadership or whatever … but the bottom line is, those new skills are of value to the company as well.

2

Gaby ... I was responsible for finalizing the new office building in Warsaw along with my manager in the Netherlands. While I was liaising with both the Polish employees and my manager I discovered our two cultures had quite different approaches.

Nico Go on ...

Gaby Well, for example, when we were finalizing the plans for the office space. My manager wanted glass partitions but the Polish employees hated the idea.

Nico Oh?

Gaby Yeah ... but then I realized they hadn't actually told him this – they told me and hoped I'd tell him on their behalf!

Nico So what did you do?

Gaby I told him! It seems that none of them wanted to question an authority figure. So that was the first problem solved.

Nico There were more?

Gaby Oh yes. Another situation occurred when I was mentoring a recent IT graduate, Magda. While we were developing a new database, I gave her the job of asking staff for their views on the database ... I even put together a few sample questions.

Nico What happened?

Gaby Well, she came back with very little information. I was extremely disappointed ... What's more, the information she had only related to the questions I'd written. She hadn't written any questions of her own to get useful information for us. I didn't know what to do. All in all it was a difficult situation.

Nico So what did you do?

Gaby Well, in the end I asked Anna, a Polish colleague.

Nico What was her view?

Gaby Well, despite Magda's qualifications, she was still the most junior person in the department, so apparently more senior people would be unwilling to answer her questions.

Nico Oh, a hierarchy thing?

Gaby Yes. It came about because of the lack of information about why we were questioning them. It seems that Magda also wasn't comfortable with the task, so she didn't add to the questions I suggested.

Nico So how did you solve the problem?

Gaby Well, I sent out a memo explaining what Magda would be doing and why. I also noted Magda's qualifications and wrote the memo in English. The reason being that Magda needed to be respected by her colleagues and English gave the note neutrality.

Nico And ...?

Gaby It really surprised me, but it worked.

57

1

A Have you read any good books recently?

B Well, I don't get much time to read, but I've just finished a novel called *Shadow of the Wind.*

C I read that – I really enjoyed it.

A What's it about?

B It's about a boy's quest to find the truth about an author who's mysteriously disappeared. It's set in Barcelona just after the Second World War. It's very atmospheric – I'd definitely recommend it.

C Absolutely. It's very well written and it's a real page-turner too. I took it on holiday with me and I couldn't put it down!

2

A ... and I must admit I'm completely hooked on it. I've watched this soap opera since it began ten years ago and I can't miss an episode!

B Sounds like you're addicted. I don't really have a favourite programme. But sometimes I just like to unwind in front of the TV, you know, after a bad day at work. The problem is I tend to channel-hop ... there are so many channels available.

C I don't have much time to watch TV. So much of it is just so bad. The live sport is good though.

A Yes ... When the World Cup was broadcast I recorded every match so I didn't miss any!

B Me too! What I really can't stand is all this reality TV. You know, like *Big Brother.*

A Oh ... I quite like that.

3

A ... It sounds great ... I mean, listen to this review ... 'A blockbuster of a movie which became a box office hit overnight. It's full of brilliant special effects with a star-studded cast and a gripping storyline that will have you on the edge of your seat from the beginning!'

B Well, I've seen it and it was really good. The whole thing is set in the future and it's about a group of historians who look back to the twenty-first century and analyse what we're doing and how we're behaving now.

C And were you 'on the edge of your seat'?

B I was, actually, yeah. I mean, OK, it's basically a science-fiction film, but it's very well done. It's very entertaining – there's quite a lot of humour in it. I don't want to spoil it for you, but there's a really surprising twist at the end – you must go and see it.

Unit 15

58

Interviewer Is it right that you've **moved on** from top-down staff appraisals to what you call 360° degree appraisals?

Manager No, we still have the more traditional top-down appraisals, but we're introducing 360° appraisals as well because they have different functions ...

Interviewer In what way?

Manager You have to think of 360° as a development tool basically ... a trigger for change ... rather than a way of deciding if anyone deserves a raise.

Interviewer So how does it work?

Manager Well, in 360°, instead of just your boss appraising you, you have several different people giving feedback ... So ... we **hand out** a feedback form to everyone you come into contact with – your manager, your colleagues, people on your team, your customers, contractors, suppliers – obviously it depends on the type of job and the organization, but we try to involve as many different people as possible ... and with this kind of peer rating, you **end up with** a more complete picture of how someone is doing in their job.

Interviewer And what do you ask them?

Manager We use a feedback form, with a scoring or value judgement system, asking them to comment on various different assessment criteria – job skills, abilities, attitudes, behaviour. Then you assess yourself using the same form to see how the two compare. ... There are two important considerations with 360° appraisal. First, it has to be completely confidential ... that way you get much more honest answers from people. And secondly, you need to make sure suitable counselling is available when you **go through** the feedback results.

Interviewer So, at the moment, you don't actually use it for appraising performance?

Manager No, it works better as a development tool. We use it as part of our overall performance management, a way of bringing about change, rather than assessing performance.

Interviewer Right. And does it really help change?

Manager Yes ... I had a new member on one of my teams recently ... I thought he was very communicative, very open, always said what he thought and I liked that. But when we did a 360° appraisal, the staff feedback was all negative, and he **came over** as domineering and forceful. As a result of this, he did change his behaviour ... and became more accepted by the team. And that's what I mean about it being different from top-down appraisals – in that example, a top-down appraisal from me would have told him to **carry on** speaking his mind ... but it was the 360° feedback that made us aware of the need for change.

59

Angelina ... I must say, we're very happy with your overall performance this year. What do you consider were your successes and failures?

Unit 12

47

1

I'm in charge of a sales team based in Lille. Most of them are French speakers, of course ... you might think I'd prefer it if everyone spoke in English, but in fact I've been anti the whole idea ever since they brought the policy in. I told them why we were worried about it, but they don't listen, they refused to modify the policy in any way ... and now that it's been implemented, we've got real problems ... just as I predicted. They know I've always been hostile to this policy ... and I'm very critical, I admit it ... but one of the reasons is that I'm genuinely concerned about misunderstandings ... and I told my manager that my team weren't sure about trying out their language skills and doing everything in English, but she was all for it ... so what can you do? But things do go wrong ... last week we had to order up 15,000 new catalogues from the Paris office, one of my salespeople phoned them and we ended up with 50,000 – a complete waste of time and money. OK, in that example, it wasn't the end of the world, but it shows the kind of thing that can happen. I say, if two people speak French, let them speak French, otherwise, you know ...

2

When they introduced the language programme a couple of years ago, I think most people were quite positive about learning English though I personally had a few concerns. Anyway, they put on lots of courses for people who needed to develop their English, but in my department – technical support – we ran into a few problems, especially just after it was introduced. Most of my team are not really natural language learners ... basically they are techies, and they weren't very keen on having to speak English all the time. They were very resistant to the idea of using English in meetings and especially on the phone. But in fact, it's OK. They found it pretty hard to start with – some of them were quite anxious about it, especially the older ones – but now they've been speaking English for a while, it's getting easier, and they've actually improved quite a lot. We can now deal with support calls from Spain, Italy and Finland, too, and I'm optimistic that we'll be able to take on more work in the near future.

3

Well, as head of the training department, I was asked to carry out a review of language use in the company, and when it was completed, we came up with the idea of a single language policy. There was a real problem ... we had three different company languages ... in meetings, you would get a mix of languages, or the majority language would dominate, and all the documentation had to be translated, so we had an army of translators and interpreters, and there was just so much paperwork, so much waste. So that was basically why we were in favour of the new policy. At the start, people were naturally apprehensive and a few people were against it – but it was nothing serious. I think most of the staff appreciated it was the right thing to do and they were very receptive to the whole idea. Now ... I think it's all working out very well. Very few people have dropped out of the courses. We've already achieved a lot, and our different offices are communicating much better as far as I can tell ... Ask me again in a year.

48

Rachel ... OK. I've spoken about our consultants' findings and we're well aware of your concerns regarding how the changes will affect our staff. As you all know, it is likely there will be some job losses but we'd like to assure you that we will keep these to an absolute minimum and try to reduce headcount through natural wastage. Decisions will definitely have been made by March as to how big the cutbacks will be. Many of you have asked about a rumoured pay freeze ...
We aren't counting this out, but this is something we'd like to avoid. Over the next few weeks, we'll be hosting departmental meetings to give more specific information ... and we plan to keep you informed about any other changes so you can answer your staff's queries with well-informed answers. Starting from next month, we'll be putting regular updates on our Intranet regarding potential changes ... but more about that later.
I'd like to pass the next point over to Imran, who has been working closely with the consultants on the subject of bottom-up management.

Imran Thanks, Rachel. Yes, bottom-up management has proven to be very successful in a number of companies and we've been working on a similar concept to implement here at FGR. Hopefully, the new model will be in place by the end of the month. Bottom-up management is quite a simple idea ...

... Normally when change takes place, this is decided and implemented by senior management. However, to make the changes work we need the enthusiasm, motivation and energy from everyone who will be affected by those changes.
Let's digress for a moment and look at this in more detail. Our idea is to give everyone the opportunity to propose changes which will benefit themselves and the company. We're proposing a Friday afternoon ideas forum where employees can put forward their suggestions for change. Each department nominates someone to present the most popular ideas to senior management, along with a business plan or some sort of proof that benefits can be gained. The first forum will be on Friday the 24th at 3.30. I'll be visiting our suppliers in Bradford on that day, so Rachel will be here to lead the session.
You may be wondering if this will work – Friday afternoons are free for most of our employees. We're convinced the opportunities outweigh the disadvantages of staying at work longer. We must see this as a step towards becoming a more effective company. It's crucial to get the employees on our side ... and we need to emphasize that there will be money available for remuneration ... which could be paid if we see real results after the changes are implemented. This last point is probably going to be difficult to administer at the beginning but the consultants had an example of remuneration scales for us to consider.
I'm sure some of you are sceptical of the consultants' proposals, but we're calling on you to be positive – pass this information on and create enthusiasm ... sell the idea of empowerment to our staff and highlight the rewards this could bring us all. Later this year we'll be reassessed to see how effective the changes are ...

49

1

A What do you think about changing the team meeting to Friday afternoons?
B I have some reservations about it. People on flexitime often choose to leave early on Fridays. And concentration probably won't be as good at the end of the week.

2

A If you ask me, this is just a way of getting rid of staff.
B I can see both sides of the argument. Management want to streamline the company's operation but employees are naturally worried about possible job cuts.

3

A I can't believe they're going to make us all learn Spanish.
B It sounds interesting – I like the idea of having a common language for the company – but people who aren't confident in their language skills might find it difficult.

4

A Do you think this latest proposal is a good thing?
B Mm. I'm not sure about it. Is management confident that extending our office hours will actually improve the service?

machines start talking to machines – we saw it first in the Wall Street crash in '87 when program trading caused complete chaos – computers were cutting prices, selling stock to other computers, and people didn't know how to stop it. It's a scary scenario because it takes us into a whole new area of experience ... and when that comes it's going to have a big impact on all of us.

Speaker 3 ... Yeah, I think maybe we're getting ahead of ourselves here ... this kind of speculation's all very interesting, but communication systems are no good if people can't use them. Now ... at the moment ... everyone you know may well have access to the Internet, subscribe to satellite TV and use a mobile phone, but that's just not the case for most people in the world. We need to focus on spreading around the basic technology we have now more fairly. As it is, more than half the population of the world has never even made a telephone call. Think about it – how good is a communication system if half the world is excluded from it?

44

Jimmy ... So this tool and service is offered to large-sized companies only. Are you with me?
Angelika OK ... Yes, I've got that.
Jimmy Mirela?
Mirela OK. I'm with you.
Jimmy Good. When you acquire your key account customer you must set up regular meetings. It's a good idea to plan these for once a quarter, every three months.
Angelika This is Angelika. What exactly do you mean by meetings? Do we still need to meet them face to face?
Jimmy Yes. We regularly bring out offers for key accounts. For example, at the moment, we're offering a special price for three job postings, one-month resumé access and logos on job ads ... so there's always something new to discuss.
Mirela Jimmy, you're very faint. Oh, this is Mirela by the way.
Jimmy Hang on ... Is that better?
Mirela Yes, it's fine again now.
Jimmy Can we speed up a little and discuss first meetings with the key accounts? There's another conference call booked for this room in ten minutes, so we can't run over.
All Yeah, no problem. / Fine. No problem.
Jimmy In your initial meeting, you need to make sure they've seen the demo for posting ads. What's useful is to send it to them on a CD a few days before the meeting.
Angelika So you're saying we don't have to go through the demo in the meeting?
Jimmy Normally not ... no. A few years ago, we always had to train them on the software, but now it's much more user-friendly and people are more familiar with form-filling and making payments online.
Mirela This is Mirela again. What do we do about price?
Jimmy OK. What happens is ... an offer is made according to the approximate number of postings the client will make in a month. Is that clear?
Mirela Yeah, that's clear. We've already started putting offers together but I just wanted to check ... And how is all this packaged?
Angelika Hello? ... I can't hear Mirela!
Mirela ... Is that better?
Angelika Yes, you're back again now.
Jimmy Well, to answer Mirela's question ... Basically, it's essential to tell them about our advantages over newspaper ads, the resumé and candidate filtering tool, the fact that responses received to ads can either be accessed online or directly sent to their email address – that's to name just a few.
Angelika Jimmy, could you slow down a bit? We're having problems following you.
Jimmy No problem. I'll email you our key account marketing information. You should read this through thoroughly and contact me if anything's still unclear.
Mirela OK. There's one last thing I wanted to ask ...

45

1

A ... So as I was saying, any chance of getting it to me by tomorrow?
B I'm afraid I didn't catch that last bit.
A I said, any chance of getting it to me by tomorrow?
B Sorry Veronica, this is hopeless. It's a really bad line.
A OK. I'll hang up and call you on the landline in five minutes.

2

A ... So can we discuss the transport arrangements for the Japanese visitors?
B Sorry, but this'll have to be quick, Renée, I'm about to board a plane!
A So now's not a good time to call?
B Not really, no. I'll be there in two hours. Can you call me again then?
A Sure, no problem.

3

A Beatriz? Is that you?
B Yes, how did you ...?
A I recognized your number on the display. Look, I'm sorry, but I have someone on the other line. Can I call you back?
B Yes, I'm around for another hour, then I have a meeting.
A OK, speak to you in a few minutes then.

46

Visitor ... So, Robert, what measures have been taken to improve your communication procedure with your clients, now that you've expanded and introduced shift work?
Robert Well, one long-term measure has been to invest in some help-desk software. But until that arrives we're working with quite a new, but ... er ... basic idea.
Visitor Can you tell me something about that?
Robert OK. Each day we have a 'man of the day'. This is always one person from the early shift and one from the late shift, one on each, yeah? These two employees check the emails and prioritize them. They also handle all the phone calls from the clients.
Visitor So how do they prioritize them?
Robert Well, at the moment, the emails are simply prioritized by being flagged. This does have its disadvantages, though. When more employees have access to the inbox, some emails get filed away and overlooked! Then we're in trouble ...
Visitor Oh ... yes, I see your point.
Robert ... Right. So our 'man of the day' has to prioritize the emails by content. If an email is connected to our auto warning system – that's a system that monitors our interfaces and feeds our clients with critical information – erm, that email has to be dealt with immediately. Then the employee checks and works on emails that the client has flagged as high priority ... and finally ... emails which are so-called 'show-stoppers' are highlighted.
Visitor Show-stoppers?
Robert Yeah, those problems that are going to affect our client's daily work and could cause delays, which obviously costs a great deal of money in the airline industry.
Visitor And how do you know what's been worked on and what's still outstanding?
Robert At the moment I speak directly to the 'man of the day'.
Visitor I see. What sort of difference will this new help-desk software make?
Robert Well, it should make a tremendous difference. It will assign a so-called 'trouble ticket' to each task or open item. As the item is being worked on, the status is updated and we can track what's being worked on, how it's being worked on, and what's already been done to it. So, for example, if a similar problem occurs, we can look back to see how we solved it last time.
Visitor It sounds as if this software will be very helpful for you.
Robert That's right. Not only for us, but in time it should be possible for our clients to receive the trouble tickets too, so they can follow the progress of the problem and not constantly have to call us to see how we're doing ...

Resolving an expansion crisis

Background

Cyclepods Ltd struggles to meet demand

A new product is currently on the market. It's environmentally-friendly – made from almost 100% recycled aluminium – and supports the 'green' mode of transport: the bicycle. The product is called a Cyclepod and it is an innovative space-saving cycle storage design which secures eight cycles in a two-metre diameter. The Cyclepod enables the cyclist to lock the front wheel of their cycle, frame and back wheel to the unit, securing the most expensive and highly-targeted parts of the cycle in place. And because the Cyclepod holds bicycles in a vertical position, they are high up and visible on any CCTV that may be installed for extra security. In addition, the Cyclepod is fully brandable and graphics can be applied by the purchaser.

Since it was founded, the company – Cyclepods Ltd – has been going from strength to strength. After the company's first year of trading, it had sold its product to eight major organizations and the orders have been flooding in since. The problem Cyclepods Ltd now has is meeting the demand. It doesn't have any stock – the Cyclepods are made to order. The company doesn't have the money to invest in mass production yet and because production is slow, profit margins are low. Despite its apparent success, Cyclepods Ltd isn't making enough profit to cover its overheads and is facing a cash-flow crisis.

FACT FILE

Founders: James Steward, Natalie Connell

Growth: 8 contracts in first 9 months – customers included Pepsi and Reebok

Price per unit: £3,900

Required investment: £200,000

The Expert View

When faced with making decisions, it is helpful to decide what sort of decision is required. Is the decision tactical or is it strategic? Tactical decisions offer short-term solutions to operational problems. They don't affect the broad plans of the organization. Strategic decisions will challenge fundamental principles such as the company's approach to marketing or production. Strategic decisions should help to create a long-term sustainable business approach for an organization. Tactical decisions should help to solve short-term issues within a fundamentally sound and successful business model. Make sure you know whether the decision you need to make is tactical or strategic.

Roger Delves, Programme Director, Centre for Customized Executive Development

Cranfield School of Management

Discussion

1 **What are the company's strengths and weaknesses?**

2 **What is the company's USP?**

3 **Where is the market for this product? Who would buy a Cyclepod?**

4 **What is your own opinion of the product?**

Task

Work in groups of four.

1 Establish the current situation for Cyclepods Ltd.
2 Individually, or with a partner, decide what you think the company should do to resolve its cash-flow crisis and increase its profit margin. Prepare your arguments and be ready to give your opinions.
3 Choose one person to lead the discussion. As a group, discuss all the options you think the company has.
4 Decide on the two best options and present them to the class.
5 Have a class vote to decide on the best option for the company.
6 Turn to File 12 on page 139 to find out how the company actually resolved its situation.

Case study

8 | Outsourcing

Learning objectives in this unit

- Talking about outsourcing
- Presenting factual information
- Apologizing and responding
- Distinguishing when to use the passive form

Case study

- Making a case for outsourcing

Starting point

1. What is outsourcing?
2. Does your company or a company you know outsource any of its production or services?
3. What are the advantages and disadvantages of outsourcing for the company and the customer?

Working with words | Outsourcing

1 **Many American and European companies outsource part of their production or service provision to emerging economies like Brazil, Russia, India and China.**

1. What opportunities does this provide for these countries?
2. What problems can it cause for them?

2 **Read the article about India's outsourcing market and compare your ideas in 1.**

1. What are the main opportunities and problems for India as outlined in the article?
2. Are the opportunities for India greater than the problems?

Outsourcing to earn India $60 bn

India could earn as much as $60 bn a year from information technology and outsourcing, an industry report says.

Potential market

India's IT and outsourcing market is currently worth $22 bn, and is expected to grow consistently. Within the next five years, business worth more than $110 bn will be outsourced worldwide to **offshore locations**, of which India is set to capture more than 50%. IT and outsourcing is projected to double to 7% of India's GDP and account for 44% of **export growth**.

Employment

The **sector** currently employs 700,000 people directly, and this is expected to rise to 2.3 m in the next five years. At current rates, there will be a shortfall of 500,000 **skilled workers. Indirect employment** is also set to treble over the same period, as more software and **business process outsourcing** (BPO) services are outsourced to India. Many companies are finding that using outside **expertise** for BPO enables greater concentration on their **core activities**.

Skills and infrastructure

There is an urgent need to develop at least ten 'knowledge cities' with universities and other **training facilities** to meet future employment needs. In addition, the **infrastructure** of these cities should be developed so that they have their own airports, roads, office space and housing to meet the needs of the technology firms.

3 **Match the words in bold in the article to these definitions.**

1 part of a country's economy: __________
2 basic systems like transport that a country needs to work properly: __________
3 the things done in a company that are most important for its main area of work: __________
4 secondary jobs created by the economic activity of a company: __________
5 places where people can learn new skills: __________
6 an increase in products sold abroad: __________
7 people with the training and experience to do a job well: __________
8 contracting a business task, such as payroll, to an outside service provider: __________
9 special knowledge or skill in a particular subject, activity or job: __________
10 based in a foreign country: __________

4 **30▷ Listen to three people talking about outsourcing and answer questions 1–2.**

1 What main points does each speaker make about outsourcing?
2 Is each speaker positive or negative about outsourcing and why?

Paula Dale
Politician

Christian Amiel
Sales Manager

Chitra Sampat
Call Centre Operative

5 **Complete the questions with these verbs from audio 30▷.**

improve *lead to* *take* *streamline* *achieve*
develop *get through* *gain* *free up* *create*

1 Do you think outsourcing business process tasks will __________ serious job losses in the EU?
2 What strategies could governments __________ to cope with job losses and to __________ more jobs in the EU?
3 What factors cause a company to __________ cost-cutting measures to reduce spending?
4 How do companies that outsource __________ lower overheads?
5 How does outsourcing help companies to __________ their operation and become more efficient?
6 What tasks could companies outsource to __________ resources for their core activities?
7 Why can companies that outsource __________ a bigger volume of work?
8 How can a company __________ a competitive edge over rival companies?
9 In what ways can outsourcing __________ the quality of life for workers in emerging economies?

6 **Work with a partner. Ask and answer the questions in 5.**

» For more exercises, go to **Practice file 8** on page 116.

7 **Work in small groups. Read about Company X.**

1 Would you advise this company to outsource? Why or why not? What would be the results of outsourcing for the company?
2 Present your ideas to the class.

Company X is considering how it can reduce some of its costs and free up resources to concentrate on its core activities. It has recently reviewed the quality and efficiency of its IT section. It has experienced difficulties recruiting experienced IT operatives. In addition it needs to reduce its IT budget. It is currently considering outsourcing the IT section, including its customer help desk, to a specialized computer company in an offshore location which operates 24/7. This will involve cutting 70 jobs in its home office. The offshore company (based in one of the emerging economies) would charge an annual fee for salaries, and administration and maintenance costs. This would be a saving of 45% for Company X.

ⓘ » Interactive Workbook » **Glossary**

Context

Sanjit Kundu works for Business Initiatives Bangalore. The Bangalore region has been singled out as a prime area for European companies to outsource to. Sanjit's role is to inform potential clients about Bangalore's business connections and its IT industry. Sanjit is 'on tour' in Europe and has been invited to make a presentation to GSV Chemicals in Belgium. This international company is considering outsourcing its IT Department to a cheaper location.

Presenting | Presenting factual information

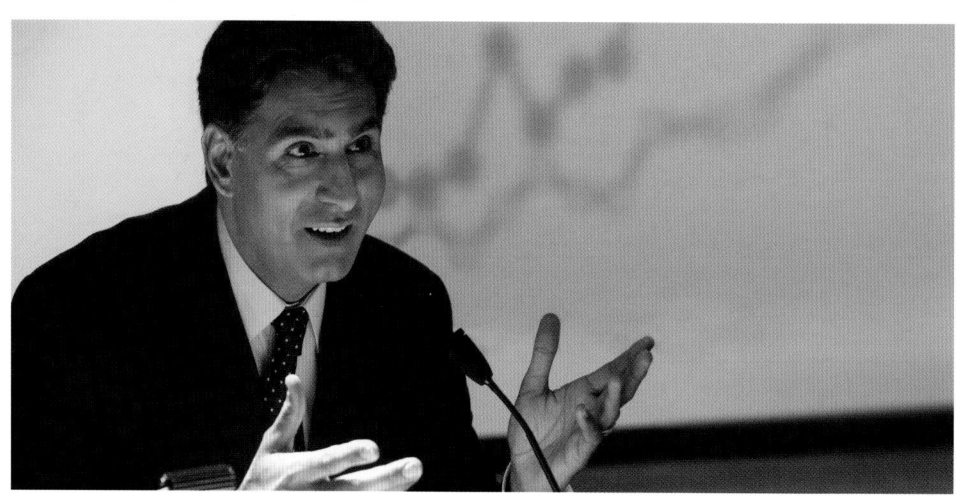

1 **31▷ Read the *Context*. Listen to Part 1 of Sanjit's presentation and answer questions 1–2.**

1 What are Bangalore's key selling points as a location for outsourcing?
2 What presentation technique does Sanjit use to keep the audience's attention?

2 **31▷ Listen again and answer questions 1–2.**

1 What two phrases does Sanjit use to prove his information comes from factual data?
2 What phrases does Sanjit use to explain the cause of
  a Bangalore's educational institutes having international recognition?
  b Bangalore becoming the fastest growing city in Asia?

3 **32▷ Listen to Part 2 of the presentation and answer questions 1–3.**

1 Is Bangalore's ability to attract industry a recent development?
2 What do these figures relate to?
  a 25–28% **b** 512 **c** 64 **d** 1,000
3 What is Sanjit's final argument for investing in Bangalore?

4 **32▷ Listen again and complete these phrases.**

1 I've ________ the background, so ________ some business facts.
2 You ________ the breakdown of traditional industries.
3 As ________, this has earned us the name 'India's Silicon Valley'.
4 Let's ________ some specific facts on the IT sector.
5 Looking ________ it is expected that Indian IT services will continue to grow …
6 And ________: more than 1,500 software and outsourcing companies …
7 ________, nearly 1,000 new staff are being taken on every month.
8 Before ________, I'd like to ________.
9 Investment in Bangalore ________ dramatic, positive lifestyle changes for its people.

5 **Put the phrases in 4 into these categories.**

a Explaining effect: ________
b Moving from one point to another: ________
c Referring backwards: ________
d Referring to visuals: ________
e Concluding on a strong note: ________

» For more exercises, go to **Practice file 8** on page 116.

6 **Work with a partner. Use this chart to prepare a short presentation about the benefits of outsourcing to Bangalore. Give your presentation to another pair.**

1 Advantages of Bangalore
- Cheap location
- Labour force
  - skilled / strong work ethic
  - multilingual
- Established international community

2 Your benefits for outsourcing
- Reduce costs
- Become more international
  - better communication
  - networking and synergies
- Invest early in emerging market

3 The facts

a
— Overheads
— IT investment

b
— Salaries
--- Start of outsourcing

c
— Shareholder value
--- Start of outsourcing

7 **Prepare a short presentation about one of topics 1–3 below (or any other topic you're interested in). Make sure you**
- introduce yourself and the topic
- include some facts and figures (these don't need to be true / accurate)
- refer to any changes and explain cause and effect
- conclude on a strong note.

1 changes in your company or in the economy of your country
2 why a particular company should relocate to your town / city
3 why a potential investor should invest in your company

Ⓘ » Interactive Workbook » **Email**

Key expressions

Presenting factual information
Statistics show …
Recent data illustrates …
Research indicates …

Explaining cause and effect
Due to …
As a result of …
The effect of this is …
(This) has resulted in …
Subsequently, …
A knock-on effect of this …

Referring to visuals
You will notice on this chart …
Looking at this slide, we can see …
Have a look at these figures …

Moving from one point to another
Let's turn our attention to …
I've (briefly) looked at … so let's move on to …
A further point to mention is …

Referring backwards
… which relates back to …
As I mentioned earlier …
… which I referred to earlier.

Concluding on a strong note
Before I go today, I'd like to leave you with some food for thought.
The message I'd like to send you away with today is …

Ⓘ » Interactive Workbook
» **Phrasebank**

Practically speaking | Apologizing and responding

1 **33▷ Listen to six apologies and answer questions 1–2.**
1 What does each person apologize for?
2 What is the reason or excuse?

2 **33▷ Listen again and answer questions 1–3.**
1 What phrase does each speaker use to apologize?
2 How does the other speaker respond?
3 Which apologies are more formal?

3 **Work with a partner. Take turns to apologize about the situations below. Follow this model and refer to the *Useful phrases* on page 134.**

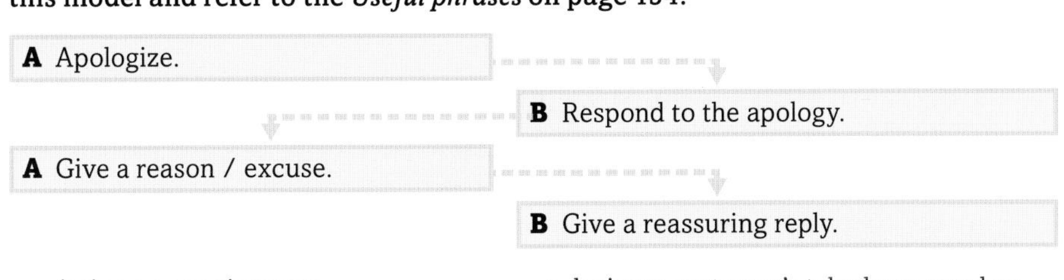
A Apologize.
B Respond to the apology.
A Give a reason / excuse.
B Give a reassuring reply.

- missing an appointment
- sending an email to the wrong person
- forgetting a birthday
- losing a customer's telephone number
- spilling a drink over someone
- not phoning someone back

Tip | Apologizing

When we apologize, we often add information to explain the situation. When we accept the apology, we often make an extra comment to help the person apologizing feel better.

Language at work | The passive

1 **Read these two sentences. Which is active and which is passive? Why is each form used?**

1 Thousands of European back-office jobs **have been outsourced** to India.
2 EU companies **have outsourced** thousands of back-office jobs to India.

2 **Read these extracts from audio 31▷ and 32▷. Why is the passive rather than the active used? How does this compare to the use of the passive in your language?**

1 Bangalore's educational institutions **have been awarded** international recognition.
2 It **is expected** that Indian IT services will continue to grow by 25–28% annually.
3 Sixty-four new offices **were opened** in the city.
4 The job market **is being fuelled** by the tens of thousands of students ...

3 **Read these sentences. Which sound natural in the active form? Which would sound more natural in the passive form? Change them into the passive.**

1 Somebody stores a lot of our sensitive information in secure remote sites.
2 Somebody phoned you while you were out at lunch.
3 Somebody must know where Jason has gone.
4 Workers will manufacture the new Mini at BMW's factory in Oxford.
5 Somebody has closed the road for repairs for two weeks.
6 You can't use the lift today because someone is servicing it.

4 **Use the passive to rephrase these sentences so they are more impersonal.**

Example: *They think* that the company will open an office in Electronics City.
It is thought *that the company will open an office in Electronics City.*

1 *People say* that Bangalore's very nice, but I've never been there myself.
2 *Everyone knows* that Indian software engineers are extremely good.
3 *Most people think* that property there is a bit overpriced.
4 *People believe* that Microsoft is interested in expanding its operations in India.
5 *Some people expect* that outsourcing to China will increase in the next five years.

5 **Work with a partner. Make a sentence giving impersonal information using the verbs in *italics* in 1–5 in 4.**

6 **Use the passive to rephrase the phrases in *italics* so you are not saying who is responsible for the action.**

Example: I'm afraid I didn't get your voicemail – *our administrator deleted it* by mistake.
I'm afraid I didn't get your voicemail – it ***was deleted*** *by mistake.*

1 I'm sorry, but you are being made redundant. *I have made the decision* and it's final.
2 I can't make a copy of the contract because *Bob hasn't fixed the photocopier* yet.
3 *John from the post room sent the package yesterday,* so it should arrive tomorrow.
4 These cuts are unavoidable, and *I am making them* to try and save money.
5 I can assure you that *someone will deal with your complaint.*

›› For more information and exercises, go to **Practice file 8** on page 117.

7 **Work with a partner. Take turns to talk about a new controversial law or regulation in your country or company. Give details of**

- what the law / regulation is about
- when it was / will be introduced
- what people think of it
- who will be affected by it
- whether it will be changed / abolished in the future.

ⓘ ›› Interactive Workbook ›› **Exercises and Tests**

Making a case for outsourcing

Background

Epam in Russia

Epam is Central and Eastern Europe's biggest IT outsourcing provider. It has development facilities in Russia, Belarus, Ukraine and Hungary. Epam has successfully developed software solutions for a wide range of industries in over 30 countries worldwide. One of its clients is Colgate-Palmolive.

To help sales representatives manage a large portfolio of customers, products and promotional material, Colgate-Palmolive wanted a software application that provided up-to-date information on demand to every salesperson in offices in 30 countries. Epam developed a software application that:

- provides sales people with customer, product, availability, promotional, order status and reporting information
- saves costs by replacing the global paper mailing of tens of thousands of product updates and reports each month
- enables a salesperson, with a laptop computer, to collaborate with internal contacts, manage customer calls, manage and track sales goals, access a product encyclopaedia, enter and monitor orders, analyse sales data and enter and process orders online with no processing delays.

As a result, Colgate-Palmolive's sales force has become more efficient and effective, especially in dealing with multiple languages, currencies and promotions. This in turn has increased staff morale. The variety of tools and options has increased sales staff's product knowledge and improved their accuracy. This has led to greater productivity.

Discussion

1 **What were the advantages of outsourcing IT software development for Colgate-Palmolive?**

2 **What factors do companies need to consider when choosing a provider of outsourcing services?**

Task

Work in groups of three. A large European company is currently considering outsourcing part of its software development work to Epam's facility in Russia. You have been asked to research the advantages of Russia as an outsourcing location and to provide an example of a successful project organized by Epam. Your task is to present your research to senior management to persuade them to outsource to Epam.

1 Read the information about Russia in File 19 on page 142 and refer to the Epam text above. Brainstorm ideas for your presentation.
2 Prepare your presentation, including one or two visuals.
3 Give your presentation to the class.

The Expert View

There are two perspectives to every outsourcing deal. Outsourcing is seen as a quick and easy way for customers to reduce their costs. The main challenge is to create a contract that allows for changes over time. Often the people who negotiate outsourcing contracts don't understand the business and its processes well enough to future-proof a contract. If changes to the original contract occur, costs savings can become cost increases. Suppliers provide a service and want to ensure a return on their investment. Their main challenge is in fully understanding their customers, so they can adapt to changes in customers' needs over time without losing revenue.

Dr Ashley Braganza, Director, Centre for Organizational Transformation
Cranfield School of Management

Case study

9 Employees

Learning objectives in this unit

- Talking about changing jobs
- Talking about ways of keeping staff
- Negotiating solutions
- Making and responding to quick requests
- Using first and second conditionals for negotiating solutions

Case study

- Negotiating a repatriation package

Starting point

1 **Why do people change jobs or careers?**

2 **What would encourage you to stay in a particular job or career?**

Working with words | Changing jobs | Keeping staff

1 **34▷ Listen to three people talking about their experience of changing jobs or careers and answer questions 1–3.**

1 Answer these questions for each speaker.

  a What was their job and what is their job now?
  b What reasons do they give for changing jobs?
  c How did they go about getting a new job?
  d What other options could they have considered?

Tyler

Fabia

Karl

2 What do you think each speaker has learnt from the experience?

3 Tell a partner about a job change you have made. Why did you make it? How did you go about it?

2 **Find these pairs of phrases in audio script 34▷ on page 157. Explain the difference in meaning between the phrases in each pair.**

1 taking early retirement / made redundant
2 temporary secondment / relocation
3 being unemployed / laid off
4 a sideways move / a change of direction
5 transferable skills / update my skills
6 a glass ceiling / opportunity for advancement
7 corporate culture / rules and red tape
8 personal development / training

3 **Choose a phrase from each pair in 2 and think of a question to ask your partner. Then take turns to ask and answer your questions.**

Example: Do you plan to take early retirement?

4 Read the interview with Ian Dickson, European HR Director for Tesco based in Prague, and answer questions 1–3.

1 What is Ian's main message?
2 What steps has the company taken to keep staff and reduce the number leaving the company?
3 Would you like to see these ideas implemented in your company? Why or why not?

What's your view on dealing with staff turnover?

I think you can tell quite a lot about a company by its **staff turnover.** If it's very high, it's probably a sign that the company's approach to **staff development** and retention isn't working well – and people believe they have to move to **get on.** As a leading retailer, with ambitious growth plans, we give a lot of attention to this area. We **invest** heavily **in** internal development programmes because we strongly believe we have talent and potential within our own workforce. If we can tap into this, it becomes our most effective way of **resourcing** for the future.

What opportunities do you provide for staff?

Wherever possible, when we have a **key vacancy**, we fill it by **redeploying** staff or **promoting** them – this is the case at all levels from departmental managers in our stores to director positions. We believe in promoting people on their **ability**, and with so many opportunities for advancement, there's a lot of **job mobility**.

Are there any other ways you try to **retain** staff?

A critical factor is how we communicate the many ways staff can develop with us. We celebrate success locally and corporately as internal people are **appointed** to key positions or successfully complete development programmes. This helps develop a culture of opportunities that stops staff from going elsewhere. It's very expensive to keep employing new people – that's a real cost – whereas, we see our internal development programmes and appointments as an investment.

Ian Dickson, European HR Director for Tesco

5 Match the words / phrases in bold in the interview to these definitions.

1 keep rather than lose something: *retain*
2 an essential job that a company is looking for someone to do: ________
3 spend money on something you think is useful: ________
4 providing something that's needed: ________
5 choose someone for a job: ________
6 be able to move easily from one job to another: ________
7 move someone to a more senior job: ________
8 move someone to a different job: ________
9 the rate at which people leave a company and are replaced by others: ________
10 the way in which companies help workers get better at their jobs: ________
11 be successful in your career: ________
12 level of skill: ________

6 Work with a partner. You have been asked to write a 50-word policy statement for your company about retaining staff. Use as many of the words / phrases in 5 as possible.

» For more exercises, go to **Practice file 9** on page 118.

7 Work in small groups and discuss the statements below, using as many words / phrases as possible from 2 and 5. Then present your views to the rest of the class, giving examples from your own experience as appropriate.

1 It is better to persuade people over 55 to take early retirement than to make people redundant based on the length of time in the company.
2 It is better to redeploy staff or promote internally than to appoint outside candidates.
3 Opportunities for advancement and personal development at work lead to greater job satisfaction than a rise in pay.

ⓘ » Interactive Workbook » **Glossary**

Context

Dermot and Johanna are leaders of two different teams in a financial services company. They have been given the task of creating a third team from their existing staff to set up a new branch in another country.

Meetings | Negotiating solutions

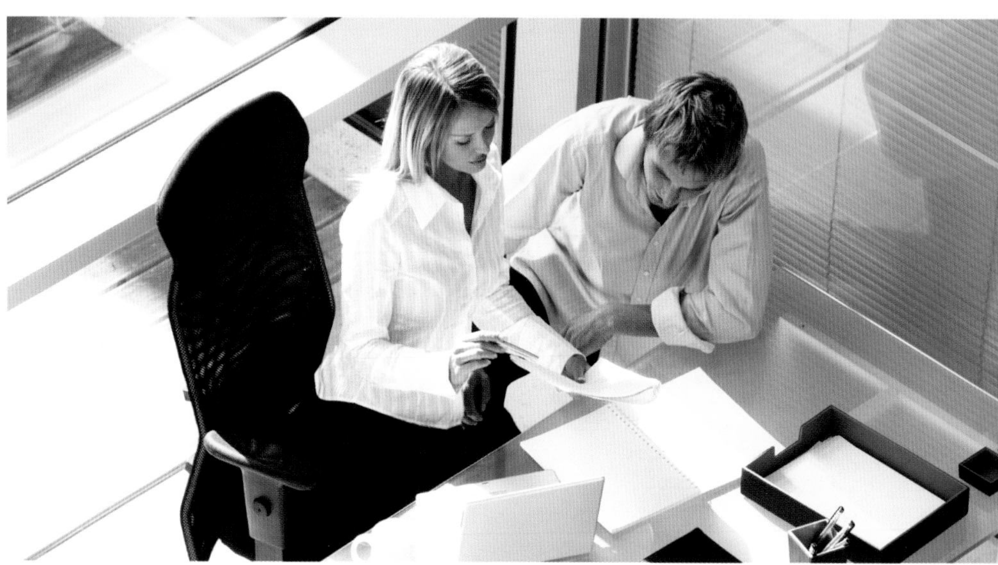

1 **35▷ Read the *Context*. Listen to the first part of the meeting Johanna had with Dermot. Who put forward these proposals? Which one did they decide on?**

1 Identify the most capable workers and send them.
2 Select three people from each team, based on their individual strengths.
3 Take on two contract workers and use just four internal staff.

2 **35▷ Match 1–7 to a–g to make phrases. Then listen again and check.**

1 What we need … ___
2 The areas we need … ___
3 If we did that, … ___
4 How about we look … ___
5 Supposing we stretch the budget a little, … ___
6 If we only have four experienced staff in the new team, … ___
7 I'm happy … ___

a we'd end up with two weaker teams …
b to discuss are …
c to decide on today is …
d with that.
e why don't we take on two contract workers …?
f at our team members' individual strengths?
g we won't lose our best workers.

NOTES FROM MEETING WITH DERMOT – TEAM FOR PROJECT VERDI

- Two people to be transferred from my team.
- Brett will do the trainees' work if necessary.
- Timo (trainee) will join the new team.
- Sabrina – good, has international experience.

Deadline from HR: team to be decided by next Monday.

3 **36▷ Listen to the second part of the meeting. Johanna and Dermot are now negotiating the new team. Correct the notes Johanna made at the meeting.**

4 **36▷ Listen again and complete these phrases.**

1 Let's ______ the situation.
2 I ______ you three, but ______ three from your team too.
3 If you ______ Brett, I ______ Jamie, Pascal and Timo from my team.
4 I ______ Brett to be on the team, ______ replace one of the trainees with …
5 ______ this list to HR before Friday, we ______ sending anyone.
6 So, ______: if I send Brett …, you'll send Sabrina …
7 I ______ that.

For more exercises, go to **Practice file 9** on page 118.

Tip | *What*

Use ***What*** at the beginning of a statement to emphasize what you're going to say.
***What** I propose is … / **What** I suggest is …* (rather than *I propose* or *I suggest*).

5 **Work with a partner. Read this information.**

A major new client has been acquired and your employer needs you to help with some training. Unfortunately this coincides with a family holiday you have booked.

Employer: Decide why you need this employee for the training at this time. What alternatives can you offer?

Employee: What alternatives can you offer your employer so you don't have to cancel your holiday?

1 Structure how the negotiation could proceed and what phrases both parties could use. Use these headings (the headings can be used more than once).
- Outline the points for discussion
- Put forward a proposal
- State a consequence
- Bargain
- Reach an agreement
- Summarize the situation

2 Choose to be the employer or employee. Carry out the negotiation, using your negotiation structure from 1 and the phrases in *Key expressions*.

6 **Work in groups of four.**

1 Pair A, turn to File 04 on page 136. Pair B, turn to File 21 on page 142. Read the information and prepare for the negotiation.

2 When you are ready, carry out the negotiation. Report the results to the class.

ⓘ » Interactive Workbook » **Email**

Practically speaking | Making and responding to quick requests

1 **37▷ Listen to six short conversations. What help does the first speaker want in each conversation? Does the second speaker agree to help?**

2 **37▷ Listen again. What does the second speaker say in response to each of these requests? How does the first speaker reply when the response is negative?**

1 Do you have a minute?
2 Could you just have a quick look at my computer?
3 Would you mind checking …?
4 Excuse me, am I disturbing you?
5 Could you spare a few minutes?
6 Can you give me a hand with …?

3 **Which of the requests in 2 are more formal (*M*) or less formal (*L*)?**

4 **Read these situations and have short conversations with a partner. Decide who you might be speaking to (e.g. your manager, a friend) and choose the appropriate level of formality. Refer to the *Useful phrases* on pages 134–135.**

- You need a client's email address.
- You need confirmation whether a business trip is taking place.
- You need help opening an email attachment.
- You need ideas for a retirement present for your boss.
- You want to swap shifts.
- You need to make an appointment for an appraisal.

Key expressions

Outlining points for discussion
What we need to decide on today is …
The areas we need to discuss are …
Let's look at what our options are.

Putting forward proposals
One option would be to …
How about we …?
What I propose is …
Let's keep our options open …
Supposing we …, why don't we …?

Stating consequences
We'd …, if we did that.
That'll solve the problem.
It just wouldn't work if …
Unless we …, we won't …

Bargaining
I could offer …, but I'd expect …
If you guaranteed …, I'd let you have …
I'll be happy … provided you …

Reaching agreement
I'm happy with that.
I can live with that.
That sounds like a plan / deal.

Summarizing the situation
Let's just summarize the situation.
So (who) have we got so far?
So, a quick recap …

ⓘ » Interactive Workbook » **Phrasebank**

Language at work | First and second conditionals

1 Read these extracts from audio 35▷ and 36▷ and answer questions 1–4.

a If I **send** Brett, Lena and Marlon, you'**ll send** Sabrina, Jamie and Pascale.
b We can't do that. If I **transferred** four people, I'**d** only **have** three left!
c If we only **have** four experienced staff …, we **won't lose** our best workers.
d If you **guaranteed** Brett, I'**d let** you have Jamie …

1 In which extracts does the speaker think that this is
- an idea / situation that is a real possibility in the future? ___
- a less realistic or imaginary idea / situation? ___

2 Which conditional is used in each case?
3 What verb forms are used in each conditional?
4 How does the use of *might* instead of *will*, and *might* or *could* instead of *would*, affect the meaning?

» For more information and exercises, go to **Practice file 9** on page 119.

2 Work with a partner. Take turns to react to these ideas. Use a first and second conditional sentence for each situation.

Example: *A I'm thinking of giving up my job and running a farm.*
B That's a great idea. If you ***move*** *to the country, you'****ll feel*** *less stressed.*
That's ridiculous. You ***wouldn't have*** *any money if you* ***gave*** *up your job.*

- having a complete career change
- relocating to another continent
- your company reducing the retirement age to 50
- HR asking all staff to work on Saturday once a month
- your team leader asking everyone to share office space

3 Read these extracts from audio 35▷ and 36▷. Match the linking words in bold to meanings 1–4.

a I'll be happy for Brett to be on the team, **provided** you replace one of the trainees …
b **Unless** we get this list to HR before Friday, we won't be sending anyone.
c We can't send all our best people **in case** we need them here.
d **Supposing** we stretch the budget a little, why don't we take on two contract workers …?

1 if not ______
2 if and only if ______
3 just imagine ______
4 because something might happen ______

» For more information and exercises, go to **Practice file 9** on page 119.

4 Work with a partner. Take turns to complete these sentences using the words in *italics* and your own ideas.

1 I can probably get you a better discount *provided* …
2 We can't give you a guaranteed delivery time *unless … / in case* …
3 *Supposing* I agree to an extra 14 days' credit …
4 *Unless / Provided that* you take out a year's subscription …
5 We offer free customer support *in case … / as long as* …
6 *Supposing* I finished those sales figures for you …

5 Work with a partner. Turn to File 20 on page 142.

1 Read the information. Work together to think of arguments that both the manager and employee could make.
2 Choose to be the manager or employee. Have a discussion and try to reach an agreement.

ⓘ » Interactive Workbook » **Exercises and Tests**

Tip | Negotiating

Use the first conditional to make a definite offer or a realistic suggestion.

If you ***agree*** *to a six-month contract, we'****ll reduce*** *the monthly service charge.*

Use the second conditional to make a less definite offer or to suggest an idea is unrealistic.

If you ***increased*** *your order, we'****d consider*** *giving you a discount.*

Negotiating a repatriation package

Background

Relocation and repatriation

GMAC Global Relocation Services is a worldwide organization with contacts in more than 110 countries. One area it specializes in is offering 'on-the-ground' support for employees who are assigned to another country. Due to the vast amount of experience gained through working with a cross section of international companies, Global Relocation Services also offers a consultancy service. It advises and supports clients on cost-effective relocation benefits and repatriation packages.

38▷ Listen to this interview with Maria from GMAC who highlights a recurring situation companies are confronted with when repatriating their staff.

Discussion

1 **What are the advantages and disadvantages for companies in developing countries of sending personnel on projects abroad?**

2 **What might be the most difficult changes that employees encounter when returning to their home country?**

3 **Would you accept the challenge of deployment abroad if your company offered it to you? If so, where would you be prepared to go, and what sort of relocation package would you expect?**

Task

1 **Read this information.**

A company has deployed a team of employees to another country for three years to oversee procedures after a takeover. The project has run smoothly and it is time to come home. While the employees were there, they experienced not only a completely different culture but a much higher standard of living compared to that of their native country. The company is keen to keep these highly-skilled employees in their workforce and needs to decide how to make returning home more attractive. A list of incentives / perks has been drawn up, which are open to discussion.

2 **Work in two groups. Group A, turn to File 17 on page 141. Group B, turn to File 39 on page 147.**

1 Read the information in the table and do tasks 1–3.
2 Work with a partner (one HR Manager and one Team Leader). Carry out the negotiation and try to reach some useful compromises to satisfy both parties.
3 After you have completed the negotiation, look at the decisions made and add up the points.
4 Report the results of the negotiation to the class.

The Expert View

International assignments are crucial for both organizations and individuals. For organizations, the investment in international mobility is high. Recent research shows that costs are twice as high as for domestic managers – and there's a lot at stake in terms of realizing organizational aims such as global coordination, finding the right skill set for vital work abroad, or the development of global managers. Individuals should think about what skills, knowledge and networks they can develop by working abroad, and how they can use these when they return. They need to make sure that they gain an adequate position with good career prospects when they move to the next (or home) location.

Dr Michael Dickmann, Senior Lecturer in Organization Studies
Cranfield School of Management

10 New business

Learning objectives in this unit
- Talking about starting up a new business
- Asking about work and life
- Asking a favour
- Avoiding saying 'no'
- Talking about activities and results using the present perfect simple and continuous

Case study
- Using contacts to help in business

Starting point

1 What attracts people to starting up their own business?

2 What are the challenges?

3 Are business start-ups in some sectors of the economy likely to be more successful than others? Why?

Working with words | Starting up a new business

1 **39▷ James Murray Wells and Jurga Zilinskiene are both very successful owners of business start-ups. Listen to them talking about their experience and complete this table. What do you think the most important factor in their success was?**

	James Murray Wells	Jurga Zilinskiene
Nature of business		
Sources of finance		
Biggest problem		
Advice		

2 **Match these nouns and noun phrases from audio 39▷ to definitions 1–12.**

gap in the market *business plan* *venture capitalist* *stake*
return on investment *turnover* *business model* *business angel*
start-up capital *network of contacts* *financial backing* *loan*

1 someone providing money for a business: ________
2 share in a business – you gain if it succeeds: ________
3 profit from shareholding: ________
4 opportunity to sell something not yet available: ________
5 document containing financial estimates for a business: ________
6 group of people who can be helpful to your business: ________
7 someone providing experience and money for a business: ________
8 support in the form of money: ________
9 money to fund a new company: ________
10 amount of business done in a given period of time: ________
11 money which is lent or borrowed: ________
12 the way a business operates to make money: ________

3 Complete this advice about funding a start-up with the phrases in 2.

When you have spotted a [1]__________ for a product or service, one of the biggest challenges is to raise enough [2]__________ to get your new business started. You may be able to get a bank [3]__________ if you can show you have a good [4]__________ for the operation of your business, plus a [5]__________ that contains detailed financial estimates. Alternatively, you could approach a [6]__________ or [7]__________ to secure the funding you need. Either way, your investors will want a [8]__________ in the new company – maybe 50% or even more – and will want to feel confident they will get a high [9]__________. Once your business is started, it is a good idea to build up a [10]__________ who might be able to help you find further [11]__________ until your [12]__________ has increased enough for you to make a profit.

4 40▷ Listen to eight extracts from James' and Jurga's talks. What adjectives come after adverbs 1–8?

1 hugely __________
2 incredibly __________
3 extremely __________
4 really __________
5 totally __________
6 completely __________
7 absolutely __________
8 really __________

Read the Tip below. What type of adjective – gradable / ungradable – goes with the adverbs

a *hugely, extremely, incredibly*? b *totally, completely, absolutely*? c *really*?

5 Arrange these adjectives into two groups that match the groups in 4. Think of other adjectives to add to each group.

kind terrible nice fantastic expensive impossible outrageous useless risky complex profitable ridiculous high wonderful

6 Work with a partner. Using an adverb and a suitable adjective, take turns to respond to these statements.

1 The bank has refused to give us a loan.
2 What's it like working for yourself?
3 I've just been nominated for the 'Entrepreneur of the Year' award.
4 Our business start-up is losing €50,000 a week.
5 One day we'll be bigger than Microsoft.
6 The venture capitalists wanted an 80% stake in the company.

» For more exercises, go to **Practice file 10** on page 120.

7 Work in small groups. Choose one of these business ideas (or think of your own) and discuss questions 1–3.

- A collapsible scooter that you can take on the train or put in the boot of your car to use in busy cities to avoid traffic. You plan to import these scooters from the US and sell them to customers in your own country.
- A fleet of self-service pay-as-you-go cars for urban commuters. Users are given a special PIN number to access the cars (which are located in designated parking places). Users pay a membership fee and then have to pay a fee based on the amount of time they use the car.

1 What's your opinion of the business idea? How successful could it be?
2 What help might someone need setting up this business? Who could they approach for finance? What advice would you give?
3 What problems or challenges might the business face?

ⓘ » Interactive Workbook » **Glossary**

Tip | Gradable and ungradable adjectives

Gradable adjectives describe qualities that can exist in different strengths, e.g. something can be more or less good or old. *Ungradable* adjectives describe qualities that can't exist in different strengths, e.g. something is either perfect or impossible or it is not.

Context

Maintaining contacts with business colleagues is important as their help or expertise may be useful at a later date. Three businesspeople have contact with former colleagues and ask for assistance with a business venture.

Socializing | Asking about work and life | Asking a favour

1 **Think of the last time you had a chance encounter with someone you hadn't seen or heard from for a long time. Describe the meeting. How did you feel? What did you talk about?**

2 **41▷ Read the *Context*. Listen to the three conversations and choose a piece of information from each column to describe each one. Write the number of the conversation in the correct space. (There are two extra pieces of information in each column.)**

Situation	Relationship	Update	Favour requested
A phone call at work ___	College friends ___	Found present job by chance ___	Contacts in Internet insurance business ___
At a trade fair ___	Ex-work colleagues ___	Married a French woman ___	New local member of staff ___
In a taxi queue ___	Business acquaintances ___	Had a promotion ___	Business contacts ___
At an airport ___	Customer / supplier ___	Business has lost customers ___	A new job ___
In a coffee shop ___	Competitors ___	Works in car industry ___	Venture capital ___

3 **Which conversation is**

a more formal? ___ b neutral? ___ c less formal? ___

4 **Match 1–8 to a–h to make phrases.**

1 I'm not sure … ___
2 I haven't … ___
3 What have … ___
4 How's … ___
5 It's good to … ___
6 That's actually … ___
7 The thing is, I'm … ___
8 I'll certainly … ___

a work?
b looking for someone to work with us …
c the reason why I'm calling.
d think about it.
e seen you for ages.
f you been doing?
g hear from you.
h if you remember me.

5 **41▷ Listen to conversation 1 again and check your answers.**

6 **Put the phrases in 4 into these categories.**

a Greeting an old friend / colleague: __________
b Asking about work / life: __________
c Changing the subject to introduce a favour: __________
d Asking a favour: __________
e Responding to a request for a favour: __________

7 **Turn to audio script 41▷ on page 159. Underline all the phrases in conversations 2 and 3 which match the categories in 6. Compare the level of formality of the phrases used in all three conversations.**

» For more exercises, go to **Practice file 10** on page 120.

Tip | *anyway*

Use *anyway* to return to an earlier topic, change the subject or end the conversation.

***Anyway**, you mentioned changes. What's been happening?*

***Anyway**, what have you been up to?*

8 **Work with a partner. Have two conversations using the flow chart. Take turns to be Student A. Use the prompts numbered 1 for the first conversation and the prompts numbered 2 for the second.**

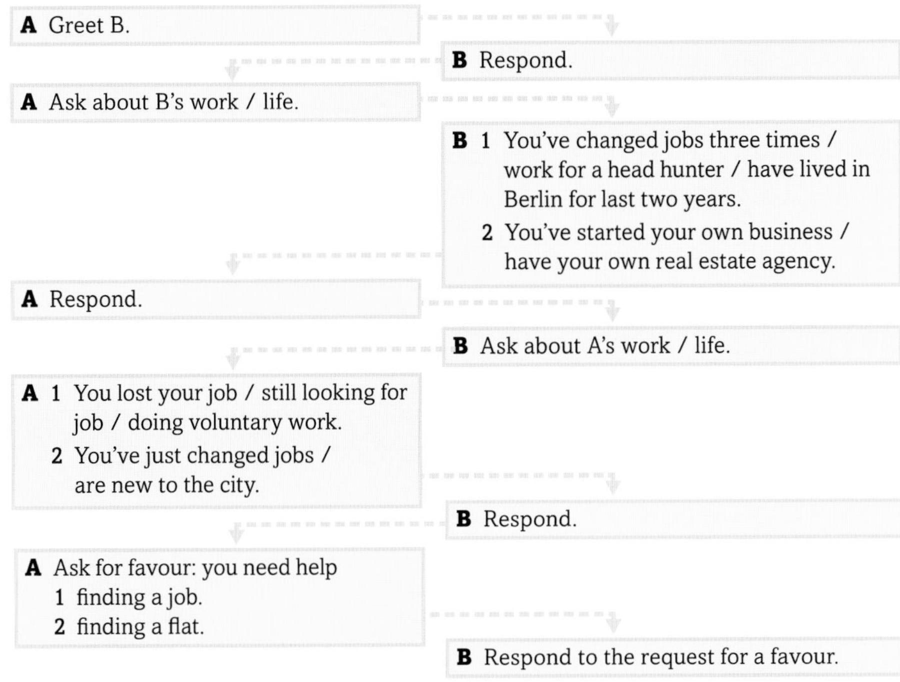

A Greet B.
B Respond.
A Ask about B's work / life.
B 1 You've changed jobs three times / work for a head hunter / have lived in Berlin for last two years.
2 You've started your own business / have your own real estate agency.
A Respond.
B Ask about A's work / life.
A 1 You lost your job / still looking for job / doing voluntary work.
2 You've just changed jobs / are new to the city.
B Respond.
A Ask for favour: you need help
1 finding a job.
2 finding a flat.
B Respond to the request for a favour.

9 **Write down three true and three untrue events which have happened to you over the last few years.**

1 Work with a partner. Have a conversation. Greet each other and find out as much information about your partner's recent past as possible.
2 Decide which information was true / untrue.
3 Check with your partner if you were correct.

ⓘ » Interactive Workbook » **Email**

Practically speaking | Avoiding saying 'no'

1 **Sometimes when we're asked a favour, we don't like to say 'no' in a direct way. Discuss questions 1–3 with a partner.**

1 How easy is it for you to say 'no' when someone asks a favour?
2 Is it easier to say 'no' to some people than to others and in different situations? Why?
3 Which of the *Useful phrases* on page 135 could you use to avoid saying 'no' in a direct way to these favours?
   a 'Could you do the on-call shift next weekend?'
   b 'Could you help me look into this customer complaint we've received?'

2 **Work with a partner. Take turns to respond to these favours. Refer to the *Useful phrases* on page 135.**

1 'Do you think you could have a look at the results from our customer survey and prepare a report for the team meeting on Monday?'
2 'I'm supposed to be making a presentation at the investor relations meeting next Friday but I want to take a day's leave. Could you stand in for me?'
3 'Could you stay late tonight and help with the stocktaking?'
4 'We need someone to help at the conference next weekend. Are you free?'

Key expressions

Greeting old friends / acquaintances
I'm not sure if you remember me.
I haven't seen you for ages …
It's good to hear from you.
What are you doing here?
When was the last time we saw each other?
It's been a long time since we've been in contact.

Asking about work / life
What about you?
What have you been doing / been up to?
How's work?
How's life treating you?
How's business with you?
Are you still …?

Changing subject to introduce a favour
That's actually the reason why I'm calling.
By the way, could you do me a favour?
With that in mind, maybe I could ask you for a favour.

Asking a favour
The thing is, I'm looking for someone to …
Could you put me in touch with … since you …?
We are looking for … and I wondered if …

Responding to a request for a favour
I'll certainly think about it.
Let's chat / talk about that over dinner.
It sounds an interesting proposal.
Send me the details …
That isn't something I can decide on right now.

ⓘ » Interactive Workbook » **Phrasebank**

Language at work | Present perfect simple and continuous

1 **Match these extracts from audio 41▷ to situations 1–3. What tense is used in each situation?**

a Our company **has secured** a huge contract with Mobelitec.
b GBF **have been keeping** me very busy.
c Since you left GBF, life**'s been** extremely hectic.

1 a state that started in the past and is unchanged ___
2 a continuous activity that started in the past and is still going on ___
3 a finished activity with an end result ___

2 **Read these two sentences. Which suggests that something is temporary? Which suggests that something is permanent? What tenses are used?**

1 **Since** last month, I**'ve been commuting** between France and Belgium.
2 She**'s lived** in Brussels **for** years.

3 **What is the difference between the use of *for* and *since* in the sentences in 2?**

» For more information and exercises, go to **Practice file 10** on page 121.

4 **Choose the best ending (a or b) for each sentence and explain your choice.**

1 I've worked out a final price,
I've been working out a final price
a but I'm still waiting for a couple of figures.
b and it's lower than the original estimate.

2 I've been calling Mrs Fischer
I've called Mrs Fischer
a but I can't get through to her.
b and left her a message.

3 I've worked with Karen
I've been working with Karen
a because her supervisor is on sick leave.
b for over 30 years.

4 We've been hiring
We've hired
a a manager and three supervisors.
b people for the new factory.

5 **Work with a partner. You are planning to set up a new business. You have both been responsible for doing various tasks. Student A, turn to File 22 on page 142. Student B, follow the instructions below.**

Student B

1 Use these prompts to ask questions about the progress your partner has made. What two tasks has your partner actually completed?
- sort out insurance
- decide on company name
- phone solicitor
- do anything about accounting system
- set up website

2 Use the information in the table to answer your partner's questions. Say what you have been doing this week and what tasks you have / haven't done.

Ongoing this week	Done	Not done
• Contact estate agents in all possible locations. • Check local newspapers for business premises to rent. • Research transport links in all the possible locations.	• Discuss required features of a business location with business adviser. • Make list of possible business locations.	• Go to any of the possible locations.

6 **Give a short presentation about three or four current activities that you or your company are involved in. For each activity, say how long it has been going on, what has already been achieved and what remains to be done.**

ⓘ » Interactive Workbook » **Exercises and Tests**

Using contacts to help in business

Background

Miho brings bagels to Tokyo

Miho Inagi, an IT graduate, resigned from her safe office job to run her own New York bagel company in the heart of Tokyo. It was a risky decision as bagels weren't well known in Japan when she came up with the idea. To begin with, the company struggled due to lack of advertising. However, this all changed when an enthusiastic customer wrote a rave review on @ bagel café – a website which rates the bagel bakeries in Japan. What differentiates Miho's bagels from others in Tokyo is the authentic choice of toppings – she doesn't bow to Japanese tastes but offers exactly what you'd expect to get in New York.

42▷ **Listen to Miho describe how she moved from computer programming to baking bagels.**

Discussion

1 **Can you think of any Eastern products that have been successfully introduced into Western culture and vice versa?**

2 **What factors might businesses need to consider when introducing a product from another culture?**

3 **How important were contacts and 'favours' for the success of Miho's business venture?**

Task

Work in groups of four. **Student A, turn to File 25 on page 143. Student B, turn to File 38 on page 146. Student C, turn to File 43 on page 148. Student D, turn to File 50 on page 149.**

You and your colleagues have been chosen to help set up a new division of a company. You have been asked to set up the new division as fast as possible so you need to work together. However, you all have a lot of individual tasks to do to get things up and running. Unfortunately, money, time and resources are tight. You each have three favours you'd like to ask of each other. Read the rules below and try to get the favours granted by your colleagues as fast as you can. The person with all three favours granted first is the winner.

Rules

1 Read your card. You have three favours to ask.
2 Ask one favour per person then move on. If someone agrees to do the favour, write the name of that colleague in the grid.
3 You must say 'yes' to two favours.
4 There are three favours listed on your card which you must refuse to do. With any other favour asked, you can decide if you want to do the favour or not.

The Expert View

Starting up a new business requires two kinds of 'personal asset'. Firstly, you have to be tough, and prepared to work long hours, face setbacks, and overcome challenges and disappointments. Secondly, you need some specific business skills. Perhaps the single most important personal quality is the ability to sell. Finding the money to support a new venture is vital, so you must persuade people to invest in your business. Suppliers must be convinced to supply the goods and services you need. And you have to persuade customers who don't know you to buy from you. No matter how good the business idea, without customers it will never succeed.

David Molian, Bettany Centre for Entrepreneurial Performance & Economics
Cranfield School of Management

Case study

11 | Communications

Learning objectives in this unit
- Talking about communications
- Explaining procedures
- Teleconferencing
- Dealing with situations on the phone
- Talking about obligation and prohibition

Case study
- Solving a communication problem

Starting point

1 **Is the world a better place with communications technologies? Why or why not?**

2 **What communications technology could you personally not live without? Why?**

Working with words | Communications

1 **43▷ Listen to an extract from a discussion programme looking at developments in the world of communications. Answer questions 1–3.**

1 How does speaker 1 see communications systems developing?
2 What three stages in communications development does speaker 2 mention?
3 What is speaker 3's main point about communications systems?

2 **Match phrases 1–9 from audio 43▷ to phrases a–i with a similar meaning.**

1 have access to ___ a communicate with
2 connect to ___ b give attention to
3 focus on ___ c combine with
4 interact with ___ d affect
5 have an impact on ___ e have something near you which you can use
6 be involved in ___ f work together with
7 subscribe to ___ g join to a supply or network
8 collaborate with ___ h be part of
9 integrate with ___ i pay regularly for

3 **Complete these questions with the correct form of phrases 1–9 in 2.**

1 Do you have the opportunity to ______________ projects run by other departments in your company?
2 Do you ______________ colleagues based in another country to put on exhibitions or conferences?
3 What equipment, if any, have you bought to ______________ your computer system at home?
4 Is it easier to ______________ other people in a teleconference if you can see them on screen?
5 Do you ______________ any teleconferencing facilities in your office?
6 How much does the Internet ______________ the lifestyle of you and your family? Do you think you spend less time together?
7 How do you ______________ the Internet at home – dial-up or broadband?
8 Do you ______________ any satellite, cable or other services at home?
9 Are there any problems your company needs to ______________ in order to improve communications between departments?

4 **Work with a partner and ask and answer the questions in 3.**

5 **Read the texts quickly. Which text is about**

1 an unexpected use of an existing technology?
2 a new combination of two different technologies?

Mercy Ships

The global charity Mercy Ships uses its growing fleet of hospital ships to deliver free health care to developing nations. Now, with the help of an innovative new microscope, the 'Nikon Coolscope', and a satellite communication system, volunteers on board can analyse blood and tissue samples with the help of experts in distant locations around the world. Still images of samples obtained from patients are loaded onto the Internet. Experts log in to a secure web page, gain access to the samples and provide immediate diagnoses or consultation by email. The Coolscope can also be used for 'live' sessions during an on-board operation. With remote access to clear digital images, expert doctors can immediately suggest a course of action to follow – by telephone, from their own home, perhaps thousands of miles away.

Africa Calling

In many parts of the world, mobile phones aren't a convenient alternative to landlines but the only means of communication: they provide connection with the outside world where there was none before. In Africa, mobile phones mean real change. If you live in rural Africa, your payment options are limited and so, therefore, is your participation in the wider economy. If you don't live within a hundred miles of a bank, don't have a chequebook and have never even seen a credit card, how do you send money to someone else? Mobile phones provide an instantly transferable form of payment. You buy a pre-pay card, obtain the voucher number and then text that number to your counterpart. And the person you sent it to can start using it right away. This enables the development of small businesses without banks and contributes significantly to the growth of the local economy.

6 **Read the texts again and answer questions 1–2.**

1 How has technology improved the service Mercy Ships can provide?
2 How have mobile phones made a difference in Africa?

7 **Complete the word families for these words from the texts.**

Verb	Personal noun	Noun	Adjective
communicate	*communicator*	communication	*communicative*
analyse			
	volunteer	–	
			innovative
		consultation	
		economy	
		development	
	–	connection	
	–		transferable
		participation	

» For more exercises, go to **Practice file 11** on page 122.

8 **Work in small groups. Discuss the changes that communications technology has brought about in your job / company / industry. Present your views to the class, giving examples from your own experience as appropriate.**

ⓘ » Interactive Workbook » **Glossary**

Context

Job Seeker is an international e-company serving both people looking for jobs and companies looking for staff. It has recently introduced services in Romania and Austria. Two new positions have been created in each country to look after key account customers. Job Seeker has arranged a teleconference with the two countries to inform them about procedures for working with key accounts. The participants are Jimmy from the US, Angelika from Austria and Mirela from Romania.

Meetings | Explaining procedures | Teleconferencing

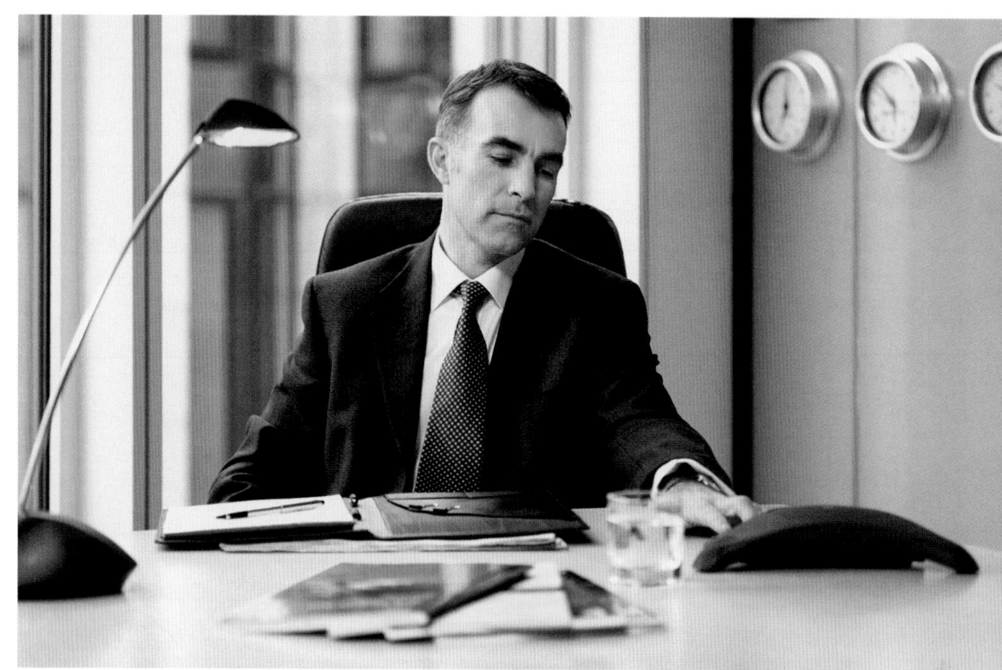

1 **44▷ Read the *Context*. Listen to the teleconference and answer these queries Angelika prepared before the call.**

How often do we contact / meet key account customers?
Do we have any offers for key accounts?
How do we calculate the price?
Can we get information about key accounts in writing from the US?

2 **Put these phrases used for explaining procedures into categories a–c.**

1 You must set up regular meetings.
2 It's a good idea to plan these for once a quarter …
3 You need to make sure they've seen the demo …
4 What's useful is to send it to them on a CD …
5 What happens is … an offer is made according to …
6 It's essential to tell them about our advantages …

a Referring to a necessary measure: ________
b Making a recommendation: ________
c Giving an explanation: ________

3 **Work with a partner. Explain the procedure for teleconferencing calls in your company (use File 23 on page 143 if necessary). Make sure you state what's necessary and what's recommended.**

4 **44▷ Listen to the teleconference again and answer questions 1–4.**

1 What two phrases did Angelika use to ask for clarification?
2 What two phrases did Jimmy use to check the participants had understood him correctly? How did the participants show they had understood?
3 What did Jimmy say to keep the meeting to time?
4 What two communication problems did they encounter during the teleconference? What did the participants say to indicate there was a problem?

» For more exercises, go to **Practice file 11** on page 122.

Tip | Teleconferencing

In a teleconference, it can be difficult to know who is speaking, especially if there is more than one woman or man present. It helps to identify yourself when you speak.

This is Angelika (speaking).
This is Mirela again.
This is Jimmy, by the way.

5 **Work with a partner. Decide what you would say in these situations, using phrases from *Key expressions*.**

1 One of the speakers is talking too fast and you can't keep up.
2 You're not exactly clear what one of the speakers on a teleconference means.
3 It's a bad line and you can't hear.
4 You're running the teleconference and you're behind time with the agenda. You want to finish on time.
5 You're facilitating the teleconference and want to make sure everyone is following what's been said.

6 **Work in groups of three.**

1 Think of a procedure you do at work or in your free time (e.g. sending a meeting request by email / decorating a room in your home).
2 Explain the procedure to the rest of the group.
3 When you are listening to the explanation, ask for clarification as necessary.

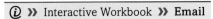

ⓘ » Interactive Workbook » **Email**

Key expressions

Explaining procedures
You must ...
It's a good idea to ...
You need to ...
What's useful is to ...
What happens is ...
It's essential to ...

Asking for clarification
What exactly do you mean by ...?
So you're saying ...?
Can you run through that again?

Checking listener understands
Are you with me?
Is that clear?

Showing you've understood
Yeah. That's clear.
OK ... Yes, I've got that.
OK. I'm with you.

Teleconferencing
Technical problems
You're very faint. / You're breaking up.
I can't hear (Mirela).
There's an echo on the line.
Hang on ... Is that better?
Yes, it's fine again now.
Yes, you're back again now.
Timing
Can we speed up a little ...?
Could you slow down a bit? We're having problems following you.

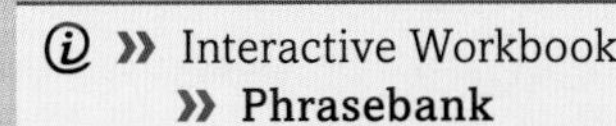

Practically speaking | Dealing with situations on the phone

1 **45▷ Listen to three conversations. Answer questions 1–2 for each conversation.**

1 What is the situation?
2 How is each situation resolved?

2 **45▷ Match statements 1–4 to the best response a–d. Listen again and check.**

1 Sorry, but this'll have to be quick, Renée, I'm about to board a plane! ___
2 This is hopeless. It's a really bad line. ___
3 I'm afraid I didn't catch that last bit. ___
4 Look, I'm sorry, but I have someone on the other line. Can I call you back? ___

a Yes, I'm around for another hour, then I have a meeting.
b So now's not a good time to call?
c OK. I'll hang up and call you on the landline in five minutes.
d I said, any chance of getting it to me by tomorrow?

3 **45▷ Which statements in 2 indicate that there is a problem in communication? Which indicate that it isn't a good time to call?**

4 **Work with a partner. Have four short phone conversations. Use these situations or think of your own. Refer to the *Useful phrases* on page 135.**

- You're on holiday in the Caribbean when your manager calls about an unfinished report.
- You've gone to visit a client in a remote country location. You call your PA for some figures.
- You're at the cinema and have forgotten to turn off your mobile. Your partner / a colleague calls to remind you about an appointment.
- You're at a crowded sports event. You need to call someone to rearrange a meeting.

Language at work | Modal verbs – obligation and prohibition

1 Read these extracts from audio 44▷.

a We **don't have to** go through the demo …
b You **must** set up regular meetings.
c You **should** read through this thoroughly …
d There's another conference call booked … so we **can't** run over.

Which extract means that

1 something is obligatory? ___
2 something is not possible or not allowed? ___
3 something is not necessary? ___
4 something is advisable or preferable? ___

2 Which of these phrases can you use in place of the modal verbs in bold in the extracts in 1?

have to *mustn't* *needn't* *ought to* *don't need to* *aren't allowed to*

3 Match these present tense forms to the past tense forms below.

have to *don't have to* *must* *are allowed to* *have got to*
mustn't *needn't* *don't need to* *hasn't got to* *can't*

1 had to: ______________
2 didn't have to: ______________
3 could(n't) / was(n't)/were(n't) allowed to: ______________

» For more information and exercises, go to **Practice file 11** on page 123.

4 Work with a partner. Ask and answer questions about your obligations at work, using *Do you have to …?* or *Can you …?*

- paying for phone calls
- working at weekends
- signing in and out of the office
- taking holiday at any time
- recording use of the office photocopier
- carrying an identity card
- working at home
- taking time off in lieu for working overtime

5 Work with a partner. Choose two of these problems that you have experience of. Explain what the problem was and how you resolved it, using the past modals in 3.

- forgetting an appointment
- running out of money
- missing a work deadline
- losing an important document
- missing a train / flight
- forgetting a ticket / passport
- sending an email to the wrong person
- having a car breakdown / accident

6 Work with a partner. Choose one of the topics below (or one of your own) and draw up a list of guidelines. Prioritize the guidelines according to their importance. Then present your guidelines to another pair.

- making a complaint about your superior at work
- making a good impression at an interview
- health and safety procedures at work
- arranging time off
- dealing with a difficult customer

ⓘ » Interactive Workbook » **Exercises and Tests**

Solving a communication problem

Background

New procedures at FWZ

FWZ is a company specializing in flight planning and flight optimization software. It has expanded rapidly and over the last few months has found its clients (airlines) are not only based in Europe, but the US and Asia too. This means shift work has had to be introduced into the small Support Department due to the time difference between its working hours and those of its different customers. Measures have had to be taken regarding the communication procedure because the team of ten employees seldom meets together as a group now. A system has had to be devised for dealing with client queries and problems via email. The task has been to determine who does this, and when, and how jobs are prioritized.

Discussion

1 **What internal communication problems might a company face when it is expanding rapidly?**

2 **What communication problems could occur when your working day is nine hours ahead or behind that of your clients'?**

3 46▷ **Listen to Robert Turner, head of the Support Department, talking about the new procedures FWZ has developed to deal with communication from clients.**

1 Do you think the prioritizing system will work at FWZ?
2 What will be the benefits of using the new software for dealing with customer communication?

Task

1 **Work in groups of four. Turn to File 24 on page 143 and read the information.**

2 **Your task is to decide on a possible procedure so that communication with clients is easier, and more efficient for clients. Discuss the problem and create a procedure to present to the rest of the class. Consider the following points.**

- Who prioritizes jobs?
- How are they prioritized (i.e. which type of calls / emails are most urgent)?
- How do the employees on a different shift know what's urgent when they arrive at work?
- When are emails checked?
- What happens to the queries / emails after someone's read them?
- What happens to phone calls? Are they documented? How?
- Who checks that jobs have been done?
- How do the employees on the different shifts know when the jobs have been done?

3 **Each group presents their procedure to the class. When you are listening, ask for clarification as necessary and make notes under the following headings for each group's procedure.**

- How does the communication flow work?
- How easy is the implementation?
- Other details / notes.

4 **Decide as a class which procedure should be implemented and why.**

The Expert View

Managing customer service effectively in an international context and across different time zones requires established procedures, and the ability to respond quickly to customer needs around the clock. A key human resources priority for such organizations is the development of team members who can manage the increasing complexity of running a global service. While they may recruit top-level managers from outside the organization, developing the skills of existing key workers is a priority to ensure consistency, and an in-depth understanding of the business. It is essential that staff are encouraged and helped to acquire a global mindset, cross-cultural experience and the relevant business insights.

Dr Hilary Harris, Programme Director, Centre for Customized Executive Development
Cranfield School of Management

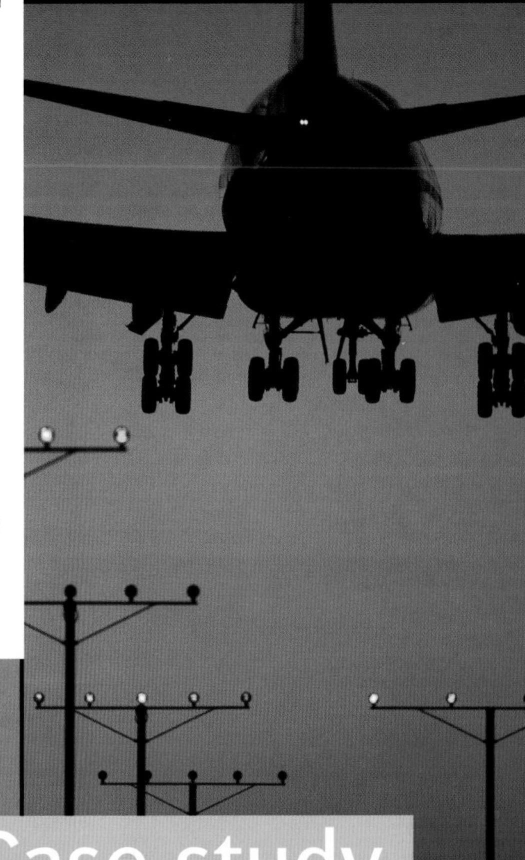

Case study

12 | Change

Learning objectives in this unit
- Talking about change
- Presenting future plans
- Being negative diplomatically
- Using future continuous and future perfect to talk about plans and changes
- Talking about probability

Case study
- Increasing operational efficiency

Starting point

Choose one of the possible changes at work below. Say

1 what problems your company might have bringing in the change
2 how you or your colleagues might react
3 what arguments your company could give to make it more acceptable.

- a new system of working hours
- using English only in meetings
- a camera monitor system to prevent time-wasting / petty theft

Working with words | Talking about change

1 **Read the first paragraph of the article and answer these questions.**

1 What is the most critical part of organizational change and what happens during that period?
2 What are the three main responses to proposals for change?

2 **Read the rest of the article. How might employees behave if they**

1 support the change?
2 are not sure about the change?
3 are against the change?

Adapting to change – or resisting?

Getting any organization to change is a slow process, but it's the initial stage – when the change is first announced – that is by far the most important. That's when the people in an organization start thinking about how the change will **affect** them personally. They weigh up the pros and cons and ask questions about its usefulness. Reactions will range from enthusiastic support, to apathy, to rejection. The people affected by the change will typically fall into the following three groups.

The supporters

If they can see the advantages of the change, your supporters will try to persuade their colleagues to **accept** it. They'll take an active part in the process and will do their best to understand the new procedures and **adapt** to new programmes.

The ambivalent

They can see that the proposals have good and bad points, but they may be nervous about the idea of change and feel anxious about changes to their current situation. They may **oppose** some of the ideas, but, given enough pressure, they'll eventually accept the changes as necessary. They won't be antagonistic, but they won't be committed either, so you'll need to lead them through the exercise – which they'd prefer not to do.

The opponents

These are going to be your biggest problem. They'll be difficult, rebellious and unwilling, and will try hard to **resist** the change. If they do eventually agree to it, they will still feel resentful and will be constantly watching for the slightest mistake. If they can't sabotage the new ways of working, they may **react** by becoming apathetic and doing as little work as possible.

Clearly, it's an advantage to have few 'opponents' in an organization, and the challenge is to create real enthusiasm and commitment, and get enough people 'on board' in support of the change. The key thing is to involve staff at the very beginning in the problem-solving phase. If you do, they're much more likely to be positive and enthusiastic about the solution.

3 **Match the words in bold in the article to these definitions.**

1 disagree with something and try to stop it from happening: ________
2 respond to something by showing feelings or taking action: ________
3 cause a change in someone or something: ________
4 agree to do something that's been suggested: ________
5 refuse to accept or comply with something: ________
6 become used to a different environment or new way of doing things: ________

4 **Work with a partner.**

1 Which of the three groups in the article would you put yourself in?
2 Use the words in **3** to make statements about how you react to change.

5 **47▷ A multinational engineering company recently introduced a policy of using only English in all meetings. Listen to three employees talking about their reactions to the change. Which of the three groups in the article in 1 does each speaker belong to?**

6 **Match phrasal verbs 1–8 from audio 47▷ to verbs a–h with similar meanings.**

1 *trying out* their language skills ___
2 they *put on* lots of courses ___
3 we'll be able to *take on* more work ___
4 *working out* very well ___
5 they *brought* the policy *in* ___
6 we *ran into* a few problems ___
7 *deal with* support calls ___
8 *dropped out of* the courses ___

a handle
b encounter
c leave
d accept
e have a (successful) result
f arrange
g practise
h introduce

7 **Work with a partner. Make a sentence with each of the phrasal verbs in 6.**

8 **Which of these words / phrases from the article and audio 47▷ describe**

1 worry / uncertainty? *concerned*
2 hostility? *antagonistic*
3 enthusiasm? *receptive*

~~antagonistic~~ *~~concerned~~* *~~receptive~~* *resistant* *worried* *nervous* *committed* *ambivalent* *hostile* *anxious* *in favour* *critical* *resentful* *enthusiastic* *keen* *against* *positive* *apprehensive* *optimistic*

9 **Which of the words / phrases in 8 are followed by these prepositions?**

about *of* *on* *to* *towards* *(no preposition)*

10 **Work in small groups. Discuss whether you would support or oppose the following changes and how you would feel about them. Use the words / phrases in 8.**

- a rise in taxation to support environmental initiatives (e.g. higher air passenger tax)
- compulsory car-sharing (e.g. several families / people own a car together)

» For more exercises, go to **Practice file 12** on page 124.

11 **Work with a partner. Think about a past or current change at work. Talk about**

- the proposals for change
- the reactions of you and your colleagues during the different stages of the change
- positive or negative outcomes of the change
- how well you feel you have adapted to the change.

ⓘ » Interactive Workbook » **Glossary**

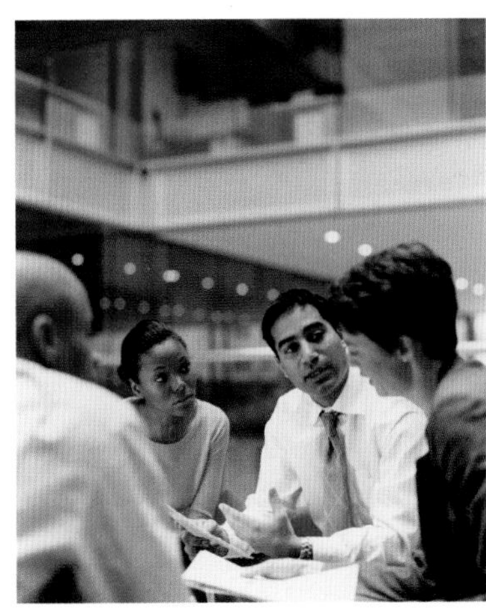

Context

FGR is a textiles company based in Northern England. Due to fierce competition from the Far East and Asia, FGR's management called in business consultants to see what changes could be made to help the company work more efficiently. Rachel and Imran are department leaders and have attended the consultants' final meeting. Their task now is to present the consultants' proposed changes to the other heads of department.

Presenting | Presenting future plans

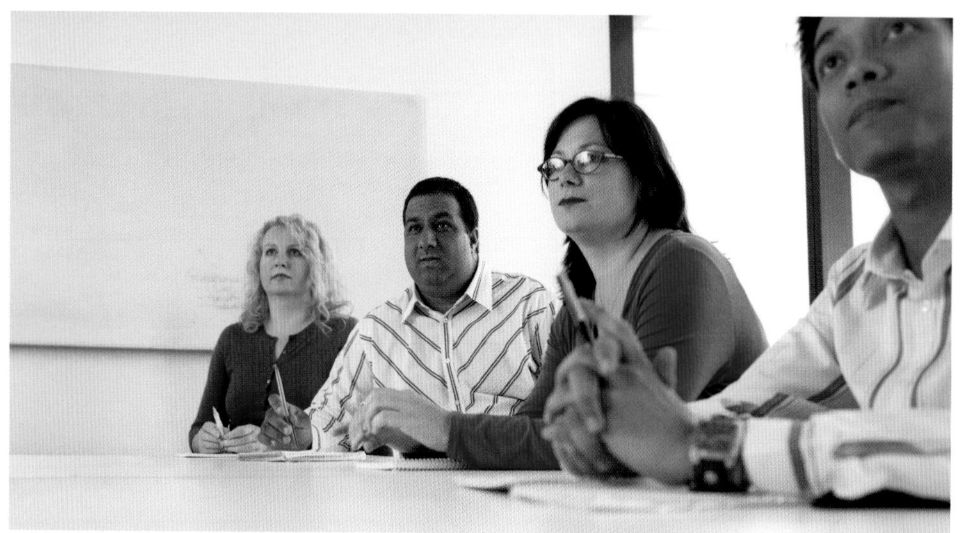

1 **Some teams, departments or even whole companies operate a bottom-up management approach where employees are involved in decision-making and policy-making. Work in small groups and discuss questions 1–2.**

1 Who proposes ideas for change and makes the decisions in your company?
2 What role, if any, do employees play in helping implement change?

2 **48▷ Read the *Context*. Listen to the presentation given by Rachel and Imran. Complete the missing information in these notes.**

CONSULTANTS' FINDINGS

Job losses? Yes.

How will job cuts be made? [1] ________

Pay freeze? Probably.

How will we be informed? [2] ________

New management model: bottom-up management

When will it be implemented? [3] ________

Friday afternoon ideas forum: potential problem: [4] ________

Will employees get remuneration? [5] ________

3 **48▷ Listen again. Put these phrases into categories a–d below.**

1 As you all know, it is likely …
2 We'd like to assure you that …
3 Decisions will definitely have been made by March …
4 Over the next few weeks, we'll be hosting departmental meetings.
5 Starting from next month, we'll be putting regular updates on our Intranet.
6 We're proposing a Friday afternoon ideas forum.
7 You may be wondering if this will work.
8 It's crucial to get the employees on our side …
9 This last point is probably going to be difficult to administer at the beginning.
10 We're calling on you to be positive – pass this information on …

a Explaining planned future events / activities: ________
b Making predictions about a future situation: ________
c Referring to audience knowledge and concerns: ________
d Making a call for action: ________

Tip | *Let's*

Use *Let's* … rather than *I'd like to* … in a presentation to involve your audience and make the situation more personal.

***Let's** digress for a moment and look at this in more detail.*

4 **Turn to audio script 48▷ on page 162. What do the speakers say to**
1 hand over to someone else?
2 indicate that they are going to give more details?

» For more exercises, go to **Practice file 12** on page 124.

5 **Work with a partner. Take turns to present these situations using an appropriate phrase. (Each person should use a different phrase for each situation.)**
1 Explain a future planned event, e.g. increase of staff numbers by 5%.
2 Make an informed prediction about the financial status of your / a business area.
3 Refer to your staff's concerns that the company may close and reassure them.
4 Indicate that you are going to expand on a point about a new flexitime system.
5 Hand over the presentation about your department to a colleague from a different department.
6 You've made a presentation about new, higher sales targets. Give your audience a 'call for action'.

6 **Choose one of the topics below and prepare a mini-presentation (two minutes) about proposed changes. Include at least one phrase from each category in *Key expressions*. The content doesn't have to be true for your job or company.**
- your department
- use of the Internet in work time
- your company's product / service
- holiday procedures
- overtime rules
- working hours

7 **Give your presentation to a partner. Your partner should listen and check which phrases you used from *Key expressions*.**

ⓘ » Interactive Workbook » **Email**

Practically speaking | Being negative diplomatically

1 **49▷ Sometimes, when you have negative feelings about an idea or proposal, you want to be diplomatic or neutral in your response rather than say what you really think. Listen to five short conversations. What idea or proposal is being discussed in each one?**

2 **49▷ Listen again. What does the second speaker say in conversations 1–5 to express the following?**
Conversation 1 I don't fully agree with the idea.
Conversation 2 I can understand the ideas of the two groups involved.
Conversation 3 My impression of the idea is positive but I have some doubts.
Conversation 4 I'm uncertain about the idea.
Conversation 5 I want more time before I give my opinion of the idea.

3 **Work with a partner. Take turns to express a diplomatic response to these ideas. Refer to the *Useful phrases* on page 135.**
- introducing a car-sharing policy and reducing the number of car parking spaces
- providing only decaffeinated coffee and tea in the company cafeteria
- introducing a shift system to make communication easier with clients worldwide but employees are concerned about the impact on their private lives
- changing from business class to economy class for all business trips
- centralizing secretarial support services (previously each department had their own service)

Key expressions

Explaining planned future events
Over the next few weeks, we'll be …
We plan to keep you informed about …
Starting from next month, we'll be …
Our idea is to …
We're proposing …
Later this year we'll be …

Making informed predictions
Decisions will definitely have been made by …
Hopefully, the new model will be in place by …
We are fairly certain this will have been carried out by …
(This) is probably going to be …

Referring to audience knowledge and concerns
We're well aware of your concerns regarding …
As you all know, …
We'd like to assure you that …
Many of you have asked about …
You may be wondering if …

Call for action
It's crucial to …
We're calling on you to be …

Giving more details
Let's digress for a moment and look at this in more detail.

Handing over to someone else
I'd like to pass the next point over to …
(John) will now deal with …

ⓘ » Interactive Workbook » **Phrasebank**

Language at work | Future continuous, future perfect and probability

1 **Match these extracts from audio 48▷ to situations 1–3. What tense is used in each situation?**

a Decisions **will** definitely **have been made** by March.
b Over the next few weeks, we'**ll be hosting** departmental meetings.
c I'**ll be visiting** our suppliers in Bradford on that day ...

1 an activity that is part of a future programme ___
2 an activity that will be in progress at a particular time in the future ___
3 an action that will be finished by a particular time in the future ___

» For more information and exercises, go to **Practice file 12** on page 125.

2 **Work with a partner. Look at the picture and answer questions 1–2. Use the prompts and / or your own ideas.**

1 What will be happening over the next six months?
clear / ground cut down / trees take on / temporary workers damage / environment
2 What will have happened by this time next year?
complete / project build / new supermarket create / local jobs ruin / countryside

3 **50▷ Listen to extracts 1–3. What is being discussed in each extract?**

4 **Turn to audio script 50▷ on page 163. Underline the following phrases that the speakers use to talk about the probability of things happening. Write *0%*, *25%*, *50%*, *75%* or *100%* to show how probable the things are.**

Extract 1		Extract 2		Extract 3	
might	*50%*	it is doubtful	___	definitely won't	___
bound to	___	is certain to	___	'll probably	___
probably won't	___	are likely to	___	perhaps	___
there's a good chance	___			will definitely	___

» For more information and exercises, go to **Practice file 12** on page 125.

5 **Work with a partner. Using as many phrases from 4 as possible, talk about your activities in and out of work.**

1 What activities will / might / won't you be doing
- next week?
- next month?
- in six months' time?
- next year?

2 What do you think you will / might / won't have achieved
- by the end of next week?
- between now and the end of the year?

6 **Work with a partner. What developments do you predict for working life? What will be happening in twenty years' time? What changes will have taken place?**

Example: *A lot more people **will be working** from home.*
*The retirement age **will have been raised** to 75.*

7 **Work with another pair. How probable are their predictions in 6?**

ⓘ » Interactive Workbook » **Exercises and Tests**

Increasing operational efficiency

Background

Change initiatives at Medstin

Medstin produces hi-tech diagnostic machines for hospitals. It has manufacturing plants and sales offices around the world. Recently the company has lost orders because its biggest competitors are manufacturers in China who can produce similar products for a considerably lower price. The management board brought in a business consultancy to analyse the company and suggest changes to make it work more efficiently. Their findings were as follows.

The company

- Least profitable sales / manufacturing offices
  - Mannheim Sales office, Germany: losing 5% of clients each year
  - Los Angeles, US: overheads highest of all locations
  - Oslo, Norway: highest payroll costs and smallest number of staff
- Old manufacturing technology slows down production
- Highly hierarchical structure – too many layers of management

The staff

- Trend for open-plan offices results in a high level of noise with constant distractions for workers and subsequent lack of concentration
- 12-hour shifts in manufacturing plant too long – the last 2 hours are unproductive
- Flexitime in office is unmonitored – those working 40–50 hours a week resent employees who 'bend the rules' – problematic in 8 out of 10 locations
- Office staff lunch hours last on average 80 minutes
- Computer system downtime means that each employee is unproductive on average 1 hour a week

The Expert View

All organizations recognize the need to change, but many experience difficulty in delivering the anticipated benefits of any change initiative. One of the main causes of failing to deliver a return on investment is the poor quality of the original business case. Early planning is critical to successful change, and needs to include a clear and measurable statement of anticipated benefits, plus an outline of the internal resources required. It also needs to consider the implications of the proposed change, both for the business and for employees. To ensure a smooth transition, organizations need to develop a consistent way of initiating and implementing change.

Dr Rob Lambert, Senior Lecturer in Management Information Systems
Cranfield School of Management

Discussion

1 **Is there anything companies like Medstin can do to secure jobs and the industry against cheaper and more competitive regions in the world?**

2 **What action might Medstin consider taking in response to the findings about the company?**

Task

1 **Work in groups of three. You are going to decide how Medstin could increase its efficiency. Discuss questions 1–3 and make notes.**
   1 What changes could be made to increase efficiency?
   2 When should these changes be implemented?
   3 What might be the staff reaction to these changes? Receptive, hostile, concerned?

2 **Use your notes in 1 to prepare a presentation to give to Medstin staff. You should each present one part of the presentation. Include the following points in your presentation.**
   - Explain the current situation and plans for future change.
   - Give an idea of the time schedule.
   - Refer to possible concerns and reassure the staff.
   - Give a call for action.

3 **Give your presentation to the class. Compare your suggested changes with the other groups. Have a class vote on the best suggestion for change for Medstin.**

13 Facts and figures

Learning objectives in this unit
- Talking about numbers and trends
- Asking for and explaining factual and numerical information
- Talking about news at work
- Reporting back

Case study
- Reaching target markets

Starting point

Discuss these questions. Choose one of the answers (if you disagree with the options, give an answer of your own).

1 When is the best age to retire?
50 60 65 70

2 How long should the working week be?
20 hours 45 hours
35 hours 60 hours

3 What is a fair total income tax rate?
10% 25% 40% 60%

4 What proportion of a year should working people have as holiday?
1/2 1/3 1/4 1/5

5 What was the most interesting decade to be born in?
the 1890s the 1970s
the 1940s the 1990s

Working with words | Numbers and trends

1 **Look at the three pictures in the text. These are all examples of 'killer' technologies. Why are they called this? Read the text quickly and find out.**

'Killer' technologies

When the steamship was introduced, it was known for blowing up. Eventually, however, the technology improved and it mostly replaced its predecessor, the sailing boat. Then along came the internal combustion engine, and the steamship in turn became redundant.

The petrol engine proved to be by far the most important technology of the early 20th century and car ownership grew by **approximately** 50% each year between 1910 and 1930. As well as replacing what came before it, this 'killer' technology revolutionized the entire world economy in **just over** 20 years with its impact on transport, trade, road-building and oil.

In the second half of the 20th century, the transistor experienced a similar extremely fast growth. The number of transistors produced in the world has reached 10^{18}, compared to just over a million in 1955. The average price per transistor has fallen steadily from 1/10 of a cent in 1975 to about one ten-millionth of a cent this year. In addition, chips'* critical dimensions have shrunk from 5,000 nm* to **slightly less than** 90 nm since 1974 and are continuing to fall.

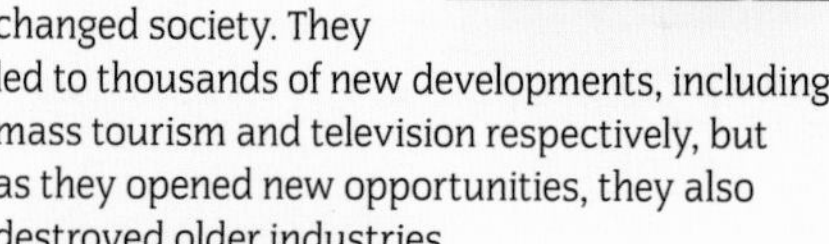

The combustion engine and transistor were core technologies that changed society. They led to thousands of new developments, including mass tourism and television respectively, but as they opened new opportunities, they also destroyed older industries.

At the beginning of the 21st century, the Internet promises to bring about as much change as anything in history, and is developing fast. Internet speeds have increased **substantially**. We have moved rapidly from 28.8 kbps connections to broadband, and in Europe, there was 206.2% growth in Internet usage between 2000 and 2007, thus reaching **fractionally** less than 40% of the population, or **somewhere in the region of** 322,000,000 people.

* chip = silicon chip which contains invisible transistors * nm = a nanometre = one billionth of a metre

2 **Read the text again. Which of these statements are made or implied?**

1 The steam engine was not a reliable technology initially.
2 The petrol engine was the dominant technology between 1900 and 1950.
3 Transistor production peaked in 1955.
4 The transistor was indirectly responsible for mass tourism.
5 Internet connection speeds were slow to improve.

3 **What do these numbers refer to in the text? How do you say them?**

1 10^{18}	6 20th
2 28.8	7 206.2%
3 1910	8 21st
4 2007	9 5,000 nm
5 $^1/_{10}$	10 322,000,000

4 **Match the words / phrases in bold in the text to these words / phrases with a similar meaning.**

1 marginally: ______
2 a little more than: ______
3 a great deal: ______
4 just under: ______
5 roughly: ______
6 about: ______

5 **Work with a partner. Ask and answer questions 1–5. It is unlikely you will know the exact figures so use the words / phrases in 4 to give an estimate.**

1 What's the average price of a car (economy, mid-range, luxury) in your country?
2 How much does your family spend on travel costs each month?
3 What percentage of items in your home contain electronic chips?
4 What Internet connection speeds are currently available?
5 How many emails do you get in a week? What percentage of these are useful?

6 **51▷ Listen to an Irish music producer being interviewed about music downloads on the Internet. What does he say about**

1 downloads of singles in Ireland?
2 sales of singles in music stores in Ireland?
3 sales of albums in music stores in Ireland?
4 the Internet being a threat?
5 the Internet being an opportunity?

7 **Where would you put these phrases from audio 51▷ on the line?**

grow gradually *crash* *rise substantially* *drop slightly*
stay the same *grow rapidly* *a significant drop*

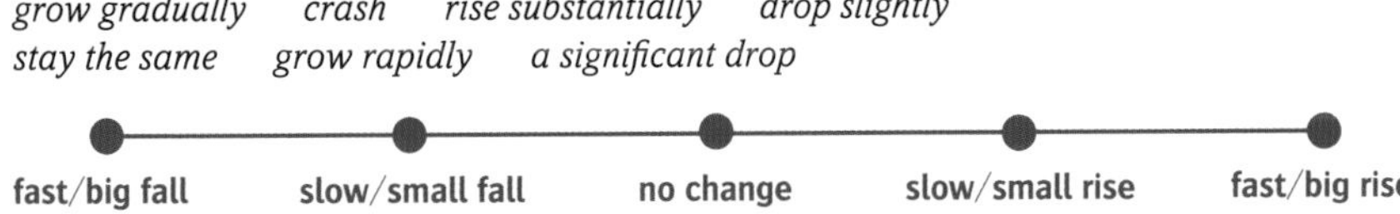

8 **Where on the line would you put the phrases in *italics* in these sentences?**

1 Oil price *shoots up* by 30% on Middle East worries.
2 Gold *plummets* to all time low.
3 There are worrying signs of *a significant increase* in unemployment.
4 Doctors express concern at *a noticeable rise* in teenage smoking.
5 We'll see *a slight fall* in house prices as mortgages rise.
6 All quiet as FTSE *levels off.*
7 *A substantial drop* in exports predicted as euro rises.
8 Cost of borrowing *rockets* as interest rates double.

» For more exercises, go to **Practice file 13** on page 126.

9 **Work with a partner. Using as many different phrases from 7 and 8 as you can, talk about changes in the cost of living in your country in the last ten years.**

10 **Work with a partner. Prepare and present a short talk about a company. Turn to File 27 on page 144 for instructions.**

ⓘ » Interactive Workbook » **Glossary**

Tip | *by* and *from ... to*

Use *by* to refer to a difference.
Car ownership grew ***by*** *approximately 50%.*
Use *from* to refer to an initial figure and *to* to refer to a final figure.
The price has fallen steadily ***from*** *$^1/_{10}$ ...* ***to*** *about one ten-millionth of a cent.*

Context

Caroline Rodgers works for SurAuto.com, a motor insurance company specializing in affordable insurance for young drivers. The company is considering new ways of reaching its target audience and Caroline recently attended a seminar on online advertising.

Exchanging information | Asking for and explaining factual and numerical information

1 **Do you look at the ads and pop-ups that you see on websites or do you ignore them? How influential are they?**

2 **52▷ Read the *Context*. Listen to Caroline reporting back on the seminar. What do these figures refer to?**

1 18–30 **2** 198.4% **3** 81.4% **4** \$300.4 m **5** 154.4%

3 **Match 1–10 to a–j to make phrases.**

1 Could you fill us … ___
2 Apparently, a recent … ___
3 What's that … ___
4 Simon claimed … ___
5 Roughly … ___
6 So how should we … ___
7 Can we look … ___
8 According to a recent … ___
9 So the bottom line … ___
10 The overriding trend … ___

a in terms of growth?
b is that user-generated media will be our new advertising platform …
c speaking, by 2010 it'll only be 39.7%.
d interpret this drop?
e in on the most relevant information from the seminar?
f is for technology, car and media brands to use this.
g that last year blog advertising accounted for …
h at the figures?
i study shows a huge increase in advertising investment via this media …
j survey, total projected expenditure …

4 **52▷ Listen again and check your answers.**

5 **Put the phrases in 3 into these categories.**

a Asking for factual or numerical information: ___________
b Reporting factual or numerical information: ___________
c Summarizing findings / trends: ___________

» For more exercises, go to **Practice file 13** on page 126.

Tip | *supposedly* and *apparently*

Use *supposedly* when a fact is not proven and to add an element of doubt to the claim.

Supposedly, *podcast advertising will be the front runner over the next four years.*

Use *apparently* to quote or repeat something you have heard from someone else.

Apparently, *a recent study shows a huge increase in advertising.*

6 Work with a partner. You and your colleague have been researching the popularity of blog advertising and have collected some information. Student A, turn to File 26 on page 143. Student B, use the information below. Read your information and report it to your colleague. Request the missing information 1–8.

Student B

	Facts and figures	Comments
No. people surveyed	1	
Type of people	Professional, global companies, different jobs / industries / segments	Provide reliable results – a good cross section
Survey results		
read blogs	2	3
read blogs once a week	51% (approx. 2,300)	
read blogs weekly for business information	53%	Need more information about who these people are and which blogs
read weekly on technology topics	4	
pass on information or content from blogs	5	6
indicate that blogs influence their purchase decisions	53% (approx. 2,385)	Very important information for us!
are thinking of starting their own blogs	7	8

ⓘ » Interactive Workbook » **Email**

Key expressions

Asking for factual / numerical information

Could you fill us in on …?
Can you give us the low-down on …?
Can we look at the figures …?
So what are the facts and figures?
How do these figures compare …?
What's that in terms of (growth)?
How should we interpret (this drop)?

Reporting factual / numerical information

According to (a recent survey), …
Apparently, a recent study shows …
Supposedly, …
Roughly speaking …
(Simon) claimed that …
(Simon) assured us that …

Summarizing findings / trends

The bottom line is …
The overriding trend is …
In general, …
Overall, things are looking positive / up / gloomy.

ⓘ » Interactive Workbook » **Phrasebank**

Practically speaking | Talking about news at work

1 53▷ **Listen to three short conversations about news at work. Which one is about**

1 relationships? ___
2 a missing item? ___
3 leaving the company? ___

2 53▷ **Listen again. Which of these phrases can you use to introduce the topic of news, repeat news you have heard or respond to news?**

1 Rumour has it …
2 Surely not!
3 I spoke to (Robert) and he told me that …
4 Did you hear the latest about …?
5 According to (Sam), …
6 That's nonsense!
7 (Anna) says that …
8 Have you heard the news?
9 Apparently, …
10 You'll never guess what I heard …

3 **Work in groups of four. Each person thinks of two pieces of news. Work with a partner and share your first piece of news. Change partners and share your second piece of news. Refer to the** ***Useful phrases*** **on page 135.**

Language at work | Reported speech review

1 **Work with a partner. Discuss how you could report these things your manager said to you using *say*, *tell* or *ask*.**

1 'Contact Helen immediately if you have any problems.'
2 'Could you come back a little later? Is that OK?'
3 'Do you know when Jan is getting back?'
4 'Have you seen Mr Smith?'
5 'I always feel a bit nervous when I get on a plane.'

2 **We can use other reporting verbs that summarize what people said. Discuss how to report the following in as few words as possible. Use the summarizing verbs in brackets.**

1 'I'm really grateful for your help.' (thank)
He thanked me for helping him.
2 'Go on, apply for the promotion.' (encourage)
3 'I'm afraid I haven't finished the report yet.' (apologize)
4 'No, no – this mistake was not my responsibility at all.' (deny)
5 'I won't do your shift on Friday.' (refuse)
6 'I can reduce the price by €200.' (offer)
7 'OK. I see your point and I'll look at the terms and conditions again.' (agree)

» For more information and exercises, go to **Practice file 13** on page 127.

3 **54▷ Work with a partner. Listen to four extracts from a meeting at a cable company.**

1 Student A, make notes on what the speakers said in extracts 1 and 3. Student B, make notes on what the speakers said in extracts 2 and 4.
2 Ask and answer questions about the meeting. Student A, ask about extracts 2 and 4. Student B, ask about extracts 1 and 3.

Extract 1
a What did John say about Lisa?
b What excuse did Peter give for missing the meeting?
c What did Anna say about the airport?

Extract 2
d What did John ask Peter?
e What did Peter say about the Europe figures?
f What did Peter say about the Venezuelan issue?

Extract 3
g What did Anna ask Peter?
h What did Peter say about the US figures?
i What did Peter promise to do?

Extract 4
j What did Anna want to know?
k What was Anna's main complaint?
l What did Peter guarantee?

4 **Work with a partner. Take turns to report a conversation you have had, saying who said what. Choose one or two of these situations (or think of your own situations).**

- a difficult situation with a customer or colleague
- an encounter with a policeman or someone in authority
- a misunderstanding with a colleague or friend
- a meeting you attended that a colleague has missed
- a piece of exciting / interesting news from a friend or family member

ⓘ » Interactive Workbook » **Exercises and Tests**

Reaching target markets online

Background

New venture at MPS

Digital music sales will more than double in the next few years and the majority of the revenue generated will be from the ringtone industry. According to business analysts, personalized data services for mobile devices, from ringtones to screensavers, are currently a $20-billion global business. However, competition is strong in this area and companies have to be willing to pay premium prices to advertise on websites which will attract their target market.

MPS is based in Germany – one of Europe's biggest markets for personalized mobile phone accessories. Its core business is acting as a 'middleman' between the music industry and the mobile phone companies. MPS negotiates rights for music recordings with the music industry and then enters into contracts with the mobile phone service providers who in turn offer the music as downloadable ringtones on their corporate websites.

MPS is aware how huge the ringtone industry has become and has decided to set up a division dedicated to offering ringtones direct to the end-user. Their Internet platform is ready to do business, but they need to decide where to advertise.

Discussion

1 **What is the target market for mobile phone accessories?**

2 **Is it 'ethical' to encourage people to spend their money on these types of accessories?**

3 **What sort of websites would provide the best advertising platform for ringtone companies?**

Task

Work in groups of three. You have each researched facts and numerical information about one Internet site which could be suitable as an advertising platform for MPS. **Student A, turn to File 28 on page 144. Student B, turn to File 35 on page 146. Student C, turn to File 44 on page 148.**

1 Read your information. Decide how the facts and figures may influence your decision to advertise on the site (e.g. continuous growth of visitors = more exposure to potential customers). Make notes under these headings.
   - Name of site
   - Facts
   - Figures / Trends
   - Interpretation / Comments

2 Report the facts / figures / trends to the rest of your group.

3 While you listen to your colleagues, record the information under the same headings as in 1.

4 Check you have understood everything correctly. Ask for interpretation of the facts / figures where appropriate and add these to your notes.

5 In your groups, decide which site would be most suitable for MPS to advertise on and why.
   - Is the website well established?
   - Will it survive and be worth investing in?
   - Does it attract enough visitors?
   - Do its visitors fit your customer profile? (Read between the lines!)

The Expert View

Consumers are no longer the passive recipients of advertising messages delivered through TV, radio and print media. Many advertisers try to reconstruct the old, one-way mode of communication over the Internet by using banner advertising, email campaigns, pop-up adverts and text messaging. But in the new media environment, communication is increasingly interactive and controlled by consumers, who direct their own information searches, participate in online communities, use RSS feeds and create blogs. The challenge for advertisers is to adapt their approach, to create a real dialogue that meets consumers' changing expectations.

Dr Stan Maklan, Senior Lecturer in Strategic Marketing
Cranfield School of Management

Case study

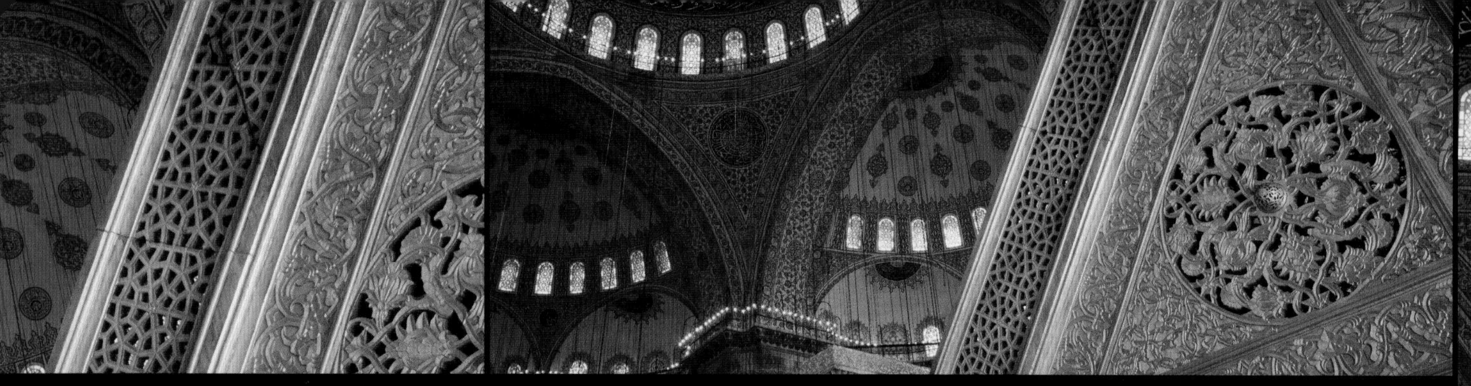

14 | Culture

Learning objectives in this unit

- Talking about cultural differences
- Narrating past events
- Giving explanations
- Talking about films, TV and books
- Talking about past events using past continuous, past simple and past perfect

Case study

- Investigating an intercultural communication problem

Starting point

1 **A common piece of advice to people travelling to another country is 'When in Rome, do as the Romans do'. What does this expression mean?**

2 **How much do you change your behaviour if you visit another country for work? Or as a tourist? Why?**

Working with words | Cultural differences

1 **If you do business with a different culture, what is it useful to know about that culture? Read the text and compare your ideas.**

Working across cultures

Professor Geert Hofstede of the Netherlands conducted a study of how values in the workplace are influenced by culture. His research, based on a large database of employees' values collected by IBM, covers 74 countries and regions.

Working, entertaining, negotiating and corresponding with colleagues from different cultures can be quite difficult. One misunderstanding could have a negative effect on months of work. Understanding intercultural differences can help communication with colleagues from other cultures. According to Hofstede, if we compare the key factors in our own culture with those in another culture, we can predict possible difficulties.

Hierarchical or egalitarian?

Some cultures, like Malaysia and Indonesia, are **hierarchical** with a caste or class system; and there is often a big difference in wealth between individuals. At work, employees respect authority, don't usually take responsibility and have a **formal** relationship with their manager. Other cultures, like Australia and Denmark, are more **liberal** and **egalitarian**. Managers give their employees responsibility and often socialize with them.

Individualistic or collectivist?

Individualistic cultures, such as the US and the Netherlands, think that individual rights and freedom of speech are important. Personal goals, choices and achievements are encouraged. In more **collectivist** cultures, such as Korea and Colombia, this self-centred approach is discouraged. The group, such as the family, has a big influence on people's lives and is often seen as more important than business. Companies have a strong work group mentality and praise is given to teams rather than individuals.

Masculine or feminine?

In 'masculine' societies, like Brazil and Mexico, the male dominates the power structure. Competitiveness and assertiveness are encouraged, and the accumulation of wealth is important. Many employees 'live to work' and take short holidays. In 'feminine' societies, such as Sweden and Finland, family, personal relationships, and quality of life are more important. Conflicts are resolved through negotiation, and people 'work to live', enjoying longer holidays and flexible working hours.

Cautious or risk-taking?

Some cultures, especially those with a long history such as Greece and Portugal, are quite **cautious**. They often have religious backgrounds and resist new ideas. At work, people prefer to follow **strict** rules and do things as they always have been done. Other cultures, like Jamaica and Singapore, often have a younger history and are willing to take risks. They are more **open** to new ideas, are less **accepting** of rules and regulations, and are more likely to welcome change.

2 **Read the text again. According to Hofstede, which culture(s)**

1 think family life is important?
2 like to be very polite to their manager and / or follow rules and regulations?
3 adapt easily to change?

3 **Which of the key factors would you use to describe your own culture?**

4 **Work with a partner. Match the adjectives in bold in the text to these definitions.**

1 very polite: ________
2 organized in levels: ________
3 classless: ________
4 careful: ________
5 receptive of new ideas: ________
6 allowing freedom: ________
7 shared by all the group: ________
8 must be obeyed: ________
9 do something without complaint: ________
10 focusing on one person: ________

5 **Discuss how each adjective in 4 could be seen as both positive and negative.**

6 **55▷ Listen to two people talking on the subject of culture.**

1 Summarize the main points of the first speaker's story.
2 What type of course is the second speaker talking about? What do people learn about on the course?

7 **Use these words from audio 55▷ to complete the sentences.**

aware *sensitive* *familiar* *respectful*
tolerant *informed* *adjust* *used*

1 People from the Czech Republic don't like to offend other people, so they're always very ________ to their guests' feelings.
2 I found it quite hard to ________ to the hierarchical culture in Thailand – my culture is much more egalitarian.
3 I wasn't very ________ with the way business is done in Romania so I was surprised by the amount of bureaucracy.
4 I wasn't ________ of the custom of greeting the oldest person first in China so I'm afraid I offended my host.
5 Mexico is a hierarchical culture so it's important to be ________ of people of a higher rank.
6 My boss sent me on a cross-cultural training course so I was ________ about business etiquette in Brazil before I was seconded there.
7 I'm ________ to people being direct in my own country so the indirect communication of Singaporeans seemed strange to me.
8 My colleague is always very punctual so he wasn't very ________ of the Greek custom of arriving late for dinner!

8 **Use five of the words in 7 to make questions to ask a partner.**

» For more exercises, go to **Practice file 14** on page 128.

9 **Work with a partner. Prepare some information for someone from a different culture who is coming to work in your company. Think about the things below and explain how aspects of your culture influence expected behaviour.**

- how people behave in meetings
- relationships between different members of staff, e.g. formality
- individual efforts and teamwork
- responsibility
- company policy
- social events

ⓘ » Interactive Workbook » **Glossary**

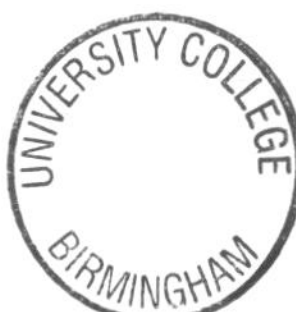

Context

'Critical incidents' are communication situations which the participants find problematic or confusing. They often consist of a misunderstanding, a linguistic mistake, or some kind of cultural faux pas. They are events that can highlight different cultural beliefs and values. They are about ways of behaving that might be interpreted in different ways by different people, particularly when people from different cultural backgrounds communicate with each other.

Exchanging information | Narrating past events | Giving explanations

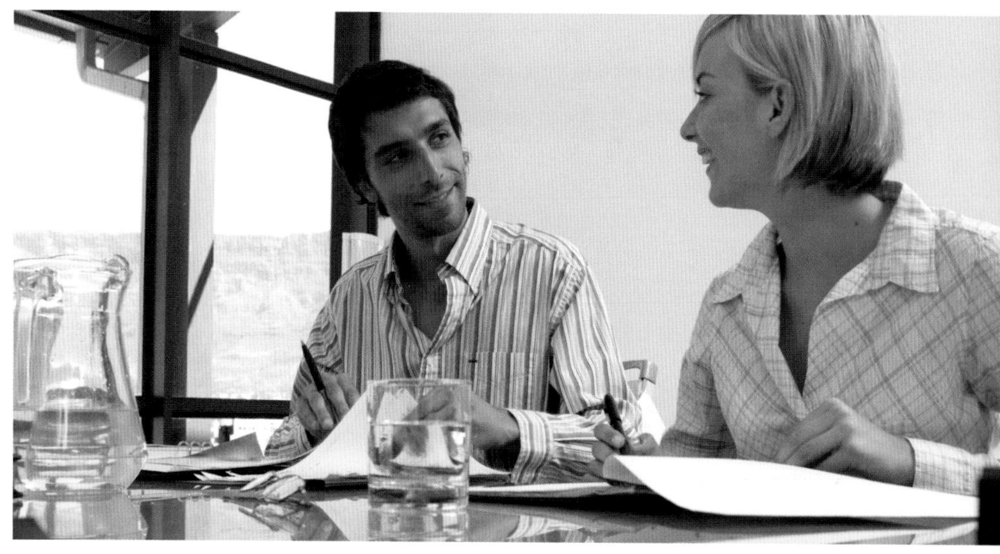

1 **56▷ Listen to two conversations describing critical incidents. Which two of these situations is mentioned in each conversation?**

1 importance of punctuality
2 questioning an authority figure
3 importance of seniority and titles
4 small talk before meetings
5 saying 'yes' to avoid loss of face

2 **56▷ Listen again. Complete the sentences with these phrases.**

in the end *that's* *but then* *it came about because of* *as time went by*
so that was *it wasn't until* *due to* *so what* *that was when*

Critical incident 1

1 … for years. ______, I noticed that things weren't being done that I'd requested …
2 … it wasn't done. ______ I was aware we had a problem.
3 Well, ______ understandable.
4 And ______ I talked to a Korean friend that I realized what was wrong.
5 My team didn't want to refuse my request ______ respect for my seniority.

Critical incident 2

6 Yes … ______ I realized they hadn't actually told him this.
7 … authority figure. ______ the first problem solved.
8 ______ did you do?
9 Well, ______ I asked Anna, a Polish colleague.
10 Yes. ______ the lack of information about why we were questioning them.

3 **Which of the phrases in 2 do the speakers use to**

a help tell the story of the incident and indicate the sequence of events? ______
b explain the reason for the incident? ______
c show they are listening / encourage more information? ______

» For more exercises, go to **Practice file 14** on page 128.

4 **Work with a partner. Read the culture tip about Indonesia on page 87. Look at the pictures and work together to tell the story of the critical incident.**

Tip | *It seems (that) …*

Use *it seems (that) …* to depersonalize a situation or avoid blaming.

__It seems that__ none of them wanted to question an authority figure.

Doing business in Indonesia

It's important to offer refreshment to guests. This is seen as respectful and polite. Guests should wait before drinking – their host will indicate when drinking can commence. Often there is a pause between receiving the drink and being asked to drink. The sign to drink may indicate that business is over. Make sure you wait and follow your host's example.

Last year – Indonesia with colleague – meeting to negotiate new contract

Near end of meeting – refreshments offered

Picked up my cup – colleague said 'wait'

Negotiation completed – host invited us to take refreshments

5 Work with a partner. Think of a situation where there was a misunderstanding between you and someone from a different culture. It could be when on business or on holiday. Tell your partner about the incident. Use these ideas if necessary.

- in a restaurant – ordering food and drink
- asking for directions
- on the telephone
- talking about own country and background
- deadlines and dates
- being unaware of traditions and cultural differences

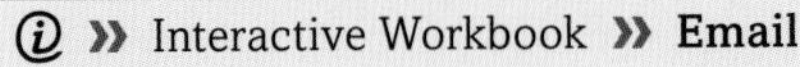
ⓘ » Interactive Workbook » **Email**

Key expressions

Giving an explanation
... due to ...
It seems that ...
The reason being that ...
It came about because of ...

Linking the narrative
It wasn't until ... that ...
Luckily ...
And / But then ...
What's more, ...
Despite ...

Time expressions
While / When ...
At first ...
After that ...
As time went by, ...
In the end ...

Encouraging more information
So what did you do?
What had you done?
And what did (she) say?
What happened (next / then / after that)?
That's (understandable).
Go on. / Oh?
What was (her) view?
So how did you ...?

Summarizing the narrative
That was when ...
So that was the first problem ...
All in all ...
It really surprised me, (but it worked).
I was extremely disappointed.

ⓘ » Interactive Workbook » **Phrasebank**

Practically speaking | Talking about films, TV and books

1 **57▷ Listen to work colleagues chatting in a break. What are they talking about in each of the three extracts?**

2 **Which of these phrases can you use to talk about**

1 a film?
2 a TV programme?
3 a book?
4 all three?

I don't get / have much time to ... *There's a ... twist at the end.* *(It's) a blockbuster.*
I'm completely hooked on it. *It's a real page-turner.* *I can't miss an episode.*
I'd definitely recommend it. *(It's) a box office hit.* *I couldn't put it down.*
I tend to channel-hop. *It's set in ... / It's about ...* *I've just finished ...*
What I really can't stand is ... *It's very well written.* *... a star-studded cast ...*
I just like to unwind in front of ... *(You'll be) on the edge of your seat.*

3 **57▷ Listen again and check your answers.**

4 **Work with a partner. Choose a film, TV programme or book and tell your partner about it. Find out what your partner likes. Refer to the *Useful phrases* on page 135.**

Language at work | Narrative tenses – past continuous, past simple and past perfect

1 Read this supposedly true story about a billionaire entrepreneur. Number the events a–i in the order they happened.

One evening in December, an American billionaire was driving down the motorway in New Jersey. It was raining hard, but the road was busy as thousands of people were leaving for their Christmas holidays.

Suddenly, the car had a flat tyre, and the chauffeur pulled over to the side. When he opened the boot, he realized that he had left the tool kit behind. While he was standing there in the rain, wondering what to do, another motorist saw him and stopped.

Together, they changed the wheel, and as the man was leaving, the billionaire wound down the window. He asked if there was anything he could do to thank him, and the man said his wife might like a small bunch of flowers.

Two weeks later, a bunch of flowers arrived at the man's house. With it there was a small note from the billionaire, thanking the man for his help and telling him that the whole of his mortgage had been paid off.

___ **a** The chauffeur and the motorist changed the wheel.
___ **b** The car had a flat tyre.
___ **c** The billionaire set off down the motorway.
___ **d** The chauffeur realized he couldn't change the wheel.
___ **e** The chauffeur left the tool kit behind.
___ **f** The billionaire paid off the mortgage.
___ **g** A passing motorist stopped to help.
___ **h** Some flowers arrived at the house.
___ **i** The billionaire spoke to the man.

2 Underline all the verb forms in the story. What tense is used to

1. set the scene and give background information at the beginning of the story?
2. describe the main action and events in the story?
3. talk about an action in progress that is interrupted by another action?
4. talk about an action that happened before another past action?

» For more information and exercises, go to **Practice file 14** on page 129.

3 Complete these sentences with the past continuous, past simple or past perfect form of the verbs in brackets.

1. They cancelled my flight because it ________ (snow) so I ________ (sleep) in the airport lounge.
2. I didn't want to interrupt my colleague while he ________ (talk) on the phone so I ________ (send) him an email instead.
3. I felt very embarrassed when I realized that I ________ (forget) my host's name so I ________ (apologize) quickly.
4. During the time I ________ (stay) in Denmark, I didn't know whether to arrive on time for dinner so I ________ (decide) to arrive five minutes late.
5. My host offered me a small gift just as I ________ (leave) for the airport and I ________ (give) her a souvenir from my own country.
6. I didn't know if the party was formal or informal because I ________ (lose) my invitation so I ________ (wear) a smart outfit.

4 Work with a partner. Take turns to talk about one of the situations below. Give some background information about the situation, explain how it came about, what happened and how it was resolved.

- a time when you had a minor accident or injury of some kind
- a time when you had car problems
- a time when you were extremely late for something

ⓘ » Interactive Workbook » **Exercises and Tests**

Investigating an intercultural communication problem

Background

Frustrating time for PCR

PCR is a medium-sized company based in Germany. It produces software solutions for banks and has acquired a new client – a large, well-established bank in Malaysia. Since finalizing contracts well over a year ago, very little progress appears to have been made. Employees working on the project at PCR are frustrated because everything is taking so long and 'cut over' (the transfer from the old system to the new system) has been postponed for the fifth time. There seems to be reluctance from the Malaysian bank to take on the new system. Constant changes are being made to suit the customer – something that PCR normally works on once the system is up and running, so users can input their problems. Training has taken place on an ad hoc basis and hasn't run very smoothly – it has often been decided on at the last minute so PCR doesn't have much time to prepare. Communication has been unpredictable and difficult, and critical decisions haven't been made.

Discussion

1 **What problems might a company face when changing to a new IT software system?**

2 **What could be the reasons for the difficulties that PCR is experiencing with its Malaysian client?**

Task

Work in groups of four. You each have some further information about PCR's situation. Student A, turn to File 32 on page 145. Student B, turn to File 40 on page 147. Student C, turn to File 45 on page 148. Student D, turn to File 29 on page 144.

1 Read your information and make notes on the problem. Think of one or two possible reasons why the problem has occurred.

2 Take turns to report your information to your colleagues using your notes. Give reasons why you think the problem occurred. While you listen to your colleagues make notes under these headings.
   - Problem
   - Possible reasons for problem

3 Discuss and analyse the situation. Try to establish what went wrong and why, and what lessons can be learned. (Read the cultural information about Malaysia in File 49 on page 149 to help you.)

4 Compose a short verbal report about the situation. Give your report to the class and compare your analysis of the situation.

The Expert View

We have a natural tendency to interpret the behaviour and attitudes of individuals from different cultures according to our own pre-conceived ideas of cultural norms. But if we focus selectively only on actions or words that appear to fit these pre-formed views, this can lead to a serious misinterpretation of interactions. To understand other people's cultural frames of reference and value systems, we need to be self-aware and, by watching and listening for all the signals, remain sensitive to the nuances of communication. If we are patient and respectful, make an effort to 'put ourselves in another person's shoes', and to build trust, we can minimize the potential for misunderstanding.

David Simmons, International Development Director & Graham Heard, Lecturer in Languages

Cranfield School of Management

Case study

15 | Performance

Learning objectives in this unit

- Talking about staff appraisals
- Discussing and evaluating performance
- Making people feel relaxed
- Talking about hypothetical past events using third and mixed conditionals
- Pointing out alternative courses of action using *could have* and *should have*

Case study

- Overcoming business setbacks

Starting point

1 **What criteria could you use to measure the performance of 1–3?**
  1 a company
  2 a project
  3 an employee

2 **Which criteria are the most important for each one?**

3 **Which criteria are the easiest to measure?**

4 **How is performance measured where you work?**

Working with words | Staff appraisals

1 **Read the article about one company's approach to staff appraisal. Match these headings to paragraphs A–G.**

1 Sharing the responsibility ___
2 A worthwhile effort ___
3 Developing an appraisal system ___
4 Monitoring performance ___
5 Don't rush it ___
6 How we conduct the appraisal ___
7 Discussing targets ___

Use appraisals to manage performance

Sea Zoo is Wales' largest marine aquarium, which attracts over 75,000 visitors a year. Director and partner, Alison Lea-Wilson, describes how the company introduced an appraisal system that has proved to be a key motivator for its 25 staff.

A When we started, our appraisals were more of an informal chat. As we grew, we decided to implement twice-yearly formal appraisals. We wanted to make sure that employees' contributions fitted the goals of the business and we also wanted to have the chance to recognize good performance and address any issues.

B We invite staff to appraisals in writing, including a copy of the appraisal form to fill in. The completed form is discussed during the appraisal itself, with an emphasis on giving constructive two-way feedback.

C The majority of our performance objectives aren't as easily quantifiable as, say, sales targets, so we use a scoring system to monitor performance. The manager and employee rate each objective on a scale of one to four and compare the results, which can be very helpful.

D Appraisals also provide an opportunity to set performance objectives. We base ours on each employee's job description. We talk to staff so that we can agree the objectives with them and they know what to expect.

E I used to think that it was my responsibility to conduct all appraisals. I've learnt that delegating to line managers is equally effective and demonstrates trust in their abilities.

F In the early days, we also underestimated how long a thorough appraisal takes. It's counterproductive if the appraisee feels their manager has one eye on the clock. We now allow a minimum of an hour and a half for each employee.

G Providing an opportunity for staff to express their views and address any issues is a real morale booster, as is giving praise where it's due. It does take time and hard work, but it enables us all to have real communication and really motivates people.

2 **Read the text again and answer questions 1–3.**

1 What were the three aims of having formal appraisals?
2 What things are discussed in the appraisal and what style of feedback is preferred?
3 How do they deal with performance objectives which aren't easy to measure?

3 **Match the verbs in A to the noun phrases in B to make phrases used in the text.**

A		B	
monitor	give	issues	performance
conduct	rate	views	objectives on a scale
agree	express	objectives	constructive feedback
address		an appraisal	

4 **Match the phrases in 3 to these definitions.**

1 carry out an assessment of how well someone is doing at work: ________
2 talk about your opinion of something: ________
3 think about a problem / situation and decide what to do about it: ________
4 tell someone in a positive way how they are doing at work: ________
5 give points to measure how well someone has been doing at work: ________
6 check regularly how someone is doing at work: ________
7 decide with someone else what you hope to achieve at work: ________

5 **Using four of the phrases in 3, make questions to ask your partner about appraisals in their company. Then ask and answer the questions.**

6 **58▷ Listen to a human resources manager describing a system of 360° feedback. Work with a partner and answer questions 1–3.**

1 What is the central idea of 360° appraisals? How do they work?
2 What do raters comment on?
3 What two important things do you need to consider if you use 360° feedback?

7 **Complete the phrases in *italics* from audio 58▷ with these words.**

criteria appraisal judgement tool management rating

1 How does 360° differ from a more traditional top-down *staff* ________?
2 In what ways is 360° a *development* ________?
3 What sort of *assessment* ________ might be used for 360° appraisal?
4 Who would carry out the *peer* ________ in your situation?
5 As a rater, how honest would you be in your *value* ________ of your peers?
6 Do you have a role in *performance* ________ in your company?

8 **Work with a partner. Ask and answer the questions in 7.**

9 **Match the phrasal verbs in bold in audio script 58▷ on page 165 to these definitions. Then make a sentence with each of the phrasal verbs.**

1 get as a result: ________
2 give an impression: ________
3 stop doing one thing and start another: ________
4 distribute: ________
5 look at very carefully: ________
6 continue: ________

» For more exercises, go to **Practice file 15** on page 130.

10 **Choose one of the jobs below or another job you know about. Think of any job skills (e.g. knowledge of medicine) and any other abilities (e.g. ability to talk to patients) that could be used as assessment criteria. Then discuss the usefulness of top-down and 360° appraisals for the job.**

- doctor
- teacher
- salesperson
- accountant
- human resources worker

ⓘ » Interactive Workbook » **Glossary**

Context

Thomas works in the back office of an international car rental company. His team undertakes a range of administrative duties including working with the call centre shift rota. The company's policy is to carry out annual staff appraisals with all its personnel. Its philosophy is that appraisal involves staff in their personal development, allows them to take some responsibility for their work and provides an opportunity for two-way feedback.

Meetings | Discussing and evaluating performance

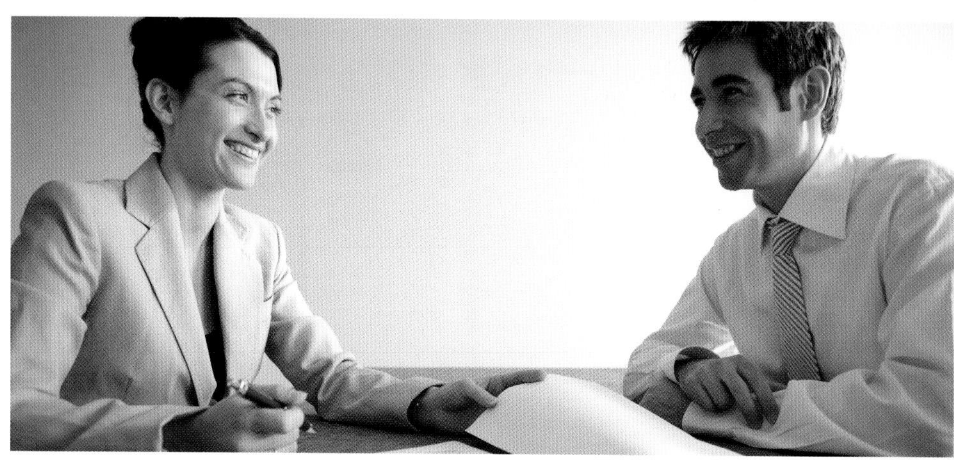

1 **59▷ Read the *Context*. Listen to Thomas having his annual appraisal with his superior, Angelina, and complete this table.**

	Appraisee feedback	Appraiser comments	Action to be taken
Positive achievements			
Areas for improvement / development			
Areas of concern			
Resources required			

2 **Work with a partner. Read these phrases. Who said them: the appraiser, Angelina (*A*) or the appraisee, Thomas (*T*)?**

1 I must say, we're very happy with your overall performance … ___
2 Can I identify that as a personal goal for the coming year? ___
3 You shouldn't have been expected to take on so much. ___
4 Are there any areas you feel you need to improve on? ___
5 If I'd known that … I might have done it. ___
6 You certainly need to focus on gaining some more qualifications. ___
7 Were there any constraints that affected your performance? ___
8 What's the best way to solve this? ___
9 We could do with some training on the new program … ___
10 If there's enough money, I'd also like another software program. ___

3 **59▷ Listen again and check your answers.**

4 **Put the phrases in 2 into these categories.**

a Asking about performance: ______
b Giving feedback on performance: ______
c Setting goals: ______
d Requesting / Giving advice to improve performance: ______
e Justifying / Explaining results: ______
f Negotiating time / resources: ______

» For more exercises, go to **Practice file 15** on page 130.

Tip | *really, certainly* and *I must say …*

Add emphasis to what you are saying by using words such as *really, certainly* and the structure *I must say*.

*You **really** should have done that course.*
*You **certainly** need to focus on gaining some more qualifications.*
***I must say** we're very happy with your overall performance …*

5 **Work with a partner. Student A, turn to File 31 on page 145. Student B, use the information below. (+ = positive, – = negative)**

Student B

1 You are the appraiser. Conduct the appraisal interview. Comment and ask questions as appropriate to complete this form.

Achievements / Failures	Explanation / Comments	Requests for resources / Advice
+ Presented new office procedures at Europe-wide meeting – v. good!		A presentation skills workshop?
+		
– Dropped out of company English course – we're disappointed		Try again – we can help with some self-study ideas
–		

2 Change roles. You are the appraisee. Discuss your team's performance over the past year with your appraiser, using this information.

Achievements / Failures	Explanation / Comments	Requests for resources / Advice
+ Organized successful kick-off meeting for international salespeople	Enjoyed it, real change to normal routine	
+ Reduced overall overtime hours	Job-sharing scheme and better delegation	More staff would help – is this possible?
– Rejection of trainee mentoring scheme	If more money for mentors – scheme been implemented	
– Slow response time to internal emails	Not 'cc-ed' into everything – could see which were important faster	Help / advice to change this?

Ⓘ » Interactive Workbook » Email

Key expressions

Asking about performance

What do you consider were your successes and failures?
Are there any areas you feel you need to improve on?
Were there any constraints that affected your performance?

Setting goals

Can (I) identify that as a personal goal …?
Let's put … on your list of goals …

Giving feedback on performance

I must say, we're very happy with …
You demonstrated …
You should have …
You shouldn't have …
You've managed to …
One area I'd like to mention is …
On a less positive note …
You could have …
Feedback from … has been (positive / satisfactory / poor).

Justifying / Explaining results

If (Katy) hadn't (left), I probably would have (done the course).
If I'd … I might have …

Requesting / Giving advice to improve performance

How can I improve my chances of …
How should I do this?
What's the best way to …?
You ought to …
(I think) you need to …

Negotiating time / resources

We could do with …
If there's enough money, I'd (also) like …
While we're talking about money, could we discuss …?

Ⓘ » Interactive Workbook » Phrasebank

Practically speaking | Making people feel relaxed

1 **60▷ Listen to three conversations. What themes / topics are being used to make the second person feel relaxed?**

2 **60▷ Listen again and tick the phrases you hear in the *Useful phrases* on page 135.**

3 **Choose one or two phrases you would like to practise from each section in the *Useful phrases* on page 135. Work with a partner. Take turns to make each other feel relaxed in these situations.**

You've been performing badly at work and have arrived for your annual appraisal with HR.
You've been invited to head office to explain why your team isn't performing very well.

Language at work | Third and mixed conditionals | Perfect modals

1 Read these extracts from audio 59▷ and answer questions 1–4.

a If you**'d started** a language course then, you**'d be** quite proficient now.

b If Katy **hadn't left**, I probably **would have done** the course.

1 Which sentence describes
- an imagined past action and an imagined past result? ___
- an imagined past action and an imagined present result? ___

2 Which conditional is used in each case?

3 What verb forms are used in each conditional?

4 What other modal verbs besides *would have* are possible in the result part of the sentence? How does each verb affect the meaning?

» For more information and exercises, go to **Practice file 15** on page 131.

2 Work with a partner. Discuss what you might say in each of these situations. Use the third conditional and at least one mixed conditional.

1 You took the company car without authorization. You drove to the project meeting and arrived on time. There was a possibility of losing the contract. Present result: the company is expanding its business.

2 You ordered some office equipment from your usual supplier who always delivered on time. A new supplier offered a discount on the same order. The new supplier didn't have a good reputation for delivering on time. Present result: you have enough paper for the current mailshot.

3 Read these extracts from audio 59▷ and answer questions 1–2.

a You **could have thought** a bit more about the call centre rota.

b You really **should have done** that course.

1 In which sentence is the speaker
- pointing out what someone has done wrong? ___
- pointing out what it was possible for someone to do? ___

2 Which modal verb could be replaced by *might have* and which one by *ought to have*?

» For more information and exercises, go to **Practice file 15** on page 131.

4 Work with a partner. Discuss how you could respond in the following situations using *could have* or *should have*. Your colleague

1 invested savings in a company tipped on the Internet and eventually sold them at a very small loss

2 arrives an hour late for an appointment without bothering to phone you

3 offers a discount to a customer without checking with the manager first

4 forgot to let you know that a meeting had been changed

5 made a very costly mistake but did not get the sack

6 wrote an angry letter to an important customer.

5 Work with a partner. Talk briefly about some of the topics below. Say what actually happened to you in the past. Then say what might or would have happened in different circumstances, or how things would be different now.

Example: *I decided to become an artist because I loved painting. If I'**d followed** my father's advice, I **would have become** an accountant or **might have become** a banker. I'**d be** richer but I'm not sure I'**d be** any happier.*

- why you chose your current career
- a narrow escape or lucky break
- a good or bad financial decision
- a mistake or misjudgement

ⓘ » Interactive Workbook » **Exercises and Tests**

Overcoming business setbacks

Background

Maximuscle – Sports nutrition

- The owner wrote a best-seller about which products help build muscle and burn fat – 24,000 copies were sold and this capital was used to finance the company.
- The owner's knowledge in gym instruction, nutrition and health led to his own-brand products being created, focusing on quality and not price (approx. €75 per Maximuscle product). Food technologists and doctors were consulted so it was ensured the product worked, tasted and looked good. The company was so confident in the brand that a money-back guarantee was offered to customers.
- After highly successful trade and Internet sales, the company opened its own retail outlets but too much time and money was spent on running shops and managing personnel, and not enough on promoting the brand. This idea was later scrapped.
- The next important step was finding a reliable, trustworthy supplier. A small health food chain was chosen which was able to build a trusting and loyal customer base.
- Steady growth took place but problems arose when athletes started blaming the product for poor performance and positive drug tests.

Innocent Drinks – Fruit smoothies

- The idea for fruit smoothies came from the owners realizing they had a bad diet and there was no time for healthy eating in their busy lives.
- They had no experience in the drinks industry. They created the drinks themselves, mixing different fruits together and trying their concoctions out on friends.
- They started their business unconventionally: offering free smoothies at a jazz festival and getting customers to put their empty cups in buckets labelled 'yes' or 'no'. 'Yes' meant they should quit their well-paid jobs and produce smoothies for a living. The 'yes' vote won and they left their jobs in the same week.
- After many months of no income and increasing costs and debt, they managed to secure funding from a business angel.
- It wasn't easy to convince people about the product: it was made from fresh juice (not concentrated), contained no preservatives (so was difficult to distribute efficiently) and was therefore relatively expensive (€3 for 250ml).
- The biggest argument against the drinks was their high cost and short shelf life, and distributors were not interested. The biggest argument for the drinks was their freshness and packaging – clever slogans, 'cool' looking bottles.

Discussion

1 What are the main strengths of each company?

2 What is the biggest challenge each company faces?

Task

Work in two groups. Choose one of the companies. You are going to discuss how the company can improve its current situation.

1 Evaluate the performance of the company and its approach and decide what you would advise the company to do now.
2 Present your evaluation and suggestions to the class.
3 Turn to File 34 on page 146 to find out how the two companies improved their situation and compare this with your suggestions.

The Expert View

Two broad ways of evaluating and improving performance are inside-out and outside-in evaluation. Inside-out evaluation answers the question, 'How well do I think I am doing?', and requires you to set benchmarks for performance drawn from industry standards. Performance must be measured against these benchmarks in a formal and regular way, and as frequently as is appropriate. Outside-in evaluation answers the question 'How well do they think I am doing?', and requires you to seek 360° feedback from customers, suppliers, and any other significant stakeholders in the value chain. This feedback is best obtained through a formal questionnaire, which should be administered regularly.

Roger Delves, Programme Director, Centre for Customized Executive Development

Cranfield School of Management

Case study

16 | Career breaks

Learning objectives in this unit
- Talking about taking a career break
- Presenting a personal case
- Talking about taking time off
- Choosing between *-ing* form and infinitive

Case study
- Applying for a community placement

Starting point

1 In your country, do young people have a gap year (a year off) between school and university?

2 How common is it for adults to have a career break? What do they use the time for?

3 What practical problems might a career break cause for both the employee and the employer?

Working with words | Taking a career break

1 **Read about three people who took career breaks. Which two people**
1 went to the same part of the world?
2 are back working for the same company?
3 give similar advice about taking a career break?
4 spent time helping other people?
5 have changed in similar ways?

Freya, Advertising Manager

Stage in career: 'I'd worked in marketing for ten years and had just completed my Advanced Certificate. I resigned.'

My career break: 'I travelled around the world for 18 months and did voluntary work in Australia. My career break **revitalized** me – it has given me a new **perspective** on life and reordered my priorities; quality of life is more important to me now. I'm also more confident. If you're **hesitating** about taking a career break, the best **piece of advice** I'd give is to make sure you've got good relevant career experience before you leave – so it's easier to get back on the career ladder.'

Effect on career: 'The break acted as a catalyst for me to change career. I **put off** looking for a permanent job for a while, but now I've applied to join a government office.'

Roberto, Business Analyst

Stage in career: 'I'd worked for the bank for 14 years, so they offered to keep a job open. I **postponed** my planned departure for a year to suit them.'

My career break: 'I spent a year travelling through south-east Asia and Australia, doing a series of scuba-diving courses. I also learnt to ride a motorbike and fly a helicopter. My **tip** for anyone considering a career break is: take it after you've worked for at least five years. That way you'll really **appreciate** the time off and have enough money to enjoy it. It's the best thing I've ever done.'

Effect on career: 'I came back with my batteries **recharged** and new enthusiasm; and now I'm doing a better version of my old job.'

Jenny, Management Consultant

Stage in career: 'I was with my company for nine years and having a mid-career crisis. I intended to resign – they said they'd hold my job open.'

My career break: 'I was in Bangladesh, attached to a **voluntary organization** working with local communities to improve education and health care, and to develop new skills and earning potential. It broadened my **outlook** and I experienced a completely different pace of life. I'm now less materialistic, and I **feel grateful for** the things I have got. If you're **feeling uncertain** about a career break, just do it – life's too short.'

Effect on career: 'I went back to exactly the same job, but I now do four days a week, spending the fifth volunteering with a children's **charity**.'

2 **Work with a partner. Which career break would you most like to take and why?**

3 **Put the words / phrases in bold in the text into pairs that have similar meanings.**

Example: *revitalized / recharged*

4 **Complete these sentences using some of the words / phrases in bold in the text.**

1 How would you enjoy working for a ________________ like the Red Cross or Médecins Sans Frontières?

2 Would you return from a career break feeling ________________ and ready to get back to your old job or would you be uninterested in going back to work? Explain why.

3 Have you got any unfulfilled ambitions that you have had to ________________ for career reasons?

4 Have you ever done anything that has given you a new ________________ on life?

5 Are you constantly seeking new things / opportunities or do you ________________ the things that you have?

6 What's the most useful ________________ anyone has given you about dealing with boredom or stress at work?

5 **Work with a partner. Ask and answer the questions in 4.**

6 **61▷ Listen to an employer talking about the benefits of career breaks. Work with a partner and answer questions 1–5.**

1 Why did the company originally introduce flexiwork?

2 Why was flexiwork particularly suited to this company?

3 What are the current benefits of flexiwork?

4 Why is flexiwork described as a win-win situation?

5 Would the same arguments for flexiwork apply in your company? Why or why not?

7 **Choose the correct answer from the words in *italics*.**

1	A break might help me to head *off / round* in a new direction.	1 2 3 4 5
2	I would like the opportunity to develop some *light / soft* skills.	1 2 3 4 5
3	I think I would return to work with *renewed / improved* enthusiasm.	1 2 3 4 5
4	I would like to *broaden / enlarge* my horizons through travel.	1 2 3 4 5
5	My boss would see a break as an important part of my career *development / improvement*.	1 2 3 4 5
6	Allowing career breaks will at some stage become our official company *policy / doctrine*.	1 2 3 4 5
7	Allowing career breaks would help the *maintenance / retention* rate in my company.	1 2 3 4 5

8 **For each statement in 7, look at the scoring system below, then circle one of the numbers 1–5. Compare and discuss your answers with a partner.**

1 = agree very much 2 = agree 3 = unsure 4 = disagree 5 = disagree strongly

›› For more exercises, go to **Practice file 16** on page 132.

9 **Think of a career break that might appeal to you and your employer. Give a short presentation of your idea, outlining**

- the basic proposition
- what the benefits would be for you
- what the benefits would be for your company
- what financial arrangements you would propose.

ⓘ ›› Interactive Workbook ›› **Glossary**

Context

Lena Johnson currently works for an IT company leading a team of technical writers. She has a diploma in photography and has decided to request a nine-month sabbatical to act as photographer for journalists making a documentary in the Antarctic.

Presenting | Presenting a personal case

1 **62▷ Read the *Context*. Listen to the meeting between Lena and her manager. Which of these benefits and arguments did she use for taking a sabbatical?**

- I've been a loyal employee.
- I'll have to resign if I'm not allowed to take the sabbatical.
- I'll be more motivated after the trip.
- I'll gain experience I can bring to the company.
- It's a lifelong ambition of mine.
- I'm feeling burnt out!
- If you sponsor my trip, the company will gain advertising opportunities.
- My creativity is being suppressed in my present job.

2 **62▷ Read phrases 1–9. Then listen again and <u>underline</u> the phrases that mean the same in audio script 62▷ on page 167.**

1 It's something I've wanted to do for a long time.
2 The people I studied with have given me the desire to do this.
3 I'll never get this opportunity again in my life.
4 It's a situation where we'll both gain something.
5 I'd obtain skills that would be very useful for managing the team.
6 I know you'll have a lot of worries.
7 If I don't take up this opportunity, I'll regret it.
8 That's not very reasonable – I've always taken on extra work.
9 I'd be very grateful if you could talk to HR.

3 **Put the phrases you underlined in 2 into these categories.**

a Stating what you want: ________
b Explaining benefits: ________
c Stating motivation: ________
d Arguing persuasively: ________
e Dealing with objections: ________

» For more exercises, go to **Practice file 16** on page 132.

Tip | *valuable* and *invaluable*

Make sure you are clear what you want to say when using *invaluable* and *valuable*.

The experience was ***invaluable.*** (= something very useful)
It was a ***valuable*** *piece of equipment.* (= worth money)

An experience can also be *valuable*, meaning 'useful'; however, the meaning is not as strong as that of *invaluable*.

4 **Work with a partner. Read this information.**

> You left your college course halfway through for personal reasons. You have performed extremely well in your job, especially since most of your colleagues are better qualified than you. You would now like to go back to college and complete your studies, but the only way to do this is to take a career break for a year.

1 Decide what type of job you have and what type of course you want to complete (use your own job if you like).
2 Discuss how you would present your case for a career break to your manager. Make sure you think of two phrases for
   - stating what you want
   - stating your motivation
   - explaining the benefits
   - arguing persuasively.
3 Think of two objections your boss might have and counter these with appropriate phrases.
4 Work with another pair. Talk them through your case and arguments.

5 **Choose one of these things that you would like to do (or an idea of your own) and prepare your case.**

- take paternity leave / extended maternity leave (assuming it isn't a legal option in your country)
- restructure your department
- introduce a new procedure in your office
- apply for a better position internally in your company
- take a temporary transfer abroad with your company

6 **Work with a partner. Take turns to present your case. When you are listening, object to some of the proposals you hear.**

ⓘ » Interactive Workbook » **Email**

Key expressions

Stating what you want
It's been a long-term goal of mine to ...
I intend to ...
I'd really appreciate it if ...

Stating motivation
I've been inspired by ...
I'd like to do this because ...
My motivation for this comes from ...

Explaining benefits
It's a win-win situation.
The experience I'd gain would be invaluable for ...
The plus points are ...

Arguing persuasively
It's a once-in-a-lifetime opportunity.
This is a chance I can't (afford to) miss.
I'll never be satisfied unless I do it.

Dealing with objections
I understand your misgivings but ...
That's hardly fair. I've never refused to ...
But there are also (other) benefits for (you / the company).

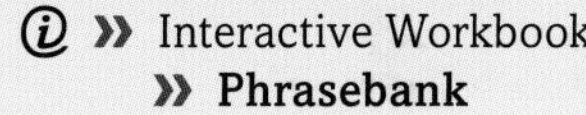

Practically speaking | Talking about taking time off

1 **63▷ Listen to three conversations. How did each speaker spend their time off?**

2 **Which of these phrases refer to the period of time taken off (*T*), the activity (*A*) or what the experience was like (*E*)?**

1 We visited my partner's family. ___
2 We just had a long weekend away. ___
3 It made a real change. ___
4 I didn't really enjoy it, but it needed doing. ___
5 It poured with rain the whole time! ___
6 I took the day off. ___
7 I caught up on some DIY jobs. ___
8 It was great for relaxing and switching off. ___
9 We managed to get away for the day. ___
10 We were on a three-day spa break. ___

3 **Work in groups of four. Think of three examples of recent time off (you can invent the information if you like). Have a different conversation about your time off with each member of the group. Refer to the *Useful phrases* on page 135.**

Language at work | *-ing* form and infinitive

1 Read these extracts from audio 62▷.

a You want **to take** an extended holiday.
b And you'd like several months off **to accompany** her?
c It's certainly worth **thinking** about.
d It's not going to be easy **to persuade** them.
e I'd enjoy **developing** my creative side …
f The experience I'd gain would be invaluable for **managing** the team.

In which extract is the infinitive being used

1 because of the verb that comes before it? ___
2 because of an adjective that comes before it? ___
3 to express purpose? ___

In which extract is the *-ing* form being used

4 because of the verb that comes before it? ___
5 because of a phrase that comes before it? ___
6 because of a preposition that comes before it? ___

2 Which of these common verbs and phrases are normally followed by the infinitive? Which are normally followed by the *-ing* form?

like	*there's no point …*	*enjoy*	*want*
would like	*look forward to*	*fail*	*decide*
refuse	*seem*	*it's very difficult …*	*miss*
it's not worth …	*risk*	*manage*	*arrange*
can't afford	*finish*	*plan*	*it's easy …*

» For more information and exercises, go to **Practice file 16** on page 133.

3 You have been asked to complete a staff survey to find out how you feel about your company. Using your own ideas, complete these sentences, starting the rest of the sentence with a verb in the *-ing* form or infinitive.

STAFF SURVEY

Good points:	I enjoy … I like …
Neutral / bad points:	I don't mind … I object to …
Commitment:	I've never refused … I've never failed …
Difficulty of tasks:	I find it quite difficult … I find it easy …
Self-assessment:	I think I deserve … I'm prepared …
Ambitions:	One day I plan … I also intend …
Fears:	I'm worried about … I'm concerned about …
Hopes:	I would like … I also want …

4 Work with a partner. Talk about your answers in 3.

5 Work with a partner. Student A and Student B, turn to File 47 on page 148 and follow the instructions.

ⓘ » Interactive Workbook » **Exercises and Tests**

Tip | Changes in meaning

Some verbs can be followed by either the *-ing* form or the infinitive, but there is a change in meaning.

Use *like* + *-ing* to mean 'enjoy'.
*I **like going** to the cinema.*
Use *like* + infinitive to mean 'I think it's good for me'.
*I **like to have** a full check-up every two years.*

Applying for a community placement

Background

Accenture – working in the community

Accenture is a global company which uses its expertise in consulting, technology and outsourcing to help its clients improve their performance. One section of the company, ADP (Accenture Development Partnerships), is involved with SPARK, a programme coordinated by VSO (Voluntary Service Overseas) to help poor rural communities in the Philippines, Thailand and Indonesia manage their natural resources effectively. The ADP team worked with SPARK to: develop a strategy for managing the programme, deal with local ownership issues, improve its overall effectiveness, and implement its successful aspects in other regions. By the end of ADP's assignment, the team had met its challenges and a pilot programme had been started in Indonesia.

Discussion

1 **What experience do employees gain from working on programmes like SPARK?**

2 **How do companies benefit from employees working on such programmes?**

3 64▷ **Listen to a consultant at Accenture who worked on the SPARK programme. Compare your ideas in 1 and 2.**

Task

A similar global company is working with a charity in Bangladesh. The aim is to provide community centres for both educational and cultural programmes. Phase 1 – building the community centres – has finished.

1 Read this extract about the project from the in-company magazine.

A Helping Hand – Phase 2

Now the community centres have been built, we are sending 40 volunteers to work alongside employees from the charity. The charity aims to provide courses on: English language for children, literacy and numeracy, computer skills, bookkeeping and basic accountancy. We are sending volunteers to teach and run the courses, as well as people to help coordinate the centres, work with back office administration and find resources.

If you are interested in a 6–12-month placement, please discuss this with your immediate superior and HR.

2 Work in groups of six. One volunteer is still required and you want to be chosen for the final place. Work with a partner and create an employee profile.
- What skills / knowledge can you offer the project?
- Why do you want to go?
- Why should you be supported in your application?

3 Present your case (in pairs) to the rest of the group. While you listen to the presentations, make notes.

4 As a whole group, hold a short decision-making meeting. Decide who should be given the final place on the project and why.

The Expert View

Career breaks offer many opportunities for personal growth, but many people are not aware of them. Developing a community of like-minded people can help individuals to define more clearly what they want to achieve or to become, and to be more aware of the opportunities that surround them. Once you've decided, it's important to stay focused on your development goals during your career break, and on your future reintegration into your company. Ask other people who have made these transitions about their strategic return to work. And ensure that you maintain contact with key decision-makers at your place of work.

Peter Fennah, Director of Career Development
Cranfield School of Management

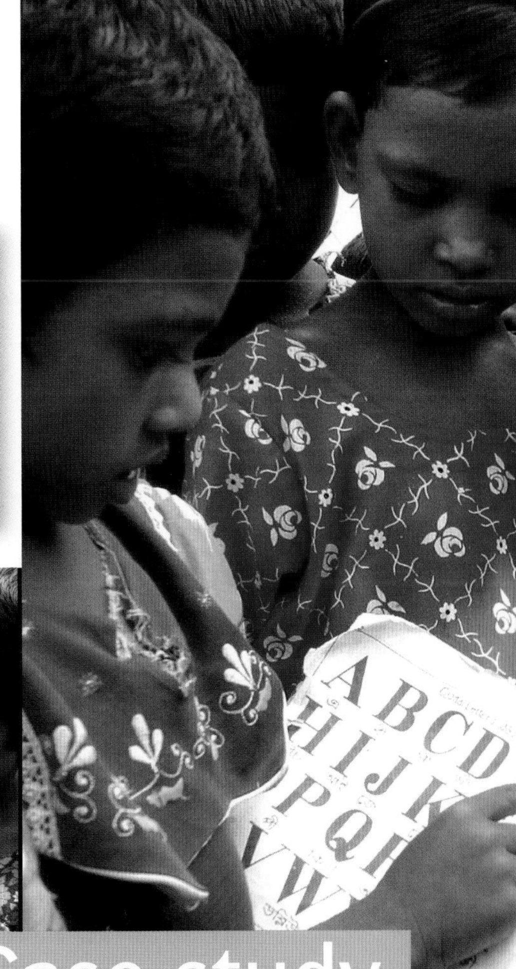

Case study

1 | Practice file

Working with words

1 Match 1–6 to a–f.

1 They'll be easy to work with – they certainly have … _b_
2 She's quite shy, but sometimes she comes … ___
3 As a financial adviser, I have to build … ___
4 I thought he was arrogant, so I took … ___
5 To attract younger customers, you'll have to project … ___
6 If your office is clean and tidy, it creates … ___

a across as being a bit unfriendly.
b a reputation for good communication with clients.
c an impression of efficiency and professionalism.
d an instant dislike to him.
e a more modern image.
f a good relationship with clients so they trust me.

2 Complete the sentences with these adjectives.

~~favourable~~ trustworthy ineffective
functional wary successful

1 Our new product got good press and _favourable_ reviews.
2 We can speak freely – my assistant is very ___.
3 The advertising campaign was ___ – our sales actually fell slightly.
4 The design is simple and ___ so the product is very easy to use.
5 Fortunately our bid was ___ so we now have funds to develop the new department.
6 It is natural to be ___ of a company that has a poor reputation for customer service.

3 Put the letters in order to make words to complete the sentences. The first letter for each answer is given.

pceslipnri prosiailonsmsef tadtnoiir
rprtoap ivatnonion ceratvtyii

1 He's a natural salesman and has a good **r**___ with clients.
2 We value **c**___, so we employ original thinkers who can come up with new ideas.
3 We couldn't fault their **p**___ – the skill and knowledge of the staff was of a high standard.
4 Their latest **i**___ is a cordless Internet phone that also has a webcam.
5 We have a long **t**___ of supporting musicians and encouraging new talent.
6 We are a 'green' company, so we should follow our **p**___ and only use 'green' suppliers.

Business communication skills

1 Complete the follow-up call from Pierre to Samir with these phrases.

would you like to meet
let's say
I'll email you a map
in from France, won't you
I suggest we meet to
responding so quickly
I wondered if you'd
can you tell me how
let me know where
see you
I'm calling about
whatever's best

Pierre Good morning. This is Pierre Jouet. [1]___ the email I sent you last week in response to your enquiry.
Samir Oh yes. Thanks for [2]___.
Pierre [3]___ had time to look at the brochure I sent you.
Samir Yes – it looks very interesting. [4]___ discuss things further.
Pierre That would be fine. When [5]___?
Samir [6]___ next Wednesday at 10.00.
Pierre Fine. [7]___ for you.
Samir You'll be travelling [8]___?
Pierre That's right. I'm planning to drive and stay overnight in Bilbao. [9]___ I get to your office?
Samir Are you familiar with Bilbao?
Pierre Not really.
Samir [10]___ you're staying and [11]___ and directions from your hotel.
Pierre Thanks. OK. [12]___ next Wednesday at 10.00.
Samir I'll look forward to meeting you. Bye.

2 Put the words in the right order to make phrases.

1 and / work / name's / UB / for / my / James Sims / I.
___
2 given / Jill Sander / your / by / I / details / was.
___
3 I / interested / offer / in / if / to / our / see / are / you / still / wanted.
___
4 Is / taxi / public / transport / by / best / or / it?
___
5 you / later / I'll / my / confirm / call / assistant / to / today / get / to.
___

Language at work | Present simple and continuous

Present simple

Use the present simple

1 to talk about routines
I usually ***arrive*** *at work at about 8.30.*

2 to talk about things we think of as permanent
I ***work*** *for IBM.*

3 to talk about states
Paris ***lies*** *on the River Seine.*

4 (with future reference) to talk about timetabled events
The next train ***leaves*** *at 11.15.*

5 to talk about future time introduced by *when, as soon as, after, if,* etc.
When I **see** *Margaret tomorrow, I'll give you a ring.*

Common phrases used with the present simple are: *as a rule, generally (speaking), on the whole, once (a week / in a while), every (winter), most of the time.*

Present continuous

Use the present continuous

1 to talk about an action happening at the moment of speaking
Mr Takashi ***is waiting*** *for you in Reception.*

2 to talk about a project that is ongoing and unfinished
I ***am writing*** *a report on the takeover, and I should finish in a few days.*

3 to talk about things we think of as temporary
I ***am staying*** *with my brother while my house is being redecorated.*

4 to talk about a gradual change or development
Because of global warming, sea levels ***are rising*** *slowly.*

5 (with future reference) to talk about an appointment or arrangement
I ***am seeing*** *Mrs Langer next Tuesday.*

Common phrases used with the present continuous are *currently, for the moment, at the moment, for the time being, tomorrow (afternoon), right now.*

Stative verbs

Verbs that describe states rather than actions are normally only used in the simple form, i.e. verbs of thinking (e.g. *know, agree*), verbs of appearance (e.g. *look, seem*), feeling (e.g. *prefer, want*), possession (e.g. *own, belong*), the senses (e.g. *taste, sound*). Some stative verbs can sometimes be used in the continuous form, but with a change in meaning.

simple: *I* ***see*** *the Eiffel Tower on my way to work.*
continuous: ***I'm seeing*** *Bob on Monday.* (= I am meeting Bob)

1 Complete these sentences with the present simple or present continuous form of the verbs in brackets.

1 A stockbroker is someone who ________ (buy) and ________ (sell) shares.
2 The M40 ________ (go) from London to Birmingham.
3 What time ________ (the last flight to New York / leave)?
4 Because of the roadworks, it ________ (take) me much longer to get to work.
5 I'm afraid Leon is out at the moment. He ________ (have) lunch with a client.
6 I can give Anne your letter. I ________ (see) her tomorrow afternoon.
7 Tell Heinrich I'll get in touch when I ________ (get back) next week.
8 We ________ (develop) a new anti-malaria drug, and hope to start trials in a couple of years.

2 Write an appropriate question for these answers, using the stative verbs from the list. (More than one correct question is possible.)

belong	taste	look
own	prefer	~~sound~~

1 Q: *Does the car sound OK to you?*
A: I think so – I can't hear anything wrong with it.
2 Q: ________?
A: He's about 2 m tall, with dark hair and blue eyes.
3 Q: ________?
A: Tea – I don't like coffee at all.
4 Q: ________?
A: It's delicious.
5 Q: ________?
A: It's mine.
6 Q: ________?
A: No, I rent it.

3 Choose the correct answer from the words in *italics*.

1 As a rule, I *catch / 'm catching* the 8 a.m. train.
2 Right now I *design / 'm designing* a new company website.
3 I *stay / 'm staying* with Clare for the time being.
4 On the whole I *complete / 'm completing* most tasks quite quickly.
5 I generally *check / am checking* my emails twice a day.

Working with words

1 Choose the best word or phrase to complete these sentences.

1 Our perks include subsidized meals, health care and a ________ car.
  a corporate **b** company **c** commercial
2 How does senior management try to ________ company loyalty among the managers?
  a develop **b** foster **c** enthuse
3 Does your company offer any kind of non-professional staff ________?
  a development **b** education **c** extension
4 We're lucky to have a non-________ pension plan.
  a contribution **b** contributing **c** contributory
5 I work for an airline, so my family gets a really good ________ on flights.
  a discount **b** decrease **c** bargain
6 Our company offers free medical ________ so we don't need to worry if we become ill.
  a assurance **b** insurance **c** reassurance
7 Non-cash ________ can often be more effective for staff motivation than extra money.
  a repayments **b** rewards **c** returns
8 Winning the prize gave me a great sense of ________.
  a realization **b** completion **c** achievement

2 Match these words to statements 1–8.

appreciation	bonus	commission
~~feedback~~	fulfilment	incentive
loyalty	morale	

1 You've done well this year, overall. There are a few things that need improvement, but you've also had some successes. *feedback*
2 My boss said he would really miss me if I left. It's nice to know he feels that way. ________
3 If I'm one of the top ten salespeople, I'll get a ten-day holiday in Florida. ________
4 The company has had a successful year. I got an extra €2,000 in November – on top of my salary. ________
5 There's a great team spirit at work. We're all enthusiastic about what we do and everybody tries their hardest. ________
6 If I can make six sales this month, that'll be 3% of €24,000 times six, which will be €4,320. ________
7 I work for a charity. The salary isn't very high but the work is interesting and I feel I'm using my skills doing something very worthwhile. ________
8 I've been with the company for 25 years; it would feel completely wrong to work for a competitor. ________

Business communication skills

1 Alain is making small talk with Kirsten at a conference. Number their conversation in the correct order 1–12.

___ **a Kirsten** Yeah. See you.
_1_ **b Alain** Hello. It's Kirsten, isn't it?
___ **c Kirsten** Yes, isn't it? I'm sure you'll enjoy the change in lifestyle. We decided to stay in the city because the house we wanted needed too much work.
___ **d Alain** How are things?
___ **e Kirsten** That's right. I thought I might see you here.
___ **f Kirsten** That's amazing! We considered that line of business too!
___ **g Alain** No, not at all. Catch you later.
___ **h Alain** No? What a coincidence.
___ **i Alain** Oh dear. Were you disappointed?
___ **j Alain** Yes, it is. In fact, we've bought a small farm and my wife runs a holiday rental business.
___ **k Kirsten** No, not really. I don't think our children wanted to move. Well … You don't mind if I go and get myself some food?
___ **l Kirsten** Very good, thanks. I've heard you've moved into the country – is that true?

2 Choose the best answer from the phrases in *italics*.

Jamal Hi, my name's Jamal. [1]*I don't think we've met. / How are things?*
Alicia [2]*No, I don't know you. / Nice to meet you.* I'm Alicia. Is this your first Nordica workshop?
Jamal Yes. My colleague is sick so my manager asked me to come instead. Do you know many people here?
Alicia Not really. I was recently transferred from Purchasing.
Jamal [3]*What a coincidence! / That's lucky!* So was I!
Alicia [4]*By the way / Apparently*, it's our new company policy – transfer rather than hire new people.
Jamal [5]*Really? / Oh dear.* We discussed the idea for our region, too, a few months ago.
Alicia [6]*Well, / By the way,* I'm sure it's a good solution for many companies.
Jamal Yes, you're probably right.
Alicia [7]*So, / In fact,* would you like a drink? I'm going to the bar.
Jamal Not at the moment, thanks. [8]*Catch you later. / Is that the time?*

Language at work | Question form review

Making questions

1 With most verbs, make direct or *Wh-* questions with a normal auxiliary verb (*be, do, have*) or a modal auxiliary (*may, will, shall*, etc.). The auxiliary comes before the subject.

__Do__ you __know__ many people here?
How long __has__ she __been working__ for Hertz?
__Should__ you __send__ that form off today?

2 With a prepositional or phrasal verb, the preposition or particle usually comes after the verb.

Where do you come __from__? (Not: ~~From where do you come?~~)
Where did you grow __up__?

3 *Who* and *what* can be the subject or the object of a question, with a difference in word order.

Who or ***what*** as subject (word order same as in a statement):
__Who__ wants to come? (Answer: Somebody wants to …)

Who or ***what*** as object (auxiliary precedes the subject):
__What__ did you say? (Answer: I said something …)

4 Make an ordinary statement into a question by using rising intonation.

A James is away, I'm afraid – he's in Rome.
B He's in Rome? What's he doing there?

5 Use negative questions to check that something is true. Put *n't* after the auxiliary, and use them when the answer *yes* is expected.

A __Didn't__ Amelie move to Marseilles a few months ago?
B Yes, that's right – when the new branch was opened.

Question tags

1 If the main verb is positive, the question tag is negative.

- With the verb *be*, repeat the verb in the negative.
  It's hot, __isn't__ it?
- With verbs in the present simple, use *don't / doesn't.*
  You work for Siemens, __don't__ you?
- With verbs in the past simple, use *didn't.*
  He left early yesterday, __didn't__ he?
- All other tenses that have auxiliaries (continuous tenses, perfect tenses, etc.), reuse the first auxiliary in the negative.
  He's been to China, __hasn't__ he?
  They would say that, __wouldn't__ they?
  You will be there, __won't__ you?

2 If the main verb is negative, the question tag is positive.

You haven't seen my keys anywhere, __have__ you?

3 If the subject is a word like *someone, no one, everybody, anyone*, use *they* in the question tag.

Anyone can use the meeting room, __can't they__?
Everybody knows that, __don't they__?

1 Put the words in the right order to make questions.

1 anyone / in / coming / is / tomorrow?
____
2 how / we / save / much / could?
____
3 about / what / you / talking / are?
____
4 with / who / you / did / come?
____
5 been / have / long / how / you / working / Diana / with / for?
____
6 to / send / the / who / you / exhibition / did?
____
7 the / to / Guy / gone / conference / hasn't?
____
8 help / manager / for / ask / we / should / our?
____

2 Correct these questions.

1 Why you didn't come to me for help?
____
2 How much costs a new one?
____
3 Don't work you for MT Electrics?
____
4 What you will do first?
____
5 How long you've been working for Cisco?
____
6 Who you did see at the sales meeting?
____
7 What means 'This program has performed an illegal operation'?
____
8 For what stands UNESCO?
____

3 Add a suitable question tag to these sentences.

1 You're from London, ________?
2 You couldn't give me a lift to the station, ________?
3 The bank shuts at 5.00, ________?
4 You didn't see Anna, ________?
5 You haven't seen Joe, ________?
6 You won't tell anyone, ________?
7 Nobody's called, ________?
8 That wasn't easy, ________?

Working with words

1 Replace the phrases in *italics* with the phrases from the list. Make any changes that are necessary.

miss the deadline	be ahead of schedule
~~set a budget~~	run out of money
allocate funds	prioritize tasks
keep track of	resolve conflicts

1 We need to *decide what we're going to spend* set a budget and try to keep to it.
2 The contractors failed to control spending and they quickly *spent everything* ________________.
3 The whole project ran very smoothly, and in the end we *finished two months early* ________________.
4 I'm responsible for the budget and *giving out money* ________________ to the different departments working on the project.
5 If you communicate well, you can usually *settle disagreements* ________________ quickly.
6 We need to *put things in order of importance* ________________ and then work steadily through the project.
7 There are strict penalty clauses, so it'll be expensive if we *are late* ________________.
8 I always look at bank statements carefully so that I *have information about what is happening with* ________________ spending.

2 Will your next project be on time and within budget? Complete these sentences. Use the answers to complete the puzzle and find the hidden answer.

1 We must ________ costs under control.
2 Don't forget to ________ contingency plans.
3 If the project ________ smoothly, it will finish on time.
4 Make sure you ________ all the facts first.
5 I'm going to ________ the course – I'm not giving up.
6 You need to ________ a realistic timescale.

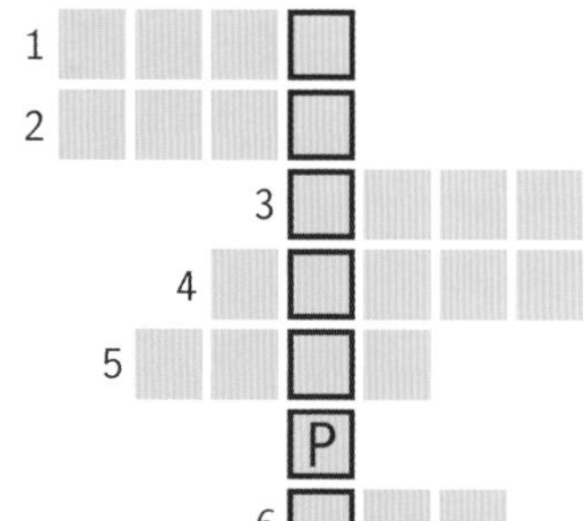

Business communication skills

1 Sondra is discussing progress of an HR project with Dimitri. Choose the best answer from 1–8 below to complete their conversation.

Sondra OK, Dimitri. What's the current [1]________ of the staff satisfaction survey?
Dimitri Well, on the whole, we're [2]________. We've received replies from the questionnaires but we haven't collated the answers yet.
Sondra You do know the regional HR conference date [3]________ for next month, don't you?
Dimitri Yes, but we've [4]________ with IT. They haven't set up the database for us yet, to collate the results.
Sondra So the real problem [5]________ IT's time management?
Dimitri Partly, yes.
Sondra How about [6]________ as much of the report as you can?
Dimitri That's [7]________, but until we have results from the survey, there's nothing to put in the report.
Sondra So what you're really [8]________ is, without the database you can't continue?
Dimitri Err, yes.

1 **a** stand **b** status **c** state **d** view
2 **a** in time **b** up to scratch **c** in the lane **d** on track
3 **a** set **b** has been already set **c** has already been set **d** had set
4 **a** hit a stop **b** knocked a problem **c** came to a problem **d** hit a problem
5 **a** lies with **b** stands with **c** sits with **d** lays with
6 **a** to prepare **b** you're preparing **c** preparing **d** prepared
7 **a** likely **b** possible **c** probable **d** possibility
8 **a** saying **b** telling **c** talking about **d** explaining

2 Match 1–8 to a–h.

1 How far are you … ___
2 Things aren't running … ___
3 We finalized the draft … ___
4 So what do you … ___
5 If you ask me, … ___
6 I'm not … ___
7 That's not … ___
8 Up to now … ___

a the venue has been booked …
b we should scrap the idea.
c as smoothly as I'd hoped.
d with the new packaging?
e an ideal solution.
f mean exactly?
g three weeks ago.
h convinced.

Language at work | Present perfect and past simple

Present perfect

Use the present perfect

1 to link a present situation with something that took place at an unspecified time in the past

*Ana **has sent** the new brochure to all our clients.*

The present situation is that all the clients have the new brochure. The past event is that Ana sent the new brochure (we don't know when).

2 with *yet* and *already* to talk about tasks expected to be done or which are done earlier than expected

*A **Have** you **finished** that report **yet**?*
*B Yes. And **I've already done** most of the next one as well.*

3 with *how long, for* and *since* to talk about duration of states and activities (see page 121)

4 with *just* to talk about things that have happened very recently

***I've just seen** Tom in the cafeteria.*

5 with unfinished time periods: *since, so far this week, up to now, recently, this month, today*

*You**'ve been late** three times this month – please be on time for the rest of the month.*

Past simple

Use the past simple

1 when referring to (or thinking of) a finished time period like *yesterday, last week, at 5.30, on 11 May, at Christmas, in 2002,* etc.

*I **went** to the sales conference last week.*

2 for questions with *When? What time? How long ago?* etc. because the expected answer is a finished time period

*A When **did** you **see** Mr Li?* (Not: ~~*When have you seen Mr Li?*~~)
*B I **saw** him yesterday.* (Not: ~~*I have seen him yesterday.*~~)

3 with many present time expressions usually used with the present perfect, like *this week, today, just,* if they refer to a time period that is about to finish or has just finished

*We**'ve made** a lot of progress this week.* (said on Wednesday – the time period is still in progress)
*We **made** a lot of progress this week.* (said at 4.30 p.m. on Friday – the time period is about to finish)

1 Complete these dialogues with the past simple or present perfect form of the verbs in brackets.

A I need to ask David if he [1]________ (decide) to set up the focus group.
B Don't worry. I [2]________ (already / speak) to him about it.
A Really? When [3]________ (you / see) him?
B I [4]________ (call) him first thing today.
A What [5]________ (he / say)?
B He [6]________ (not / make) up his mind yet. He needs some documents from head office, and they still [7]________ (not / arrive).

A [8]________ (you / finalize) all the arrangements for Mr Eng's visit yet?
B I'm dealing with it now. I [9]________ (fix) a date for him to come and visit – the 19th.
A What about Bob? I think he needs to be there.
B That's fine. I [10]________ (speak) to Anna a couple of days ago, and the 19th is fine for him too.
A [11]________ (you / arrange) the visit to the warehouse yet?
B Yes, I [12]________ (just / organize) that – for the afternoon.
A What about dinner that evening?
B I [13]________ (book) a table yesterday – at the Mill – I hope that's OK.
A Fine. That all sounds excellent. You [14]________ (be) very efficient.

2 Match sentences 1–6 to contexts a–f.

1 Has our bid for the contract been successful? __
2 Was our bid for the contract successful? __
3 Have you spoken to the caterers this week? __
4 Did you speak to the caterers this week? __
5 I've just cancelled the order. __
6 I just cancelled the order. __

a The result of the contract bids was announced last week.
b I only cancelled the order. I didn't reorder or complain.
c They're announcing the results of the contract bids now.
d I am expecting to speak to the caterers some time this week. It is Wednesday.
e I was expecting to speak to the caterers this week. It is 5.00 on Friday. I am about to leave the office.
f I cancelled the order a couple of minutes ago.

Working with words

1 Replace the verbs in *italics* with a phrasal verb from the list with the same meaning. Make any changes that are necessary.

get round	set up	come up with
take forward	pay off	carry out
bring down	take up	

1 I'm thinking of leaving the company to *start* ________________ my own business.
2 We're over budget on this project – we need to do something to *reduce* ________________ the costs.
3 That's a great idea – I knew you would *create* ________________ a plan to solve the problem.
4 The company has *responded to* ________________ the challenge of recruiting across the EU.
5 We *performed* ________________ a lot of tests before we launched this product on the market.
6 We put a lot of money into this idea – hopefully the investment will *have a good result* ________________.
7 We *avoided* ________________ the problem of relocating extra staff by recruiting locally.
8 The first stage of the project went well, and we're now *developing* ________________ our plans for the next stage.

2 Complete the phrases in bold in the text with a suitable word from the list.

technology	revolutionary	practical
advantage	potential	features
state-of-the-art		

The Cell Zone™ is a [1]________ **idea** from Salemi Industries – a cell phone booth that lets you make and receive cell phone calls without disturbing anyone. It's a [2]________ **solution** to the problem of making calls in noisy public spaces. The Cell Zone™'s **key** [3]________ are its effective sound-proofing and its unique cylindrical shape. It is both functional and stylish – a product where **cutting-edge** [4]________ is combined with [5]________ **design**. A **major** [6]________ of the Cell Zone™ is that it can be located almost anywhere – airports, nightclubs, etc. or even on the street. It also has [7]________ **benefits** for advertisers who can use the exterior to promote their product or service.

Business communication skills

1 Number these extracts from a presentation about a new product in the right order 1–10 to give a logical structure.

___ a First, I'll give you a brief overview of the product.
___ b Basically, Minute Monitor combines a department's time schedules. It …
___ c Does that sound OK?
___ d Now I'd like to move on to some of its features. I'd like to demonstrate this by using the tool itself.
___ e Then I'll talk about its benefits. After that I'd like to show you some of its features.
___ f Good. The greatest benefit of this is that all your staff's appointments are logged in one main diary so everyone can see who's in the office and when.
_1_ g What I'd like to do in this presentation is demonstrate a new scheduling tool.
___ h Have a look at the screen – with your current system you can't link everyone's calendars. However, with Minute Monitor, you'll all be able to access this central one.
___ i Is everything clear so far?
___ j OK. We call the product Minute Monitor, and it's a pretty simple concept.

2 Complete the rest of the presentation with the words and phrases from the list.

this means	the biggest potential benefit of
in the future	the other major advantage
at the moment	is another great thing about
whereas	

Minute Monitor scheduling tool can be set up with your current system immediately, [1]________________ similar tools on the market require much higher investment to make them compatible. [2]________________ is that the program is very user-friendly and doesn't require a lot of previous knowledge or training.
A drop-down user-guide helps you with every step, which [3]________________ Minute Monitor.
[4]________________, your system is able to schedule 25 employees' appointments, but with Minute Monitor you can increase this to 50. [5]________________ that project leaders can have a better overview of the activities taking place.
[6]________________ Minute Monitor is that project scheduling can be delegated to admin staff [7]________________, giving the team leader more time on the project.

Language at work | Present, past and future ability

Use *can* or *(be) able to* to talk about ability. *Can* has only two forms: *can* (present) and *could* (past). Use *be able to* when an infinitive is needed.

Present ability

1 Use *can* to talk about general or present ability.

*I **can** speak French, but I **can't** speak German very well.*
*Could you speak louder – I **can't** hear you.*

2 *Is / are able to* is possible instead of *can* but *can* is more common.

***Are** you **able to** hear me at the back of the room?*

Past ability

1 Use *could* to talk about general ability in the past and with verbs of perception (*feel, see, hear,* etc.).

*Anna **could** speak four languages when she was six.*
*I **could** see that she was upset.*

2 For a single specific action in the past (as opposed to general ability), to mean 'tried and succeeded', use *was able to.*

*I **was able to** run fast enough to catch the bus.*
*I **could** run fast when I was young.*

However, if the specific action is negative, use *couldn't* or *wasn't able to.*

*I called customer services again and again, but I **couldn't / wasn't able to** get through.*

3 To talk about a specific action in the past, especially when we succeed in doing something difficult after trying hard, use *managed to.* It can be used in the positive or negative.

*They didn't want to give us the discount at first, but we **managed to** persuade them.*

4 To refer to past ability with a connection to the present, use the present perfect form of *be able to.*

*I **have** always **been able to** learn languages quite easily.*

Future ability

Since *can* has no infinitive form, use *be able to* to talk about future ability

1 after *will* and *going to*

*Perhaps Jane **will be able to** help you.*
*I'm afraid I'm not **going to be able to** do anything for you.*

2 after modals

*I **may / might be able to** help you.*

3 after verbs like *would like to* and *want to*

*I **would like to be able to** help you.*

1 Complete these sentences with the correct form of *can* or *be able to*. Sometimes more than one answer is possible.

1 Do you think you ______ come to the launch party next week?
2 We may ______ offer you a slightly better discount – I'll try my best.
3 So far I ______ (not) contact her, but I'll keep trying.
4 As far as I ______ see, you have a valid complaint.
5 Do you know if Amanda ______ speak Spanish?
6 Do you think you are going to ______ finish on time, or will you need a few more days?
7 I'm afraid I ______ (not) come to the meeting next week.
8 We'll need an interpreter because I ______ (not) speak Chinese.
9 ______ (she) finish that report yet?
10 I ______ understand your worries, but I think we should take the risk.

2 Choose the correct answer from the words in *italics*.

1 A Did the hotel have a good view of the mountains?
B Yes, I *could / was able to* see Mont Blanc from my room.

2 A When I got to the office, the door was locked.
B How *could you / did you manage to* get in?

3 A So what happened when you missed the plane?
B Luckily I *could / was able to* take another flight.

4 A Were you late for the meeting?
B No. Fortunately I *could / was able to* find a taxi.

5 A If the safe was locked, how *could you / were you able to* get the documents out?
B One of the managers had a spare key.

6 A What did you think when you heard Jan had been promoted?
B Well, at first I *couldn't / wasn't able to* believe it.

7 A Did you renegotiate the contract?
B Yes, we *could / managed to* obtain a slightly better deal.

8 A *Could you / Were you able to* contact Katie?
B No, but I'll call again later.

Working with words

1 Match these adjectives to definitions 1–10.

attentive, loyal, discourteous, dissatisfied, existing, responsive, high-quality, efficient, repeat, sub-standard

1 a ________ customer is someone who uses your service again and again
2 ________ goods are goods which do not meet levels of quality
3 a ________ sales assistant wouldn't be very polite to customers
4 ________ customers will complain to all their friends about bad service
5 a ________ customer will buy only from you and not your competitors
6 ________ customer service is of a very good standard
7 a company is ________ when it acts quickly and in a helpful way when a customer has a problem with its service
8 your ________ customers are the ones who currently use your service
9 if a delivery service is ________, you know things will be delivered on time
10 sales assistants who are ________ are always on hand to meet your needs

2 Choose the best word to complete these sentences.

1 We'll look at how we can use the Internet to ________ feedback from customers.
a receive **b** get **c** acquire

2 We try to provide excellent service and ________ all our customers' needs.
a meet **b** fill **c** answer

3 It's a lot easier to ________ an existing customer than to find a new one.
a stay **b** hold **c** keep

4 We are continually improving our service with the goal of ________ our clients' expectations.
a passing **b** exceeding **c** beating

5 We have recently ________ customers to our main competitor so we need to attract them back.
a left **b** lost **c** dropped

6 We regularly have surveys to ________ customer satisfaction.
a judge **b** grade **c** measure

7 The manager plans to ________ an unpublicized rule – let customers in up to 6.10.
a introduce **b** create **c** begin

Business communication skills

1 A customer is calling TNC about a banking problem. Complete the dialogue with the phrases from the list.

by tomorrow
in time for the
you mean
how can I help you
could you give me
once I've looked into it I'll call you back
let me get this straight
could you explain exactly what the problem is

A TNC, Customer Service. [1]________?
B Hello. I'm calling about my online bank account. I'm having problems completing a transaction.
A [2]________?
B Well, I've entered the payment details to pay an invoice for my holiday and the computer won't let me send it.
A Hmm. [3]________ – you want to transfer some money but you can't?
B That's right. I'm trying to pay an invoice. I've left it a bit late and need to pay it [4]________.
A [5]________ your user number and the name of the account. [6]________.
B Thanks.

(5 minutes later)

A Hello. This is TNC. The account you're trying to access is a savings account and you can't use your online facility with that.
B [7]________ I can't pay my invoice online with that account?
A That's correct. You can transfer money into your current account and then pay the invoice.
B If I do that, will the invoice be paid [8]________ deadline tomorrow?
A I'm afraid you need to allow three working days for …

2 Correct the one mistake in each sentence.

1 What can I do you for?
____
2 If I understand you right, you received the wrong items.
____
3 I'll look under it straightaway.
____
4 We need the goods in time to the training day.
____
5 Once I've found your order, I'll get you back.
____
6 It should be by Friday by the latest.
____

Language at work | Direct and indirect questions

Direct and indirect questions

1 In a direct question, the normal word order is ***verb–subject***. In an indirect question, starting with a phrase like *Do you know …*, the positive form is used and the order becomes ***subject–verb***.

Direct: *When **is Mr Patel** leaving?*
Indirect: *Do you know when **Mr Patel is** leaving?*

These differences are most noticeable in the present simple and past simple. In the indirect question, the auxiliaries *do/ does* or *did* are not needed.

Direct: *Where **does** Mr Elmore **work**?*
Indirect: *Could you tell me where Mr Elmore **works**?*
Direct: *When **did** Cassie **call**?*
Indirect: *Could you tell me when Cassie **called**?*

2 For *Wh-?* and *How?* questions, we repeat the question word.

Direct: ***Who*** is Jan seeing tomorrow?*
Indirect: *Do you know **who** Jan is seeing tomorrow?*
Direct: ***How much** does it cost?*
Indirect: *Do you know **how much** it costs?*
Direct: ***Why** did Mr Peters leave?*
Indirect: *Do you know **why** Mr Peters left?*

*When *who* or *what* is the subject of the question (see page 105), there is no difference in word order.

Direct: ***Who is coming** to the meeting?*
Indirect: *Do you know **who is coming** to the meeting?*

3 For *Yes / No* questions, use *if* or *whether (or not)*.

Direct: *Is it going to rain tomorrow?*
Indirect: *Do you know **if** it's going to rain tomorrow?*
Direct: *Have you decided to go ahead?*
Indirect: *Could you tell me **whether or not** you've decided to go ahead?*

4 The most common phrases to introduce indirect questions are

Could you tell me … / Do you know … / Could you let me know … .

Language tip

Other common phrases that follow the same pattern are these reported thought phrases.

I wonder … / I'll try and find out … / I have no idea … / I don't know … / I'm not sure … / I doubt whether …

*I wonder **when** our order **will arrive.***

1 Tick (✓) the sentences that are right. Correct the sentences that are wrong.

1 Can you tell me what he said? ✓
2 Do you know what is the time? ✗
Do you know what the time is?
3 Do you know why did he leave the company?
4 Could you let me know is Sam working today?
5 Do you know what her phone number is?
6 Could you tell me who did you speak to?
7 Do you know if has the meeting started?
8 Could you tell me how much it will cost?
9 Do you know whether can we leave early today?
10 Could you tell me where is the information office?

2 Rewrite these direct questions as indirect questions starting with the words given.

1 Will he take the job?
Do you think ______________________________?
2 When did Amanda send them the catalogue?
Could you find out ______________________________?
3 Is this the train for Munich?
Do you know ______________________________?
4 Where does the bus for Place de la Concorde go from?
Do you know ______________________________?
5 Have you had anything from the minibar?
Could you tell me ______________________________?
6 Who left this package here?
Do you know ______________________________?
7 What time will you be arriving?
I'd be grateful if you could tell me ______________________________.
8 Do you have any special dietary requirements?
Please let us know ______________________________.

Working with words

1 Match 1–7 to a–g.

1 We work with local communities and take … ___
2 We have strongly held beliefs about equality and intend to stay … ___
3 We need to do more to reduce … ___
4 Environmental groups share … ___
5 We work hard to ensure that our subsidiaries all act … ___
6 The government needs to make sure that companies comply with … ___
7 As a fund-raising manager, I encourage companies to donate … ___

a regulations and follow official guidelines.
b money to our charity.
c the impact our factories have on air pollution in the local area.
d an active part in managing health and education projects.
e a strong commitment to caring for the environment.
f true to our principles.
g responsibly and follow our environmental policies.

2 Complete this text with the correct form of the words in brackets.

Choose investments carefully

1 ______________ (ethics) investments are having an increasing impact on the financial services sector. These investments, also known as socially-2 ______________ (responsibility) investments, are beginning to have more 3 ______________ (credible) than they did when they started 30 or 40 years ago.
Investing in one of these funds is meant to be a good investment choice rather than an act of 4 ______________ (generous). Fund managers invest in companies with a good reputation, which treat their workers with 5 ______________ (fair) and avoid all forms of 6 ______________ (discriminatory) or 7 ______________ (prejudiced). In theory, this should lead to better industrial relations and greater long-term profitability.
Fund managers also try to avoid unstable and undemocratic regimes where there is evidence of 8 ______________ (bribe) and 9 ______________ (corrupt), as well as companies who do things by 10 ______________ (deceptive).

Business communication skills

1 Jana at Events4U has been asked to organize an information day at RCI for key account clients. She is meeting with Xavier from RCI. Number their conversation in the correct order 1–10.

___ a **Jana** Oh, speaking of staff … We aim to have the reps available to the clients as long as possible. They're welcome to attend the whole day and the evening gala dinner too.
___ b **Jana** Well, the idea is to focus on the different products you offer and to provide interactive stands. The clients can then try out your new products and speak to you – the reps – directly.
___ c **Xavier** That makes sense. The reps can decide which shift they prefer.
___ d **Xavier** That's a great idea. I'm glad you're involving the staff.
___ e **Xavier** I'm not sure many reps will stay in the evening if they've been at the event all day.
___ f **Xavier** Thanks, you've done a great job so far. It's exactly what we're looking for.
1 g **Jana** I've called this meeting to tell you about the key account event you asked us to organize. We're planning to hold it at the Lichtenstein Palace.
___ h **Jana** Finally, we'd like to offer you two possible 'performances' during the day too. I'll email you the details next week.
___ i **Xavier** That sounds great – a lovely venue. How are you going to organize the event?
___ j **Jana** Yes, I thought that might be a problem. We recommend you arrange a shift system throughout the day, so reps attend either the afternoon or the evening.

2 Put the words in *italics* in the right order to complete the sentences.

1 *We're / you / going / provide / to* with free transport.
____
2 *You'll / to / opportunity / get / the* sample our products.
____
3 The Acto Museum *is / visit / worth / well / a.*
____
4 *It / a / would / good / to / be / idea* buy a ticket in advance. ______________
5 *We'd / to / to / like / you / invite* an information evening.
____
6 *It's / thing / need / the / just / kind / we / of* for our clients. ______________
7 *Alternatively, / show / be / you / delighted / we'd / to* our facility in Prague.
____

Language at work | Talking about the future

will

Use *will* + infinitive

1 to make predictions or talk about future facts

It looks as if the economy ***will slow*** *down next year.*

2 to make decisions at the moment of speaking

A I'm sorry – I'm really busy at the moment.
B Don't worry – ***I'll call*** *back later.*

For decisions made earlier, when you mean 'I've decided to', use *going to*, not *will*.

I should be back in an hour. ***I'm going to get*** *my hair cut.*
(Not: ~~*I will get*~~ *...*)

be going to

Use *be going to* + infinitive

1 to talk about a plan or intention where the decision has already been made

A I've asked the contractors to meet with us.
B I see. What ***are you going to say*** *to them?*

2 to make a very definite prediction based on evidence that you can see or know about

*My manager likes to start meetings on time, so he****'s going to be*** *annoyed when I arrive late.*

Often either *will* or *going to* can be used to make predictions.

When interest rates go up, people ***will / are going to*** *start spending less.*

Present continuous

Use the present continuous to talk about arrangements, appointments, social events and anything you would put in a diary, particularly when the time, place or purpose is mentioned.

I'm seeing *Bill in Paris tomorrow to discuss the project.*

Going to can almost always be used in these situations, but use of the present continuous is very common in everyday spoken English.

Present simple

Use the present simple to refer to future events that are in a timetable.

Do you know when the last train ***leaves****?*

The verb *be* is often used in the present simple when talking about personal schedules.

I'm *in Madrid on Friday and* ***I'm*** *away for a couple of days next week as well.*

1 Read the situations and the responses. Cross through the one option in *italics* that is incorrect.

1 You come to an office to see either Mr Peters or Miss Winston. The receptionist tells you that Mr Peters is away for the day. Response: That's OK. *I'll see / I see* Miss Winston.

2 A colleague asks you if you are free this afternoon. You have arranged to take Ben to the airport. Response: No, *I'm taking / I'll take / I'm going to take* Ben to the airport.

3 A colleague asks if you have any plans for the weekend. Response: Yes, *I'm meeting / I'll meet / I'm going to meet* Jack for a meal this evening.

4 A friend asks you what the future holds for property prices. Response: Most people seem to think *they're falling / they're going to fall / they'll fall* next year.

5 You are at a football match. Your team is 3–0 down and there are only two minutes to go. A friend asks why the manager doesn't bring on some new players. Response: It's too late. *We'll lose / We're going to lose.*

6 A colleague wants to arrange a meeting for Tuesday. Reponse: Sorry, that's no good – *I'm / I'm being / I'll be* in Paris on Tuesday.

7 A colleague tells you that she can't give you a lift to the station as originally planned and she apologizes. Response: Don't worry – *I'll get / I'm going to get* a taxi.

2 Complete these dialogues with the best form of the verbs in brackets. Sometimes more than one answer is possible.

A Where are you going?
B I [1]__________ (pick up) the new catalogues from Amanda today.
A Do you think Bill [2]__________ (be) there?
B Yes, I [3]__________ (see) him after Amanda. Why?
A I've got a new price list for him.
B OK, I [4]__________ (take) it with me if you like. I [5]__________ (make sure) he gets it.

A Have you decided on your holiday yet?
B Yes – we [6]__________ (go back) to Spain. I booked everything a few weeks ago.
A [7]__________ (you / stay) in the same place?
B Yes, but we [8]__________ (not / fly) this time.
A How [9]__________ (you / get) there?
B Ferry and car. There's a ferry that [10]__________ (leave) at 8 p.m. The whole journey [11]__________ (only / take) 24 hours, and it means we [12]__________ (have) our own transport when we're there.

7 | Practice file

Working with words

1 Someone is talking about their colleagues. Match these adjectives to statements 1–8.

conventional	creative	determined
impulsive	indecisive	methodical
outgoing	thoughtful	

1 First Su Li said she was going to apply for the job; then she said she would stay where she was. So I don't know what she's planning. ________

2 Tony isn't boring but … he always wears a suit and tie. He wants to get married and have two children, work from nine to five and retire at 65. ________

3 Everyone loves Bob – he's always in a good mood, and he likes chatting to new people and making friends. ________

4 I asked Bill what he was doing at the weekend. He said 'nothing'. Then, driving home, he decided to go skiing. So he drove to the airport, got a ticket and went! ________

5 When Jane has made her mind up about something, nothing will stop her. So, if she says she wants to become Sales Director, that's what she'll do. ________

6 I couldn't find the mistake in the figures, so I asked Arturo to look. He started at the beginning, read every page, and finally worked out what the problem was. ________

7 She'll be a great art editor – she's very talented. She's a musician *and* a painter. She's got good fashion sense and she's always full of bright ideas. ________

8 If you ask Jonas something, he doesn't suggest a solution straightaway. He goes away and considers it quietly, but when he does give an answer, it's usually right. ________

2 Choose the correct answer from the words in *italics*.

1 I need to show this to my line manager to get a different *perspective / attitude* on the project.

2 Let's not reject anything – we need to *think / consider* all the options and then make a choice.

3 I need time to *balance / weigh up* the information and work out what to do.

4 It's hard when you have to decide *about / between* two very good candidates.

5 In business you have to be rational and logical. You can't just *rely / trust* on feelings.

6 You're very experienced and you should have more *assurance / confidence* in your own judgement.

7 If I don't have enough information, I usually *wait / delay* my decision until I've done more research.

Business communication skills

1 Put these words in the right order to make phrases.

1 white / black / here / they're / in / and …
____

2 think / be/ it / to / crazy / I / would …
____

3 me / should / if / we / ask / you …
____

4 us / detail, / you / please / could / some / give?
____

5 Clare / to / let's / what / on, / has / hear / hang / say.
____

6 right / says / is / John / what.
____

7 facts, / look / the / if / we / at / we'll / see …
____

2 Abigail, John and Bettina are discussing offers for language training at their company. Complete their discussion with these phrases.

let's draw up some action points	in other words
I don't want to spend too long	I don't think we
what you're getting at is	it'll mean we
as far as I'm concerned	that's my view
what's your position	today, I'd like to
I'm not convinced	the fact is

A [1]________ dicuss the three offers for Spanish training. John, [2]________ on this?

J [3]________ there are two very fair offers and one that seems expensive.

B [4]________ should only consider price. [5]________, the more expensive course includes all materials plus holding the training here.

A So [6]________ the more expensive option also includes more?

B Exactly.

J [7]________. We don't know the quality of these courses – have we received any recommendations?

A The more expensive course is offered by an established institute, but the cheaper options have good marketing.

B But if we take an all-inclusive package, [8]________ ________ won't have any unforeseen costs.

J True, but we should meet with the three companies first – [9]________.

B [10]________ we need to discuss the offers with the provider before a decision is made?

J Yes. [11]________ on what we've discussed so far.

A OK, but [12]________ on this point. We have other items still to discuss.

Language at work | Countability | Expressing quantity

Countability

Countable nouns

A countable noun (e.g. *chair, cat*) can be singular or plural.

a chair, three cats

Single countable nouns have a singular verb.

My office ***is*** *in Manhattan.*

Plural countable nouns have a plural verb.

The managers ***are*** *unhappy about the new proposal.*

Some nouns are always plural (*scissors, clothes*).

The scissors ***are*** *on Jamie's desk.*

Uncountable nouns

An uncountable noun (e.g. *advice, equipment*) has a singular verb and has no plural form.

Your advice ***was*** *very useful.*

Countable and uncountable nouns

Some nouns can be both countable and uncountable, but there is a change in meaning.

coffee – the drink or the crop
two coffees – two cups of coffee

time – minutes and hours passing
four times – four occasions

Additional words can also be used to refer to parts of a whole.

a ***piece*** *of information, an* ***item*** *of furniture*

Expressing quantity

1 To talk about something in general, use

- a plural countable noun and no quantifier
  Computers are getting cheaper all the time.
- or an uncountable noun and no quantifier
  Cash is less secure than a cheque.

2 When talking about quantities, use the following quantifiers with these classes of nouns.

singular, countable: *a, an, the, one* (You must have a quantifier of some kind.)

plural, countable: *how many, (too) many, (not) many, more / fewer, (a) few, very few* and numbers (1, 2, 3)

uncountable: *how much, (too / not) much, more / less, (a) little , very little*

uncountable or plural countable nouns: *lots of, plenty of, masses of, most, most of the, some, some of the, all of the, all my, (not) enough, hardly any, (not) any, no, none of the*

1 Complete the table with pairs of countable and uncountable nouns that match together.

~~traffic~~	correspondence	training
furniture	hotel room	equipment
~~car~~	letter	money
accommodation	software	time
table	fax / photocopier	lesson
week	computer program	euro

countable	uncountable	countable	uncountable
car	*traffic*		

2 Choose the correct answer from the verb forms in *italics*.

1 The equipment you need for the presentation *is / are* at reception.
2 The people I met at the conference *was / were* very friendly.
3 The sales statistics *don't / doesn't* show a rise in demand for the product.
4 Could you turn on the TV? The news *is / are* going to be on soon.
5 Progress at the site *has / have* been slow recently.
6 My clothes *isn't / aren't* smart enough for the interview.
7 When I was in the UK, the weather *was / were* varied.
8 The new software *is / are* being developed in-house.

3 Choose the correct answer from the words in *italics*.

1 I need *many / more* time to make a decision.
2 She's managed to get *a / some* job with an insurance company.
3 There *is very little / are very few* information about this on the website.
4 I had *too much / too many* emails to reply to before the end of the day.
5 I think there are *very little / very few* people who understand the theory fully.
6 I'm sure we can find you *a / some* suitable accommodation.
7 Let me give you *a little / a few* advice about negotiating with that company.
8 Would you like *morning paper / a morning paper* delivered with your breakfast?

Working with words

1 Complete the sentences with these words.

process, employment, activities, facility, growth, location, workers

1 If we outsource the administrative tasks, our European centres can focus on their core __________.
2 If the business __________ outsourcing goes ahead, all our filing, etc. will be done in China.
3 The factory will create 500 jobs, but if you count the indirect __________ from jobs like taxi drivers and caterers as well, the figure is much higher.
4 R-It is a new training __________ for students, focusing on all aspects of information technology.
5 Karnataka has 77 engineering colleges producing more than 29,000 graduates a year so there is a large group of skilled __________.
6 We are selling more and more of our products abroad, so our export __________ is rising steadily.
7 We decided to outsource software development to an offshore __________ rather than to one in our country.

2 Rewrite the phrases in *italics* using the phrases from the list. Make any changes in form that are necessary.

take cost-cutting measures, lead to job losses, improve the quality of life for, create new jobs, streamline our operation, free up resources, gain a competitive edge

1 Some politicians argue that BPO *results in a reduction in employment* __________ at home.
2 Outsourcing has led to the building of new roads and housing in Bangalore, which has *increased personal satisfaction in life experienced by* __________ many local people.
3 Our budget deficit has increased again so we need to *do something to make savings* __________ and reduce our office costs.
4 RGM's help desk outsourcing services have helped us to *make the way we work simpler and more efficient* __________.
5 We decided to outsource our back office work in order to *make money and personnel more available* __________ for our core activities.
6 Thirty new offices were opened in the area last year – this *generated 980 additional positions* __________ in the IT industry.
7 We want to *achieve an advantage* __________ over our competitors so we aim to increase production by 10%.

Business communication skills

1 Complete the extracts from a presentation about outsourcing key services with these phrases.

due, data, have a, move on, looked at, notice on, look at, the facts, has resulted in, leave, a result, turn our attention to

Recent [1] __________ shows that outsourcing of office cleaning, catering and the customer helpline [2] __________ financial benefits for the company.

Let's have a [3] __________ this slide. On the left you can see our expenditure five years ago …

I'd like to [4] __________ to give you some background about each sector we've outsourced. Firstly, cleaning. [5] __________ to increasing personnel costs, outsourcing seemed to be our only option. You will [6] __________ this chart savings other companies achieved. We analysed these carefully and as [7] __________ decided to do the same.

OK, we've [8] __________ cleaning, so let's [9] __________ catering. After careful research, [10] __________ were clear: employing staff to run a restaurant was too expensive and not cost-effective. [11] __________ look at these figures …

Finally, I'd like to [12] __________ you with some interesting statistics regarding the customer helpline …

2 Choose the correct answer from the prepositions in *italics*.

1 Due *for / to / from* the recent large increase …
2 A knock-on effect *of / to / on* this was …
3 This relates back *for / at / to* the point I made earlier.
4 To illustrate this, let's have a look *on / at / to* this chart.
5 This resulted *to / for / in* huge financial losses.
6 You will notice *on / in / by* this chart how big our market share has become.
7 Let's turn our attention *from / to / on* the drawbacks involved.
8 As a result *from / to / of* public criticism, we stopped our ad campaign.
9 Let's consider financing the project, which I referred *to / about / of* earlier.
10 To conclude, I'd like to leave you with some food *for / to / in* thought …

Language at work | The passive

Passive forms

1 Verbs in sentences can either be active or passive. To make the passive, use the verb *be* in the appropriate tense and a past participle.

Tense	Active	Passive
Present simple	*We* ***do*** *the job.*	*The job* ***is done.***
Present continuous	*We* ***are doing*** *the job.*	*The job* ***is being done.***
Past simple	*We* ***did*** *the job.*	*The job* ***was done.***
Past continuous	*We* ***were doing*** *the job.*	*The job* ***was being done.***
Present perfect	*We* ***have done*** *the job.*	*The job* ***has been done.***
Past perfect	*We* ***had done*** *the job.*	*The job* ***had been done.***
Modal	*We* ***must*** *do the job.*	*The job* ***must be done.***
Infinitive	*We need* ***to do*** *the job.*	*The job needs* ***to be done.***
-ing form	*We object to someone* ***doing*** *the job.*	*We object to the job* ***being done.***

2 Make questions and negatives in the same way as in active sentences.

Was the email ***sent*** *to Mr Jordan?*
The email ***wasn't sent*** *this morning.*

Use

1 To change the focus of a sentence from who does something to what happens to something.

My assistant ***has prepared*** *the contract.* (The focus is on my assistant, the subject of the active sentence.)
The contract ***has been prepared.*** (The focus is on the contract and what has happened to it.)

2 To describe processes or how something is done.

When the grapes ***have been picked***, *they* ***are taken*** *to the factory.*

3 When the person who does the action is unimportant or unknown or we want to avoid saying who is responsible.

My secretary ***has lost*** *the order form.*
The order form ***has been lost.***

Use *by* to say who does the action following a passive verb.

The decision ***has been made by*** *the Managing Director.*

4 To talk about reputation and with phrases like *is said to be, is believed to be.* These phrases are often used in news reports and make the information more impersonal.

California ***is said to be*** *warm and sunny.*
The Prime Minister ***is believed to be*** *in talks with …*

1 Change the phrases in *italics* from active to passive.

1 *Somebody has lost all my important files.*
____

2 When I returned from holiday, I found that *somebody had broken into my flat.*
____

3 My colleague Jane is expecting *somebody to promote her.*
____

4 I don't like *people telling me* what to do.
____

5 *Somebody must have hacked into our computer system.*
____

6 I feel that *somebody is not telling us* the whole story.
____

7 *They are sending me* to Shanghai for three months.
____

8 When I finally arrived at the conference, *someone was putting away the chairs.*
____

9 *Somebody unveiled Microsoft's latest operating system* last month. ____________________

10 After the Games, *will they use the Olympic Village* for housing? ____________________

2 Complete the article with the active or passive form of the verbs in brackets. Use these tenses.

Paragraph A: present simple Paragraph B: past simple
Paragraph C: present perfect Paragraph D: *will* future

A A report today [1] __________ (accuse) leading stores of exploiting workers in Bangladesh: 'Workers in factories there [2] __________ (pay) low wages; the employers [3] __________ (not / recognize) unions and workers [4] __________ (often / force) to work seven days a week.'

B The author of the report [5] __________ (visit) several factories: 'On one occasion, the owner [6] __________ (tell) in advance of our visit. That time, there [7] __________ (be) 30 workers and they [8] __________ (give) regular breaks. When we [9] __________ (make) a surprise visit the next day, the same room [10] __________ (pack) with over 100 workers.'

C A spokesperson for one of the stores said: 'We [11] __________ (have) factories in Bangladesh for years and are proud of the improvements in working conditions that [12] __________ (make). The factories [13] __________ (always / produce) high-quality goods and customers in Europe [14] __________ (benefit) from low prices.'

D The report says: 'We expect the issue [15] __________ (raise) in boardrooms over the next few weeks, and we [16] __________ (get) lots of promises. But we need more than this – so we [17] __________ (keep up) the pressure. We hope that something [18] __________ (finally / do).'

Working with words

1 Match 1–8 to a–h.

1 Many women feel there is a glass ceiling … ___
2 Some banks have a corporate culture which … ___
3 I could take early retirement which … ___
4 He felt the new job was a sideways move … ___
5 When the factory downsized … ___
6 Setting up a new company involves dealing with official agencies and … ___
7 To save costs, the company made … ___
8 I can't move house because of the children's schools, so … ___

a would mean stopping work at 55 rather than 65.
b relocation is not an option.
c a lot of rules and red tape.
d rather than a promotion.
e a lot of the staff redundant.
f is very masculine and competitive.
g a third of the workers were laid off.
h stopping them from getting top jobs.

2 Complete these sentences. Use the answers to complete the puzzle and find the hidden word.

1 It's a lot cheaper to try and _________ staff than to continually find replacements.
2 Mangement failed to adequately _________ the project with experienced personnel.
3 Management want to _________ several staff to our new store on the outskirts of the city.
4 When they _________ the new Operations Manager, everyone will be informed immediately by email.
5 We believe in job _________ and giving you the opportunity to do different jobs in the company.
6 We intend to _________ a lot of time and money in the new HR department.
7 Two _______ vacancies must be filled as soon as possible.
8 You start at the bottom, and if you do well and work hard, the company will _________ you.

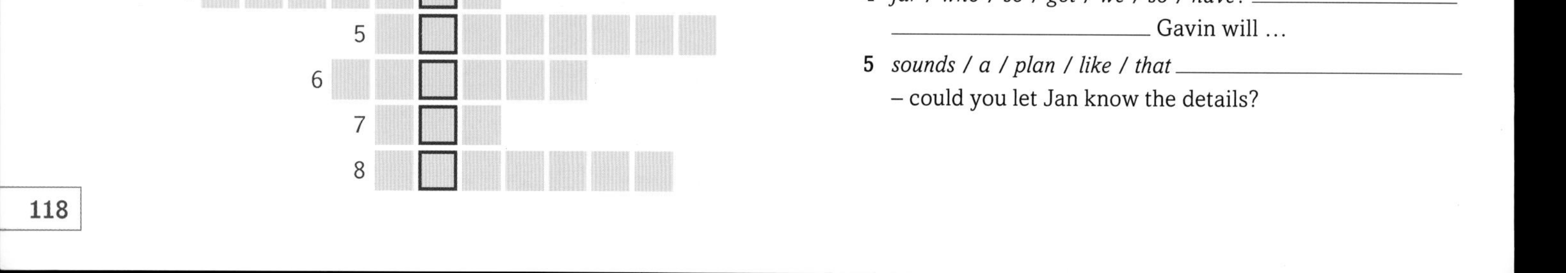

Business communication skills

1 Anton and Carolina from the workers' council are meeting with Bob from HR to negotiate the annual staff trip. Complete this extract from their meeting with the correct answer from 1–10 below.

Anton What we need to [1]_________ on today is what to do for the staff trip. Let's look at what our [2]_________ are.

Carolina [3]_________ about we charter a plane to Morocco for a weekend?

Anton We do have that on our list of options, but [4]_________ need to stretch the budget if we did that.

Carolina Yes, you're right. Bob, how does HR view things? What can you [5]_________ us?

Bob Well, the workers' council always offers a staff trip – so we can't stop this – but what we [6]_________ is it should be educational as well as entertaining.

Anton You mean, [7]_________ we include something cultural we can choose any of our suggestions?

Bob Yes. Let's say you take the Morocco option. [8]_________ you offer excursions to places of interest as part of the package, HR might veto the whole trip.

Carolina OK. We can [9]_________ with that and would organize the trip to comply with HR's wishes.

Anton So, a quick [10]_________ – if …

	a	b	c	d
1	talk	meet	decide	discuss
2	possibilities	options	opinions	alternatives
3	What's	Who	Why	How
4	we'll	we	we'd	we've
5	lend	help	propose	offer
6	plan	propose	aim	intend
7	provided	would	were	supposing
8	until	providing	unless	if
9	be	remain	stay	live
10	review	recap	repeat	outline

2 Put the words in *italics* in the correct order to complete the sentences.

1 *discuss / the / areas / we / to / need /are* _________________ _________________ the weekend rota and overtime.
2 *to / one / would / option / be* _________________ cancel the event.
3 *we / don't / on / why / take* _________________ two temporary staff for our busy period?
4 *far / who / so / got / we / so / have?* _________________ _________________ Gavin will …
5 *sounds / a / plan / like / that* _________________ – could you let Jan know the details?

Language at work | First and second conditionals

First conditional

First conditional sentences have two parts. In the *if* clause, we talk about a present or future situation that is quite likely to happen; in the other clause, we talk about the result.

Likely situation	Result
If + present tense	*will* + infinitive
If you ***order*** *20 units,*	***we'll give*** *you a 15% discount.*
If ***I'm not promoted,***	***I'll leave*** *the company.*

Variations

1 Use the present continuous or present perfect in the *if* clause.
If anyone ***is waiting*** *for you in reception, I'll let you know.*
If he ***hasn't*** *emailed them, I'll call instead.*

2 Use other modals in the result clause.
If we hurry, we ***may / might /could / should*** *arrive in time.*

Second conditional

Second conditional sentences have two parts. In the *if* clause, we talk about an imaginary present or future situation that is not likely; in the other clause, we talk about the result.

Imaginary situation	Result
If + past tense	*would* + infinitive
If we ***accepted*** the takeover bid,	*we* ***would be*** *out of a job.*

Variations

1 Use the past continuous in the *if* clause.
If you ***were applying*** *for a job, what would you put on your CV?*

2 Use *could* or *might* in the result clause.
If we got a bit more help, we ***could / might*** *finish on time.*

Linking words

1 A number of expressions mean 'if and only if', and emphasize the condition: *provided (that)*, *providing* (less formal), *as long as* and *on the condition that*.
I'll help you today ***providing*** *you do my shift on Friday.*

2 *Supposing* means 'just imagine', so it is normally used with second conditionals.
Supposing *they offered you the job, would you take it?*

3 *Unless* is similar in meaning to 'if not'.
I'll be home by 5.30 ***unless*** *the meeting finishes late.*

4 Use *in case* to talk about action taken to avoid something happening.
I'll take a spare battery ***in case*** *the main one runs out.*

1 Choose the best answer from the words in *italics*.

1 Daniela is interested in moving to your team. But if she *comes / came* to you, I *will / would* need to find a replacement here as soon as possible.
2 We can easily fulfil orders for a few hundred metres of cable. However, if you *want / wanted* 50,000 metres, say, that *will / would* take a lot longer.
3 I think you're being very rash. If I *am / were* you, I *will / would* reconsider your decision.
4 I *will / would* agree on the deal now if I *have / had* the authority, but I have to check with the directors first.
5 Can you leave this with me until tomorrow? I think I *will / would* be able to work something out if you *give / gave* me more time.
6 I *will / would* apply for the Madrid job if I *speak / spoke* good Spanish, but unfortunately I don't.
7 I can't let you have time off. If I *make / made* an exception for you, everybody else *will / would* expect the same.
8 If you *want / wanted* to read the contract again before signing, we *will / would* take a break now and resume our meeting in half an hour.

2 Which of the situations in 1 are

1 likely to happen? ________
2 not likely to happen? ________

3 Complete the sentences with these linking words.

if unless provided
as long in case

1 I'm organizing some insurance ________ I get ill.
2 I'm very busy, so please don't disturb me ________ it's an emergency.
3 ________ sales don't start falling, we'll reach our targets this year.
4 I should be able to get there by 10.30, but I'll let you know ________ there's a problem.
5 ________ as we get the funding, we can go ahead with the project in October.

4 Using first or second conditionals, complete these sentences with your own ideas.

1 If I ever had the chance, ________________________
2 I wouldn't take time off work unless ________________________
3 If it's a nice weekend, I think ________________________
4 If he hasn't come in the next five minutes, ________________________

Working with words

1 Complete these sentences with the best option.

1 It was obvious there was a ________ in the market for more affordable lenses.
 a space b break c gap

2 Unless we can secure more financial ________, we won't be able to go ahead with our expansion plans.
 a approval b backing c aid

3 My advice is to build up a ________ of contacts who can offer advice and support to your business.
 a network b system c connection

4 How much start-up ________ do you need for equipment, rent and supplies for the first year?
 a wealth b assets c capital

5 Some start-ups get funding from business ________ who can offer advice as well as money.
 a guardians b messengers c angels

6 Investors will want to look at your business ________ in detail to assess the potential of your idea.
 a map b plan c chart

7 We need a lot of funding to start the business so we're going to approach a ________ capitalist.
 a business b venture c project

8 Banks are wary of giving ________ to start-ups – they prefer to finance businesses already in profit.
 a stocks b assets c loans

9 Most investors want to be confident they'll receive a good return on ________.
 a investment b asset c speculation

10 It was announced today that SFR Ltd has bought a 60% ________ in Lin Productions.
 a portion b stake c piece

2 Choose the correct answer from the words in *italics*.

1 This proposition is *hugely / totally* ridiculous – there's no way we can agree to it.
2 So far we've had *a really / an absolutely* successful year.
3 Their demands are *extremely / absolutely* outrageous.
4 The prices you've been quoted seem *completely / incredibly* high.
5 The concept is extremely *brilliant / clever* – there's no way it could possibly fail.
6 The procedure is *really / absolutely* complex, but I'm sure you'll understand it fairly quickly.
7 It's totally *impossible / difficult* to cut costs any more.
8 Researching an appropriate business model is *completely / hugely* important before looking for funding.

Business communication skills

1 Two business acquaintances meet up at a trade fair. Correct the mistakes in the phrases in *italics* in their conversation.

Barbara Is that you Josef? [1]*What you do here?*
____

Josef Hello, Barbara. [2]*I don't see you for ages.*
____

Barbara [3]*How does life treat you?*
____

Josef I've been working on a big project for Avrim. [4]*How's you with business?* ________

Barbara Well, I've moved house, changed jobs and I'm about to set up on my own. Actually, with that in mind, [5]*could you make me a favour?* ________

Josef If I can – what do you need?

Barbara [6]*The things is, I look for someone* ________ ________ to come into partnership with me. Would you be interested?

Josef Me? [7]*That not something I can deciding on right now.*
____

Barbara OK. I'll email you the details and maybe we could discuss it over lunch.

Josef Well, [8]*I'll surely think about it.*
____

2 Match 1–10 to a–j.

1 That's actually … ___
2 Let's talk … ___
3 By the way, could … ___
4 The thing is, we're looking … ___
5 It's been a long time since … ___
6 With that in mind, maybe … ___
7 What have you … ___
8 Are you still working … ___
9 I haven't seen you … ___
10 We're looking for an investor and … ___

a for SFL?
b I could ask you for a favour.
c for someone to help us out.
d we've been in contact.
e about that over dinner.
f I wondered if you were interested.
g for ages.
h been up to?
i you do me a favour?
j the reason why I'm calling.

Language at work | Present perfect simple and continuous

Talking about duration

1 Use the present perfect continuous with *How long…?*, *for* and *since* to talk about continuous activities or repeated actions that started in the past and are still going on now.

*How long **have** you **been learning** English?*
*I've **been learning** for three years / since I joined ILS.*

2 Use *for* to talk about amounts of time (*for three weeks*, *for two months*). Use *since* to talk about points in time (*since 10.30*, *since Monday*, *since the end of May*).

3 When talking about a state (see page 103), use the present perfect simple, because stative verbs are not used in the continuous form.

*How long **have** you **known** Pia?*
*I've **known** her for five years. (Not: '~~ve been knowing~~)*

Unfinished time periods

1 Use the present perfect continuous or simple with unfinished time periods like *recently*, *all day*, *this week*.

*I've **been trying** to call her all day.*
*We've **had** six offers so far this week.*

2 Use the present perfect continuous when talking about activities that are temporary or unfinished.

Temporary activity: *I've **been staying** with my brother this week.* (I usually live in my own flat.)
Unfinished activity: *I've **been talking** to my accountant this week.* (The discussions are continuing.)

3 Use the present perfect simple for stative verbs.

*My boss **has been** away in London this week.* (It is Thursday and he is still not back.)

4 Use the present perfect simple when talking about completed actions and to give details of quantities.

*I have seen my accountant **three times** this week.* (Those three occasions are in the past.)

No time period

When no time period at all is mentioned, the difference between the present perfect simple and continuous depends on whether the action is finished (and we stress the result) or unfinished (and we stress the action).

*Sam's **read** your report.* (He's finished it.)
*Sam's **been reading** your report.* (He hasn't finished it and the activity is continuing.)

BUT the present perfect continuous can be used to talk about recent activities that are **finished** if there is some evidence of the recent activity.

*It's stopped now, but it's **been snowing** and the roads are still very dangerous.*

1 Complete these sentences with the present perfect simple or present perfect continuous form of the verbs in brackets.

1 I can certainly recommend Mr Hiro to you – I ________ (know) him for a long time.
2 The Finance Director is in Hong Kong – he ________ (stay) at the Excelsior for the last two weeks.
3 Someone ________ (use) my printer – feel how hot it is – and half the paper's gone!
4 We ________ (negotiate) the new contracts since May, but we still can't agree.
5 I ________ (read) the report, but I haven't got to the final recommendations yet.
6 I ________ (go sailing) for five or six years now – I go most weekends.
7 So far we ________ (have) over 400 complaints, so we've definitely got a problem.
8 I'm sorry for the delay – ________ (you / wait) long?
9 I ________ (try) to get in touch with customer service for days but the line is always busy.
10 It ________ (rain) for days and days – when is it ever going to stop?

2 Match 1–10 to the most likely context in a–j.

1 I've been writing the report. ___
2 I've talked to Mr Holmes. ___
3 What have you done? ___
4 The weather has been getting better. ___
5 I've written the report. ___
6 Jack's been skiing. ___
7 I've been talking to Mr Holmes. ___
8 The weather has got better. ___
9 Jack's gone skiing. ___
10 What have you been doing? ___

a I'm asking about your life in general since we last met.
b I have finished my discussions with Mr Holmes.
c It's summer now and it's warm every day.
d The report is not finished.
e It's warmer than it was, but it's not warm every day.
f I am still in discussions with Mr Holmes.
g I'm asking what tasks you've completed on your 'to do' list.
h Jack is an expert skier. Ask him about Austria.
i The report is finished. Here it is.
j Jack is on holiday in Austria at the moment.

Working with words

1 Choose the correct answer from the words in *italics*.

1 The touch screen makes it very simple to interact *in / at / with* the program.
2 With Internet banking, you can have access *for / to / in* your account at any time.
3 The new tax laws will have a dramatic impact *on / for / to* company profits.
4 More than 15 telecommunications firms were involved *in / for / on* the XB communications project.
5 We need to focus *into / over / on* our core business and the activities we do best.
6 Can you connect *in / into / to* the Internet using your mobile?
7 We subscribe *with / for / to* several trade magazines at work.
8 On this project we'll be collaborating *with / by / in* colleagues in Frankfurt and Milan.
9 More needs to be done to integrate the staff from the new company *with / on / at* our existing staff.

2 Complete these sentences with the correct form of the words from the list. Use each word twice.

analyse communicate consult
participate transfer

1 A systems ________ is an IT expert who looks at a company's needs and designs computer programs.
2 To solve the problem you need a clear, logical, ________ approach.
3 My colleague's not very ________ – he rarely talks to the rest of us.
4 Modern forms of ________ make it very easy to stay in touch.
5 The employees want more ________ in the decision-making process in the company.
6 The ________ at the conference represented a wide variety of audio technology companies.
7 An outside agency has prepared a ________ document to suggest solutions to our communication problems.
8 The charity Mercy Ships often uses ________, like Dr Arras, who specialize in trauma surgery.
9 I've applied for a ________ to the marketing department so I can learn new skills.
10 Technical skills are important, but we also want people with ________ skills like time management, creative thinking …

Business communication skills

1 Mikhail is telling a member of his staff about the new payment procedure for telephone orders. Number the dialogue 1–8 in the correct order.

___ a **Katya** So you're saying we can refuse to take an order if the caller is using their partner's credit card for example?
___ b **Katya** Yes, I've got that.
___ c **Mikhail** That's right. … OK. Then we need to ask for the identification number. It's those three digits above the signature. Is that clear?
___ d **Mikhail** Sure. You must ask for the last three digits of the number on the back of the card – it's common practice now.
___ e **Mikhail** Finally, what's useful is to ask for an email address as well as a contact number, in case there's a problem with the order. Are you with me?
___ f **Katya** Not quite. Can you run through that again?
_*1*_ g **Mikhail** First of all, it's essential to check that the caller is also the owner of the credit card being used for payment.
___ h **Katya** OK, I'm with you. I remember needing that number last time I shopped online.

2 Match the thoughts in 1–6 with the phrases a–f that you would say in a teleconference.

1 Don't whisper! ___
2 We need to hurry up – my colleagues want this room soon. ___
3 Why can I only hear every second or third word he's saying? ___
4 I can't keep up with him – it's so complicated and I'm trying to take notes at the same time. ___
5 I keep hearing myself speak as if I'm talking to myself – this is terrible! ___
6 Where's Steffi gone? She disappeared in the middle of a sentence! ___

a Can we speed up a little?
b Could you slow down a bit? We're having problems following you.
c I can't hear Steffi.
d You're very faint.
e You're breaking up.
f There's an echo on the line.

Language at work | Modal verbs – obligation and prohibition

Obligation

Use *must* or *have to* to talk about an obligation.

1 *Must* is more common when the sense of obligation comes from the speaker (i.e. when the speaker is telling someone what to do or giving an order / instruction). It is also more common in formal language.

*You **must** get to the meeting on time tomorrow.*

*Visitors **must** switch off their mobile phones.*

Should is also possible, but is not as strong as *must* (it is used to suggest something is advisable or preferable).

*It's getting late and you've worked hard, so I think you **should** go home now.*

2 *Have to* is more common when talking about rules, regulations, duties and responsibilities.

*If we want to smoke, we **have to** go out of the office.*

*When people call the helpline, I **have to** put them through to a suitable adviser.*

No obligation

Use *don't have to, don't need to* or *needn't* to talk about a lack of obligation.

1 *Needn't* is more common when the idea of the lack of obligation is coming from the speaker (i.e. when the speaker is giving someone permission not to do something).

*You **needn't** do any more work on this – I'll take care of it myself.*

2 *Don't have to* and *don't need to* are more common when the speaker is talking about a lack of obligation and saying that something is not necessary.

*The office is closed for the holidays now and we **don't have to** return until 3 January.*

Prohibition

Use *mustn't, can't* and *aren't allowed to* to talk about prohibition.

1 *Mustn't* is normally used when the idea of prohibition comes from the speaker, and is also more common in formal language.

*We **mustn't** disturb him if he's busy.*

*Passengers **mustn't** leave their luggage unattended at any time.*

2 *Can't* and *aren't allowed to* are more common when the speaker is talking about what is permitted and what is not permitted.

*I'm sorry, but you **can't** park here – it's an emergency exit.*

Past forms

1 Obligation – *had to* (*must* has no past tense)

*I couldn't come and see you because I **had to** go to Berlin.*

2 No obligation – *didn't have to*

*They offered me a free upgrade on the flight – I **didn't have to** pay anything at all.*

3 Prohibition – *couldn't, wasn't / weren't allowed to*

*For security reasons, we **weren't allowed to** take hand luggage onto the plane.*

1 A trainer is giving feedback on a speaker's presentation skills. Complete the sentences with *must*, *needn't* or *mustn't*.

1 You ________ try and speak a bit louder, or people at the back won't be able to hear you.

2 You ________ prepare your talks more carefully; they still sound disorganized.

3 You ________ spend weeks and weeks on preparation, but two or three days is a good guideline.

4 You ________ move about too much when you are talking – stay still.

5 You ________ use PowerPoint if you don't want to – a good handout will be fine.

6 You ________ try and make eye contact with the audience – it makes them and you feel more relaxed.

7 You ________ read from a script – they've come to hear you speak, not read aloud.

8 You ________ go too fast – remember that some of the audience will not be native speakers.

9 You ________ answer questions as you go along – you can ask your audience to save questions until the end.

2 Complete what Natacha says about her workplace with *have to, don't have to* or *aren't allowed to*.

Natacha We've got some strict rules about the Internet. We can use it for work, but we [1] ________________ use it for anything personal. They've also brought in new rules for phone use. We [2] ________________ use the phone for making personal calls. They check every number, and you [3] ________________ explain why you made a particular call. You [4] ________________ be as careful about incoming calls – they don't check them. It's annoying – when I want to make a call, I [5] ________________ use my mobile. It costs quite a lot, but at least I [6] ________________ ask permission when I want to contact someone.

Working with words

1 Replace the words in *italics* with the phrases from the list. Make any changes that are necessary.

bring in	work out	deal with
put on	run into	try out
take on	drop out of	

1 I'll be able to *practise* ________________ my Italian when I am seconded to our Rome office.
2 I have *accepted* ________________ some extra work because I need the money.
3 Marketing is *arranging* ________________ an exhibition to promote the company's work in Mexico.
4 We have *introduced* ________________ a new dress code for workers in our reception area.
5 The project was delayed because we *encountered* ________________ some unexpected problems.
6 Three people *left* ________________ the computer course after the first week.
7 Who *handled* ________________ all the complaints about the recent unavailability of our website?
8 The introduction of flexitime has *had a successful result* ________________ for most people on the team.

2 Match the adjectives from the list to the statements about how each person is feeling about a proposed change. Add the correct preposition.

ambivalent	critical	~~nervous~~
receptive	concerned	enthusiastic
optimistic	antagonistic	

1 'It's very worrying. How will it affect me? I felt much safer with the old system.' He is *nervous about* the change.
2 'This is the most ridiculous idea I've ever heard, and I will not tolerate it.' She is ________________ the idea.
3 'I think there are some problems with the idea. The finances haven't been worked out properly, and the implications for the staff haven't been examined fully.' He is ________________ the idea.
4 'I'm not sure … I like the idea of the extra free time at weekends but I don't like the idea of starting earlier in the morning.' She is ________________ the change.
5 'This is quite an interesting idea – I'd like to hear more, because I think it has some good points.' He is ________________ the idea.
6 'I think it'll work out well and will improve our working conditions.' She is ________________ the change.
7 'Some of these proposals worry me – I'm not sure they've been properly thought through.' He is ________________ the proposals.
8 'This is going to be absolutely fantastic – I just can't wait.' She is ________________ the change.

Business communication skills

1 Dermot is explaining to worker representatives about the proposed changes in production. Complete his presentation with these phrases.

we're calling on you to
you may be wondering
starting from February next year
as you all know
let's digress for a moment and
we are fairly certain everyone
I'd like to pass this point over to
we'd like to assure you

Dermot … [1]________________ BRT is going to diversify into manufacturing energy drinks. [2]________________ we'll be producing our new brand called Boost. [3]________________ that sufficient training will be given to everyone involved in this new product and [4]________________ look at this as a positive move. Training will take place for everyone from October onwards and [5]________________ will have been trained by the end of the year. [6]________________ why we're moving into energy drinks. There are several reasons so [7]________________ Xavier from Marketing. He can show you some interesting statistics.

Xavier Thanks, Dermot. I have a market survey comparing the sales of soft drinks across Europe. The figures are quite revealing, so [8]________________ look at these in detail. Over the last five years …

2 One of the worker representatives presents the changes to production staff. Put the words in *italics* in the right order to complete these presentation extracts.

1 *from / starting / learning / month / we'll / next / be* ________________ how the new drink will be produced.
2 *aware / well / your / regarding / we're / of / concerns* ________________ new technology.
3 *next / weeks / the / few / over / be / we'll / nominating* ________________ some of you to become trainers.
4 *also / introduce / proposing / we're / to* ________________ shift work.
5 Veronika *now / will / deal / with* ________________ remuneration …
6 *be / this / we'll / month / later / recruiting* ________________ five new workers.

Language at work | Future continuous, future perfect and probability

Future continuous

Use the future continuous (*will be* + *-ing*) to talk about

1 activities that will be in progress (and unfinished) at a certain time in the future

*I can't see you at 11.00 on Monday because **I'll be visiting** the factory.*

2 repeated or continuous activities over a period of time, often with the prepositions *for* and *until*

***I'll be meeting** Matthew regularly **until** the project is finished.* (repeated many times in the future)
*We'**ll be living** in Osaka **for** 6 months.* (continuous over a period of time)

3 activities that are part of a future programme

*Welcome to the course. Over the next few weeks, we'**ll be looking** at methods for making marketing more effective, and we'**ll be discussing** new ways of reaching customers.*

Future perfect

1 Use the future perfect (*will have* + past participle) to talk about an action that will be completed before a point of time in the future.

A How's the report?
*B It's going well. I'll definitely **have finished** it by Friday.*

2 The prepositions *by* or *before* are normally used with the future perfect. The negative future perfect + *until* is also common.

*I **won't have finished** the report **until** Friday.*

Probability

1 Use *may* and *might* to suggest some uncertainty.

*I **may** come to the party. Then again, I **might** not. It depends on how I'm feeling.*

2 Adverbs like *probably* and *definitely* give a clear indication of how probable we think something is.

*I'll **definitely** come to the meeting.* (certain)
*I'll **probably** come to the meeting.* (very likely)

In positive sentences, the adverb usually comes after *will* (*I'll definitely be there*). In negative sentences, it usually comes before *won't* (*I definitely won't come*).

3 Adjective structures like *is certain to, is sure to, is bound to, is (quite) likely to, is (highly) unlikely to* + infinitive can also be used to indicate degrees of probability.

*We won't wait for John. He's **bound to** be late.* (very sure)
*I think our application is **unlikely to** be successful.* (unsure)

1 Complete these texts with the future continuous or future perfect form of the verbs in brackets.

A We're starting our consultation process today, and over the next few weeks, we [1] ________ (talk) to you individually about how you feel about the changes. We [2] ________ (finish) our research by the end of March. During the first two weeks in April, we [3] ________ (analyse) the findings. We [4] ________ (produce) a report on the main conclusions by May at the latest. During the consultation period, we [5] ________ (also / hold) a series of meetings to debate the issues, and senior managers [6] ________ (give) a range of presentations on the key topics.

B It's proving very hard to arrange a meeting with Mr Sanchez next week. You can't do Monday because you [7] ________ (not / agree) a price with Jenny by then – you need this for your meeting with Mr Sanchez. He can't do Tuesday because he [8] ________ (visit) his suppliers. Wednesday's no good because you [9] ________ (attend) that exhibition in Paris. Thursday's out because you [10] ________ (not / get back) from Paris by 12.00 – the only time he's free.

2 Rewrite the sentences using the words in bold.

1 She'll definitely be unhappy about these proposals.
bound *She's bound to be unhappy about these proposals.*

2 To be honest, I'm unlikely to get the job. **probably**
____

3 They may very well cancel the whole order. **quite likely**
____

4 There will almost certainly be some changes in the final design. **certain**
____

5 They probably won't accept these terms. **unlikely**
____

6 I think there's a chance I'll be offered promotion.
might ________

7 There's a chance we will face some opposition to these changes. **may**
____

8 If this goes ahead, there are bound to be some job losses.
definitely ________

Working with words

1 Do the quiz by choosing the correct option in *italics*. Check your answers at the bottom of the page.

1 Count Alessandro Volta invented the first battery in the *17th / 11th / 18th* century.

2 The can opener was invented *3 / 48 / 2,000* years after cans were introduced.

3 Thomas Edison filed *11 / 66 / 1,093* patents.

4 The first electronic mail, or 'email', was sent in *1966 / 1972 / 1988* by Ray Tomlinson.

5 Half the world's population earns about *5.7% / 22.5% / 88%* of the world's wealth.

6 The sun is *4,500 / 88,000 / 330,000* times larger than the earth.

7 10^4 / 10^6 / 10^8 is the same as a million.

8 Approximately *180,000 / 180 / 180,000,000,000* emails are sent every day.

2 Now write the answers to the quiz in words.

1 ______________________

2 ______________________

3 ______________________

4 ______________________

5 ______________________

6 ______________________

7 ______________________

8 ______________________

3 Look at the graph and complete this extract about sales of XTU and WebMix music downloads. Use the words from the list.

levelled	approximately	shot
substantially	gradually	gradual
somewhere	fractionally	significant

XTU sales rose [1] ____________ in January then [2] ____________ off in February. There was a [3] ____________ decline during March and up to the end of April. WebMix sales [4] ____________ up from [5] ____________ 24% to [6] ____________ less than 58% in January. There was a [7] ____________ fall in February. Then sales dropped [8] ____________ in March and April to the previous low of [9] ____________ in the region of 25%.

Sales (%)
100
75
50
25
0
XTU
WebMix
January
February
March
April

Business communication skills

1 Choose the correct answer from the words in *italics*.

1 Roughly *spoken / speak / speaking*, by 2020 it will be up by 25 per cent.

2 *Accord / According / Accorded* to a recent study, there has been a big increase in podcast advertising.

3 So what are the facts and *numbers / amounts / figures*?

4 The *final / bottom / end* line is that user-generated media will continue …

5 So how should we *interpret / analyse / describe* this drop?

6 Can you give us the *run-down / downturn / low-down* on the types of advertising available?

7 In *generally / general / generality*, traditional forms of advertising …

2 Regina asks Project Manager, Ursula, to explain the spending on a project. Complete their conversation with these phrases.

what's that in terms of	Stani assured us that
can we look at the figures	according to
apparently, figures from	in general
overall things are looking	show

Regina [1] ____________ for the project so far?

Ursula [2] ____________ we are within budget.

Regina Are you sure? [3] ____________ Stani, you're spending a lot on external staff.

Ursula He's right. We do have a lot of contractors working for us but the fact is, we can't make the deadline date without them.

Regina I see. [4] ____________ overall expenditure then?

Ursula [5] ____________ the overspend now will be balanced out when we reach the test phase of the project.

Regina What do you mean?

Ursula [6] ____________ a similar project in our Polish office [7] ____________ that they came in under budget because they took on specialist contractors to do the programming and saved money in the testing phase.

Regina OK, so [8] ____________ positive, despite the overspend?

Ursula That's right.

1 18th 2 48 3 1,093 4 1972 5 5.7% 6 330,000 7 10^6 8 180,000,000,000

Language at work | Reported speech review

Reported speech

1 Reporting verbs used to report the exact words said:

reporting speech – *say, tell, explain, point out,* etc.
reporting thought – *think, know, believe, (not) realize,* etc.
reporting requests – *ask, wonder, want to know,* etc.
reporting orders – *tell, order,* etc.

2 Main tense changes in standard reported speech, when the reporting verb is in the past tense:

Actual words		Reported speech
present simple	→	past simple
present continuous	→	past continuous
past simple	→	past perfect
past continuous	→	past perfect continuous
present perfect	→	past perfect
present perfect continuous	→	past perfect continuous
past perfect	→	no change
past perfect continuous	→	no change
am / is are going to	→	*was / were going to*
will future	→	*would* future
imperative	→	infinitive

'I'm driving home.' → *He said (that) he was driving home.*
'I didn't see her.' → *He said (that) he hadn't seen her.*
'It's been raining.' → *He said (that) it had been raining.*
'I'm going to resign.' → *He said (that) he was going to resign.*
'Don't disturb me.' → *He told me not to disturb him.*

3 Modal verbs change as follows: *can* → *could, may* → *might, must* → *had to, need* → *needed, will* → *would.*

4 If the reporting verb is in the present tense and the situation is still current, there is no need to change the tense.

'I like working here.' → *He says he really likes working here.*

5 To report *Wh-* questions: repeat the question word, change the tense (as above) and change the word order.

When is Jane going? → *He asked me when Jane was going.*

6 To report a direct question, use *if* or *whether.*

Has Bill spoken to you? → *He asked me if Bill had spoken to me.*

7 Several verbs can be used to summarize what people say. These can follow a number of different patterns.

verb + *that* (*deny, warn, admit, advise*): *He* ***denied that*** *he had disclosed any confidential information.*

verb + *someone* + *that* (*warn, advise*): *She* ***warned me that*** *the company was not a safe investment.*

verb + infinitive (*agree, refuse, offer*): *She has* ***agreed to see*** *me tomorrow.*

verb + *-ing* (*advise, admit, deny, apologize for*): *They* ***admitted leaving*** *the factory early.*

verb + *someone* + infinitive (*invite, warn, advise, encourage*): *They have* ***invited us to visit*** *the showroom.*

1 Rewrite these sentences beginning with the words given.

1 'The plan will not work,' I thought. **I didn't think** ______

2 'I don't believe in working at weekends,' my boss always says. **My boss always says that she** ______

3 'Send the letter immediately,' he said to me. **He told me** ______

4 'Have you been waiting long?' she said to me. **She asked me** ______

5 'We had a great time on holiday,' they said. **They said** ______

6 'What do you think about the proposal?' he asked me. **He asked me** ______

7 'A lot of people are unhappy about these changes,' she says. **She says** ______

8 'Don't let anyone see these plans,' he said. **He told me** ______

9 'Have you ever been skiing?' she asked. **She asked me** ______

10 'I'll be back on Friday,' he said. **He said** ______

2 Match the actual words 1–6 to the summaries a–f.

1 'Go for it – you're an ideal candidate.' ___
2 'Let me give you a hand with that.' ___
3 'It wasn't my fault.' ___
4 'Sorry, I didn't get here on time.' ___
5 'Sorry, but no – you can't have my laptop.' ___
6 'I'm pleased to say we can offer you the loan.' ___

a deny / be responsible
b encourage / apply for the job
c refuse / let / use computer
d offer / help
e apologize / be late
f agree / lend money

3 Write out summaries a–f as complete sentences.

a ______
b ______
c ______
d ______
e ______
f ______

Working with words

1 Match these adjectives to the statements 1–10.

hierarchical	strict
cautious	individualistic
egalitarian	formal
liberal	collectivist
open	accepting

1 'I like to make my own choices about the way I live my life.' ________
2 'My parents allowed me a lot of freedom when I was young.' ________
3 'We are all the same here – there's no separation between bosses and workers.' ________
4 'My boss is a Level 1 worker, and I'm a Level 4. You're only Level 7, but you'll climb the ladder in time.' ________
5 'If they introduce a shift system, I'll take part – I won't complain.' ________
6 'I'm not going to invest the money in shares. It's going into a bank account where I know it'll be safe.' ________
7 'I would be grateful if you would call me Mr Jones rather than Barry.' ________
8 'My organization has a lot of rules that we have to obey.' ________
9 'I'm always willing to listen to new ideas and suggestions.' ________
10 'Team effort is more important than individual achievement in my company.' ________

2 Complete the sentences with the correct prepositions.

1 My last boss was sensitive ________ people's needs and treated everyone very well.
2 The company I work for isn't very tolerant ________ individualists.
3 I've just read an article about Finland, so I'm informed ________ business etiquette there.
4 I'm not familiar ________ your customs, so could you explain what I'm meant to do?
5 In some cultures, it's important to be respectful ________ tradition.
6 If you do business in Romania, you need to be used ________ dealing with bureaucracy.
7 When I moved to the US I found it hard to adjust ________ the directness of the people there.
8 What customs do I need to be aware ________ when I visit Korea?

Business communication skills

1 Jorge and Lana are talking about doing business in Ukraine. Put the words in *italics* in the right order.

Jorge I had an interesting time in Ukraine and [1]*the in end* ________ a deal was done.

Lana Was doing business there different to Greece?

Jorge Yes, very. We had a lot of misunderstanding at first. [2]*It because about came of* ________ our lack of knowledge about negotiating in Ukraine.

Lana So what happened?

Jorge We met our Ukrainian colleagues and expected to get down to business. But it seemed a long time before we even spoke about the negotiation. [3]*That problem the was first* ________.

Lana [4]*So did do you what?* ________

Jorge We made small talk – about our journey, our families and so on. Eventually we spoke about the real business. [5]*seems it that* ________ relationship-building before business is very important to them.

Lana [6]*What next happened?* ________

Jorge The Ukrainian team looked at the deal as a whole. They told us exactly what they required from the contract and [7]*when that was uncomfortable I felt really* ________. I mean, we don't negotiate like that here. We do it bit by bit.

Lana And then?

Jorge [8]*time by went as* ________, we became more aware of each other's culture and how business is done and …

2 Jorge continues his story. Choose the correct answer from the words in *italics*.

Jorge [1]*At last / At first* it seemed that the Ukrainians were very direct and abrupt, but this was just their style. [2]*What's most / What's more*, they said 'no' to us quite frequently, which was difficult to get used to. [3]*It wasn't until / It wasn't since* I read about the Ukrainian negotiating style that I found out they say 'no' about nine times more often than Western negotiators! [4]*In spite / Despite* this we became quite good friends. There were a few times when it was tough and we thought we'd lost the deal. [5]*Luckily / Happily* my colleague knew that hospitality is also very important to business relationships and he invited the Ukrainian team to dinner. The idea was that it would get our relationship back on track. [6]*It really shocked me, but it functioned / It really surprised me, but it worked*. I've certainly learnt from the experience.

Language at work | Narrative tenses – past continuous, past simple and past perfect

Past continuous

1 The past continuous (*was doing, were doing*) is often used to set the scene and give background information at the beginning of a narrative.

When I got to the trade fair, it was still early. Some of the exhibitors ***were setting up*** *their stands and others* ***were unpacking*** *their publicity materials.*

BUT the past continuous is not used with stative verbs (see page 103) or when describing permanent features.

Our stand ***looked*** *very professional and it* ***was*** *ideally placed because it* ***was*** *on the aisle that led to the main restaurant.*

2 The past continuous is also used for an action in progress that is interrupted by another shorter action. (Use the past simple for the action that interrupts.)

I ***was unpacking*** *one of the boxes for our stand when my mobile* ***rang****.*

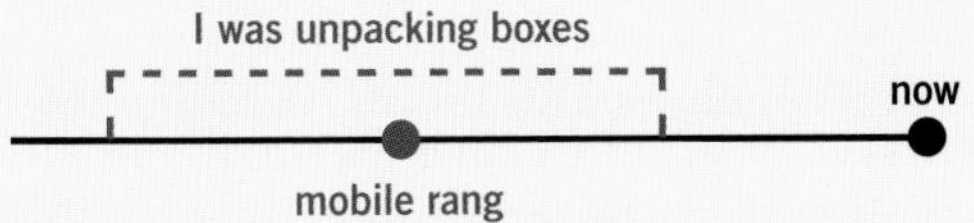

Past simple

The past simple (*did*) is used for the main actions and events in a story that happen one after the other.

He ***said*** *I was wanted back at the office immediately and* ***ended*** *the call. I* ***tried*** *to call back, but there* ***was*** *no reply. In the end, I* ***packed*** *everything up,* ***locked*** *it away and* ***left*** *the hall.*

Past perfect

The past perfect (*had done*) is used when we are already talking about the past and want to refer to an earlier action, event or state.

When I ***got*** *to the station, I realized* ***I'd left*** *my briefcase at the exhibition.*

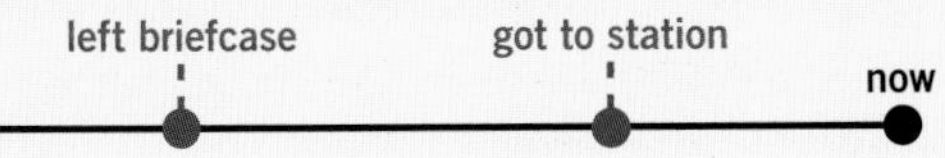

1 Complete these sentences with the past continuous, past simple or past perfect form of the verbs in brackets.

1 I ________ (not recognize) him because he ________ (change) so much.

2 While I ________ (wait) for the train, I quickly ________ (call) the office to leave a message for Joe.

3 On my way to work this morning, the sky ________ (be) grey and it ________ (rain) lightly.

4 I first ________ (meet) Harry while I ________ (work) for Morgan Stanley in New York.

5 When I ________ (get) to the checkout, I realized that I ________ (leave) my credit card at the office.

6 When they ________ (arrive) back from their holiday, they were shocked to find out that someone ________ (break) into their apartment.

7 I ________ (jump) up, ________ (run) across the room and quickly ________ (smash) the glass to set off the fire alarm.

8 I ________ (notice) a couple of small mistakes while I ________ (read) your report.

2 Complete this story about a boat trip with the past continuous, past simple or past perfect form of the verb in brackets.

A few years ago, while I [1]________ (do) a training course in Borneo, I [2]________ (go) with some colleagues to an island animal sanctuary – with lots of wild monkeys. We [3]________ (arrive) at lunchtime, and I [4]________ (decide) to explore the jungle. I [5]________ (walk) along a path when I [6]________ (see) a large monkey sitting on a branch in front of me. I [7]________ (stop) because I [8]________ (never / come) across wild monkeys before, and I [9]________ (not / know) what to do. Suddenly, the monkey [10]________ (jump) down and [11]________ (come) towards me very aggressively. I [12]________ (turn) and [13]________ (run) as fast as I could, shouting loudly as I got to the beach. When my colleagues [14]________ (look) up, I [15]________ (race) towards the water and the monkey [16]________ (chase) after me. I finally [17]________ (reach) the safety of the sea and [18]________ (dive) in. When I [19]________ (look) round, I [20]________ (be) pleased to see that the animal [21]________ (disappear) but my colleagues [22]________ (laugh) uncontrollably.

Working with words

1 **Put the letters in the right order to make words relating to appraisals. Then complete the sentences with the words.**

sadders ______ corucstetivn ______
geare ______ espxrse ______
ccdnotu ______ tjebicoev ______
imnoort ______

1 If you don't ______ performance, you may overlook important areas where change is essential.
2 Always allow yourself enough time to ______ an appraisal – don't rush things.
3 Could we set up a meeting to ______ some of the issues about the new filing procedure?
4 During the appraisal we rate each ______ on a scale of one to five.
5 The weekly meeting gives us an opportunity to ______ our views to the manager.
6 It's important to give ______ feedback rather than criticizing things that haven't been done properly.
7 Today we are going to ______ my objectives for the coming year.

2 **Complete the text with the words from the list.**

peer value performance
tool appraisals criteria

[1] ______ management is not just about carrying out top-down staff [2] ______; it's about encouraging change and making sure everybody gets the chance to perform well. A 360° appraisal system is a really useful development [3] ______ for doing this. In our department, we spend time carefully working out the assessment [4] ______ we are going to use. And people enjoy taking part in the process – they like having the chance to make [5] ______ judgements on their colleagues' performance; and if they are being assessed, they take it very seriously, because [6] ______ rating is as important as what the manager says.

3 **Complete these sentences with the correct preposition.**

1 My manager handed ______ a feedback form to all my colleagues.
2 We go ______ the form during the appraisal.
3 My manager plans to carry ______ doing 360° appraisals every year.
4 I usually come ______ as very confident at work.
5 I've decided to move ______ from learning French to learning Spanish.
6 I think I will end up ______ a good score at the end of my appraisal.

Business communication skills

1 **Sylvie is conducting an appraisal with an employee. Complete their conversation by finishing the words and phrases.**

Sylvie So, Julio, what do you consider were your [1]**s**______ and [2]**f**______ this year?

Julio I think I've performed quite well and reached my sales targets. And if I'd secured the Zipco contract, I'd [3]**h**______ **b**______ salesperson of the month.

Sylvie Yes. I must say, we're very [4]**h**______ with your achievements. Are there any areas you feel you need to [5]**i**______ on?

Julio Yes. I sometimes have difficulty closing a sale. What's the [6]**b**______ **w**______ to deal with apprehensive clients?

Sylvie There are quite a few approaches you could take. You [7]**o**______ to observe some of your colleagues and see what they do.

Julio That sounds a good idea.

2 **Complete the rest of their conversation by correcting the mistakes in the phrases in *italics*.**

Sylvie Yes, you need to focus on encouraging more teamwork. [1]*Throwback from the sales force* ______ has been rather poor.

Julio [2]*How I should this do?* ______ Perhaps I could arrange the observation as a team-building activity?

Sylvie Good idea. [3]*Can we identification that as* ______ a personal goal for next year?

Julio Yeah. But [4]*we could help with some support* ______ from our managers, so we're given enough time for team building.

Sylvie OK. Now, [5]*you delegated good* ______ interpersonal skills when working with clients, and we'd like to involve you in training new graduates in customer care.

Julio Sounds great. But [6]*if I'd known about this earlier, I would may not have organized* ______ so many business trips in the next few months.

Sylvie Oh. We'll talk about dates later then. Let's turn to the issue of remuneration.

Julio Good. [7]*While we're talking to money, could we discuss* ______ travel expenses, too?

Sylvie Hmm, I suppose so.

Language at work | Third and mixed conditionals | Perfect modals

Third conditional

1 Use the third conditional to talk about things that did not happen in the past (imagining what would have happened if things had been different). It is often used to criticize past actions or to express regrets. In the *if* clause we talk about the imagined past situation; in the other clause we talk about the imagined past result.

Past situation	Past result
If + past perfect	*would(n't) have* + past participle
If you'd ***concentrated,***	*you* ***wouldn't have made*** *the error.*
*If I'****d studied*** *harder,*	*I* ***would have*** *passed my exam.*

2 Notice how negative changes to positive and positive changes to negative.

Real past: *You* ***didn't give*** *me the information.* (negative)

Imagined past: *If you'****d given*** *me the information.* (positive)

Real result: *I* ***made*** *the error.* (positive)

Imagined result: *I* ***wouldn't have made*** *the error.* (negative)

3 In the result clause, use *might have* or *could have* to talk about a less certain result.

If you'd helped me, we ***might / could have*** *finished on time.*

Mixed conditional

Change the verb forms in conditional sentences to talk about an imagined past situation and an imagined present result.

Past situation	Present result
If + past perfect	*would(n't)* + present infinitive
If you'd ***done*** *what I advised,*	*we* ***wouldn't be*** *in trouble now.*
If I ***hadn't won*** *the money,*	*I* ***would*** *still* ***be working*** *in a supermarket.*

Perfect modals

1 Use *could have, might have* and *would have* to talk about something that was possible in the past but didn't happen.

It's a good thing you didn't invest in that company – you ***could / might / would have*** *lost everything.*

2 *Could have* and occasionally *might have* can be used to express irritation and criticism.

I was expecting you at the meeting – you really ***could / might have*** *told me you weren't going to come.*

3 Use *should have* to criticize what people have or haven't done.

You ***should have*** *asked me for authorization – you* ***shouldn't have*** *made the decision yourself.*

1 Complete these sentences with the correct form of the verbs in brackets. Sometimes more than one answer is possible in the result clause.

1 That was a missed opportunity. If we ________________ (buy) the shares in April, we ________ (make) a lot of money.

2 It's just as well we took the train to the airport. We ________ (miss) the flight if we ________ (drive), because there was an accident on the motorway.

3 If I ________ (study) harder when I was at school, I ________ (not need) to go to language classes now.

4 They called the strike off because if it ________________ (go on) for any longer, the company ________ (shut down) the factory.

5 Of course I've got my mobile. If I ________ (not bring) it with me, I ________ (not / talk) to you now!

6 This is all your fault. If you ________ (pack) the items more carefully, none of this ________ (happen).

7 If we ________ (leave) an hour earlier, we ________ (be) there by now, instead of being stuck here in this traffic jam.

8 I understand why you made that decision – if I ________ (be) in your position, I think I ________ (do) the same thing.

2 Rewrite the phrases in *italics* using *could have, should have* or *might have*. More than one correct answer is possible.

1 That wasn't a very sensible decision. *You ran the risk of being dismissed.* ________________

2 What a pity you didn't come five minutes earlier. *You have missed the chance of seeing Anne.* ________________

3 *You were wrong to speak* ________________ to her like that.

4 *I'm irritated you didn't let me know* ________________ you were coming.

5 *It was a mistake not to send* ________________ the price list with the catalogue.

6 *We're very lucky we didn't lose* ________________ the contract.

7 *I'm irritated that you didn't call* ________________ to say the meeting had been cancelled.

Working with words

1 Complete these sentences with the words and phrases from the list.

appreciate, charity, hesitate, perspective, put off, tip, revitalized

1 Going away for a year gave me a new ________ on life – I'm going to rethink my priorities.
2 I really ________ what you've done for me, so thanks.
3 If you ________ any longer, you'll lose this opportunity to see the world.
4 That was a very useful ________ you gave me about gaining more experience before I leave.
5 I had to ________ my trip for a couple of months for family reasons.
6 I've applied for a job as a fundraiser for a ________.
7 I feel really ________ after my six-month break from the office.

2 Put the letters in the right order to complete the sentences. Write the answers in the puzzle. The hidden word is something you deserve.

retnetnio, nthsmiseua, cilypo, sfto, oetdlvempne, ehad fof, bnroade

1 After a break, people return to work with renewed ________.
2 ________ skills are just as important as technical qualifications.
3 Learning a new language would help my career ________.
4 We have a very high ________ rate, which shows that our staff are happy.
5 Seeing other countries gave me the chance to ________ my horizons.
6 Time away from work can sometimes help people ________ in a new direction in their career.
7 Car-sharing is now official company ________.

Business communication skills

1 Marion is speaking to her boss, Bernhard, about taking six months off to travel. Complete their conversation with the correct answer from 1–8 below.

M It's been a long-term [1]________ of mine to travel to Australia.
B But what about your job here?
M Well, I'd like to take six months off. And I'd really [2]________ it if you could keep my job open for me.
B I'm not sure that's fair on your colleagues.
M I understand your [3]________ but none of my colleagues have shown any interest in doing something similar.
B Maybe not, but I need to know more about your plans.
M Well, I've been offered a work placement for four months and then I'd like to travel.
B Go on.
M The fact that I can travel and gain experience is unique. It's a once-in-a-[4]________ opportunity.
B OK. But what are the [5]________ for the company?
M I intend [6]________ apply for a project manager position and the experience I'd gain would be [7]________.
B It sounds interesting and you're showing promise with project work. I'll need to discuss this with HR.
M Great. Do tell them it's a [8]________ situation for us all!

	a	b	c	d
1	goal	target	point	task
2	depreciate	enjoy	appreciate	pleasure
3	warning	suspicions	misgivings	mistrust
4	life	lifetime	century	blue moon
5	wins	uses	profits	benefits
6	towards	to	for	on
7	priceless	valueless	precious	invaluable
8	win-lose	win-win	benefiting	profit

2 Put the words in the right order to make phrases.

1 finish / a / of / long-term / been / mine / to / goal / it's / my university course ________
2 and / points / more leadership experience / are / the / plus / skills development ________
3 my / this / for / from / motivation / comes / my volunteer work / with the Red Cross ________
4 I'll / satisfied / be / never / unless / do / I / it ________
5 fair / – I've / do / hardly / never / to / overtime / that's / refused ________

Language at work | *-ing* form and infinitive

-ing form

1 A number of verbs are followed by the *-ing* form. Many of these verbs are connected with likes and dislikes. Common examples are *like, dislike, enjoy, love, hate, can't stand, look forward to, avoid, miss* and others such as *consider, delay, deny, finish, involve, mean, risk, suggest.*

I really enjoyed ***seeing*** *Martha again.*

2 A number of expressions are followed by the *-ing* form. Common examples are *it's not worth, there's no point, it's no use.*

It's no use *complaining – you'll never get your money back.*

3 When a verb follows a preposition it is connected with, it always takes the *-ing* form.

I'm ***keen on*** *travelling, but I'd be* ***worried about*** *taking a whole year off.*

Infinitive

1 A number of verbs are followed by the infinitive. Many of these verbs are connected with making plans and decisions. Common examples are *agree, arrange, decide, expect, hope, manage, offer, plan, prepare, promise, refuse* and others such as *afford, deserve, fail, learn, seem, want, would like.*

We ***arranged to meet*** *the following week.*

2 The pattern 'subject (or *It*) + *be* + adjective + infinitive' is often used.

Chinese is hard to learn. / It's hard to learn Chinese.

3 The infinitive can be used to express purpose.

A *Why are you taking a year off?*
B ***To travel*** *round the world.*

A preposition (like *for*) to express purpose isn't needed. The infinitive alone is enough.

I called them ***to arrange*** *a meeting.* (Not: ~~*for to arrange*~~)

Changes in meaning

Some verbs can be followed by either the *-ing* form or infinitive and change their meaning.

I stopped going *to the gym months ago.* (I gave up the activity.)

I stopped to go *to the gym.* (I was driving and stopped in order to go to the gym.)

I remember seeing *Ken at the party.* (I saw him, and I have a clear memory of it.)

I remembered to see *Ken at the party.* (I knew he wanted to speak to me, so I went over to him.)

Other verbs like this include *try, forget, regret, like, hate.*

1 Complete this email with the correct form of the verbs in brackets.

Dear Hanno

I'm writing [1]________ (tell) you about what I'm planning [2]________ (do) next year because it will affect you, and you may want [3]________ (think) about [4]________ (find) a replacement for me.

As you know, Ingrid has arranged for me [5]________ (send*) to the Seoul office [6]________ (oversee) the new branch out there. I originally expected [7]________ (be) away for six months. However, I would like [8]________ (explore) that part of the world. I asked Ingrid if she would consider [9]________ (let) me have an extended break, and she has agreed [10]________ (give) me an additional six months' unpaid leave.

This means I'll be away for a year, which I appreciate is not ideal for you. However, it is very important for us [11]________ (keep) you as a client, so Ingrid has suggested [12]________ (take) over the day-to-day running of your account herself. I'm sure you'd enjoy [13]________ (work) with her but I thought it was important [14]________ (check) that you would be happy about [15]________ (collaborate) with her.

Please let me know your feelings about this, and contact me if there is anything you want [16]________ (discuss).

I look forward to [17]________ (hear) from you.

Dan

* TIP: active or passive?

2 Match 1–8 to a–h.

1 I stopped to have a coffee … ___
2 I stopped having coffee … ___
3 I regret to say … ___
4 I regret saying … ___
5 I don't remember signing the cheque … ___
6 I didn't remember to sign the cheque … ___
7 I'll never forget sending you a birthday card … ___
8 I'll never forget to send you a birthday card … ___

a because I didn't want to fall asleep at the wheel.
b because my computer is programmed to send me a reminder.
c that your application for secondment to Brussels hasn't been successful.
d but I must have done, because the bank didn't send it back.
e and that's why the bank sent it back.
f because I couldn't sleep if I drank it last thing at night.
g because I was stuck in the post office for three hours.
h I'd apply for secondment to Brussels.

Useful phrases

1 | Exchanging contact details

Asking for details
Let me take your name and number.
Can I have (your) name / number / email address?
What's the best way to contact you?
I have an email address for you but I'm not sure if it's current.
Can you text me your business card?

Giving details
Let me give you / Here's my card.
Thanks, and here's mine.
I'll send you (my) contact details by text.
You can call / reach me on …
Here's my email address.
The one above is my business email. I check it regularly so please use that one.
It's easiest if you just give me your email address.

2 | Exiting a conversation

Maybe see you later?
Nice talking to you.
I'm afraid I must be off.
I promised to meet someone else. But I'll come back when I've seen him / her.
I'm going to get some food. I missed lunch because of (the conference call).
Is that James over there? Excuse me, I really must go and speak to him.
Catch you later.
Well, I'm going to circulate. It was good to meet you.
Is that the time? My parking ticket runs out in five minutes!
Look, I really don't have time to chat at the moment. I'll call you tomorrow, though.

3 | Catching up with colleagues

Questions
What are you doing at the moment?
What about you?
How about you?
Are you still (playing golf)?
So how's (the new job) going?
Do you still work for the same company?
Anyway, how are things with you?
Have you been away recently?

Comments
It's a lot of fun too.
I don't play as much as I used to.
It's going well, thanks. I'm really enjoying it.
I've just come back from …
I haven't been on holiday for ages.
It's difficult to find the time. I'm always so busy.
We're really busy – as usual.
It's always different. And it keeps me on my toes.

4 | Thanking and responding

Thanking
Thank you for having me.
Thanks. / Thanks a lot.
Thank you very much.
Thanks for your time / help.
I'd like to thank you for …

Responding
It's a pleasure.
No problem.
You're welcome.
That's OK.
Thank you for coming.

5 | Reassuring and sympathizing

Asking about a situation
How did (the call / it) go?
(What's / Is something) the matter?
You seem a bit (unhappy / quiet / upset / frustrated).
How's (the new job) going?
Is there (anything / something) wrong?
Is everything OK?

Reassuring / sympathizing
How awful!
Oh no!
It sounds as if you …
You couldn't have done any more.
I know it's hard … but …
Don't worry about it.
Try to forget it.
You did the right thing.
I'm sure you did the best you could.

6 | Responding to spontaneous invitations

Inviting / Offering
How about … -ing?
What about … -ing?
Do you feel like … -ing?
Would you like to go …?
Do you want to …?

Accepting
I'd love to.
Good idea.
Why not?

Partly accepting
Maybe … Can I let you know later?
Let me just check with (my wife / boss).
OK … but I can't stay long.
Yes … but can we make it tomorrow?

Declining
Sorry – I'm heading straight home tonight, it's (my partner's birthday).
Not tonight, I've had a bad day.
(I'm afraid) I don't really feel like it today.
(I'm afraid) I need to stay behind and finish this (report / email / presentation / offer).

7 | Talking about social plans

Questions
What have you got on this weekend / this evening / tonight?
What are you up to tonight / at the weekend?
What are you doing (this weekend)?
Anything nice planned for (the weekend)?
Are you taking any time off (in the summer)?

Responses
We're off to (Italy).
We'll probably see a film / catch a movie.
I'm supposed to be (helping a friend).
Nothing special.
It depends on (my colleagues / the weather).

Reactions
Very nice.
Great!
Poor you!
Lucky you!
I see.
Sounds good.
How relaxing!

8 | Apologizing and responding

Apologizing
Sorry (I'm late) …
I'm sorry (that) …
I'm really / very sorry (about) …
I do apologize (for) …
Sorry about that.
I'm afraid (that) …

Responding to an apology
Never mind.
That's OK.
That's all right.
It doesn't matter.
Don't worry about it.
No problem.

9 | Making and responding to quick requests

Making a quick request
Do you have a minute?
Excuse me, am I disturbing you?
Could you just have a quick look at …?
Could you spare a few minutes?
Do you have a few minutes?
Would you mind checking …?
Can / Could you give me a hand with …?

Responding to requests
Yeah, sure.
No problem.
Certainly. Take a seat.
Yes, come in.
I'm a bit busy right now.
Sorry, no time!
I'm sorry, not just now.
Sorry, I'm just on my way to …
Give me two minutes and I'll be right with you.

Replying to a negative response
OK, I'll try you (tomorrow).
Never mind.
It's not that urgent.
I'll send it to you in an email then.

10 | Avoiding saying 'no'

Sorry, I'll be away on business / holiday then / when you need me.
Er … have you tried John?
Hmm, I don't have a lot of time at the moment.
I'd love to help, but …
It may be a bit problematic …
Try me again when (I've finished the project / I'm back from holiday / the kids are back at school).
I'm afraid I've got too much on at the moment.
I suppose I could look into it.
I'll give it some thought.

11 | Dealing with situations on the phone

Problems in communication
You're breaking up … I haven't got a very good signal.
Sorry, it's a really bad line.
I'm afraid I didn't catch that / that last bit.
You're very faint. Can you speak up a bit?
Hold on while I go somewhere quieter.
I'll hang up and (call you on the landline / try again later / go outside to call).

Not a good time to call
I'm sorry, but I have someone on the other line. Can I call you back?
Sorry, but this'll have to be quick, I'm about to (board a plane / go into a meeting / enter a tunnel).
So now's not a good time to call?
I'm afraid I really don't have a lot of time today. Can you call again tomorrow?
I'm just on my way out. Can you call again later?

12 | Being negative diplomatically

I have some reservations about it.
I can see both sides of the argument.
It sounds interesting but …
I'm not sure about it.
I need to think about it.

13 | Talking about news at work

Introducing news
You'll never guess what I heard, …
Have you heard the news?
Did you hear the latest about …?

Repeating news you have heard
According to (Sam), …
Rumour has it …
Apparently, …
(Anna) says that …
I spoke to (Robert) and he said / told me …

Responding to news
Really?
Surely not!
No!
You're joking!
That's really (childish).
That's nonsense!
Wow!
I don't believe it!
That's incredible!
Are you sure?

14 | Talking about films, TV and books

Books
It's a real page-turner.
I couldn't put it down.
It's very well written.
It's been on the best-seller list for weeks.
Have you read any good books recently?
I don't get much time to read.
I've just finished …

Films
I was on the edge of my seat.
It's a blockbuster of a movie.
It's full of brilliant special effects.
The computer animation is extremely clever.
It's an absolute classic with a star-studded cast.
It became a box office hit overnight.

TV
I'm completely hooked on it.
I tend to channel-hop.
I can't miss an episode.
I record (the live sports programmes).
What I really can't stand is reality TV / soap operas / sport.
I just like to unwind in front of the TV.
I don't have much time to watch TV.

Describing the story from a book, film, TV drama
It has a gripping storyline / a really fast-moving plot.
The main character(s) is / are …
It's a story about …
(There's) a twist to the plot / story / at the end.
It's set in (Venice / the 18th century).

General comments
It's very atmospheric / exciting / entertaining / enjoyable / well done.
I'd definitely recommend it.
I really enjoyed it.

15 | Making people feel relaxed

Offering a seat / drink
Please have / take a seat.
Let me get you a tea or coffee.
Can I get you something to drink / a tea or a coffee?
A (coffee / cup of tea) would be nice.
Could I have a (tea)?
Coffee, white no sugar, please.

Dealing with bags / coats
I'll put your coat / bag / umbrella over there, but don't forget it!
Let me take your coat.
You can leave your bag over there.
Let's put your bag / suitcase out of the way.
Would you like to leave it (behind reception).

Talking about the journey
How was your journey?
Very straightforward thanks. / The traffic was terrible.
You've (driven over / flown in) from … today?
Did you have any trouble finding us?
It was quite easy. / No problems. / No, not at all.
I hope you managed to avoid the roadworks / find a parking space / follow my directions.

Talking about the weather
What was the weather like when you left?
Much worse / better / warmer / colder than this.
It's absolutely freezing out there!
It's quite warm / cold for this time of year, isn't it?

16 | Talking about taking time off

Talking about a weekend or short holiday
I took the day off.
We managed to get away (for a weekend / without the kids / for the day).
We just had a long weekend away.
We booked a last-minute holiday.
We visited my partner's family.
I caught up on some DIY.
We were on a three-day spa break.
I did some (household chores / shopping).

Commenting on what the experience was like
It poured with rain the whole time!
We had lovely weather.
We had a great time.
It made a real change.
I'd highly recommend it.
It was just what we needed.
It was great for relaxing / switching off.
I didn't really enjoy it, but it (had to be done / needed doing).

Information files | 01–08

File 01 | Unit 1

Case study, Task, page 11

Name: Silent Systems

Product: cabinets for servers / audio / technical equipment

Information for your networking colleagues:
Cabinets reduce the noise and keep equipment cool. They can be positioned in the office, avoiding the need for a purpose-built computer room.
We provide demonstrations, customized units and value for money. Recent clients include government agencies and several multinationals.

Current activities: breaking into the US market

Name: Languages Today

Product: translation, interpreting and proofreading services

Information for your networking colleagues:
150 languages can be translated and interpreted at this agency by linguists around the world. Specialist / technical subjects can also be translated.

Current activities: setting up a database of clients and translators; producing specialist glossaries for key clients

Name: Sitemagic.com

Product: all-in-one website design for small- to medium-sized businesses

Information for your networking colleagues:
Provide a website, domain registration and email at very reasonable prices. We can start your website after one phone call.

Current activities: expanding to fifteen staff and moving to new premises; offering websites in other languages

Name: Reisinger & Taylor

Product: independent corporate caterer

Information for your networking colleagues:
Provide catering for offices, schools and colleges – USP = fresh ingredients. We offer value for money and a large distribution network. No company is too small.

Current activities: expansion into more regions; new events catering service; special banquet service available

File 02 | Unit 2

Practically speaking, Exercise 2, page 15

1 You meet a client by chance at the theatre during the interval. The bell for the second half has just rung.
2 You meet your old manager at your child's football match. You have a lot of friends there so you don't really want to talk to him / her for long.
3 You're at a conference and have been talking to an acquaintance for five minutes. You've run out of small talk topics.
4 You're just leaving your friend's birthday party. It's been a long day and you want to get home. You bump into a colleague who's just arrived and wants to chat.

File 03 | Unit 3

Language at work, Exercise 3, page 22

Student A

1 Your colleague is in a project team which is converting an old building to provide new company premises. Ask how the project is going. As your colleague is speaking, comment on what he / she says and ask additional questions.
2 Your company is building a new warehouse and office complex. Update your colleague, using these prompts and / or your own ideas. Use *already* and *yet* and appropriate time expressions.
- finish the main building work
- have problems with some of the suppliers
- not install the IT system
- not complete electrical wiring
- reschedule the opening date

File 04 | Unit 9

Business communication skills, Exercise 6, page 57

Pair A: Managers

Your company is finding it difficult to keep staff – apparently your competitor has better working conditions. Two members of staff have recently told you that they are thinking of leaving. Hold a meeting with them to discuss working conditions. Find out what they want. Then decide what you can offer them and what you are willing to compromise on. Likely areas of discussion are

- flexible hours / home working
- better travel expenses
- more perks: fitness club membership, lunch vouchers, new computer
- increased salary (this should be no higher than 1% more than inflation)
- less bureaucracy in the job
- more training for future promotion.

You will lead the discussion. Make sure that you outline the situation, put forward proposals, state the consequences of these, bargain as necessary, and summarize your progress.

File 05 | Unit 2

Case study, Task, page 17

Student A

PROSPECTS / TRAINING

1 Overall, employees felt their job lacked prospects, and personal development has not been consistently encouraged throughout the company.

'dead-end job' 'not going anywhere'
'no encouragement to better ourselves'

'I've been at the company 6 years and have only been offered a training course once – when I began the job.'

'When I asked for a training course, I was told I'd have to take holiday or time in lieu to do it.'

2 There is a clear difference between what's offered to employees in different departments – this depends very much on management of department and where their priorities lie.

'unfair if you're in a "disinterested" department'

'not fair if you're in one (department) where no importance is given to staff well-being'

'differences between departments' spending priorities is quite demotivating if you're in a department that never invests in its staff'

File 06 | Unit 3

Working with words, Exercise 7, page 19

Project: increase plant space of factory by 25% and install new production train

Total cost of the work: estimate = 1 million; actual cost = 1.3 million

Target date for completion of project = 18 months; actual date = 2 years

- Project meetings not held on regular basis – communication often by email (not everyone copied in)
- Clearing of site took place quickly and easily – met deadline
- Production manager changed specification of production train to increase capacity but didn't tell project manager – software program had to be rewritten quickly – resulted in errors in program
- Problems during construction – discovered length of new building 2 m short (due to changes in specification – suppliers not told of change)
- Production train delivered two weeks late – not able to install power connections at scheduled time – loss of several weeks of production
- All other new equipment ordered arrived on time
- Kept to budget for first six months but overspending after construction problems

File 07 | Unit 2

Language at work, Exercise 5, page 16

Student A

Over lunch with a colleague in the canteen, you suggest a tourist attraction that a visitor to your company might enjoy (think of a tourist attraction that you personally know very well). However, you are not in a talkative mood today. Be prepared to answer your colleague's questions, but make him / her work a bit harder than normal to get the information and keep the conversation going. When you have finished, change roles.

Student B

Over lunch in the canteen, your colleague suggests a tourist attraction that a visitor to your company might enjoy. You think it sounds like a great idea, and want to find out more, but your colleague is being uncommunicative today. Ask questions

1 to check that what you have heard about the place (if anything) is correct
2 to get factual information, e.g. location, opening hours
3 to show surprise or interest in what your partner says.

When you have finished, change roles.

File 08 | Unit 3

Business communication skills, Exercise 5, page 21

Student A

1 Read the 'To do' list you sent to Ian and the notes you have written under your tasks (M).
2 Begin by calling Ian. Ask Ian to update you on his tasks (I).
3 Answer his questions about your tasks.
4 Make and respond to suggestions as necessary.

Launch date 'To do' list

Bring Anvikon merchandise to venue (I)
Finalize timetable of day with sound engineers (M)

Meeting with them later today.
Suggestion: sound check night before?

Brief Anvikon staff about handset demonstration (I)
Check replies from the press – who's coming? (M)

Behind schedule! Some invitations sent only 2 days ago!
Suggestion: we plan for more people than expected?

Send Anvikon PR manager's speech to MMT-Tec (I)
Make sure Sarah's briefed on everything (I / M)

Suggestion: Wait till last minute – want to give her positive information! Make good impression!

File 09 | Unit 4

Case study, Task, page 29

Entrepreneurs

1 Decide on your new business idea. It can be a new product, a new service, or any other kind of business idea. Use your own idea, or one of the ideas below.

2 Prepare your presentation.
- Introduce yourself and preview the presentation.
- Introduce your business idea – what it is and how it works.
- Explain its benefits to users.
- Compare the future benefits for the users with the present (or past) situation.
- Explain what stage of development it is at, why you need the investment and how much profit you expect to make in the next three years.

3 Give your presentation.

Investors

1 Listen to the presentations.

2 After each presentation, ask any questions that seem important, such as: why their idea is different; whether they have already made any sales; what the competition is; who their customers are; what experience they have of running a business of this kind.

3 At the end of all the presentations, decide how much you will invest in each idea. Explain to the group which ideas you've chosen to invest in, how much you will invest, and why. **Important!** Do not tell the other groups how much you are prepared to invest until the end of the activity.

The result

1 Entrepreneurs – the winner is the idea which attracted the biggest total investment from the investors.

2 Investors – the winner is the one with the most money at the end. Double the amount of money you invested in the winning idea, and add it to any money you did not spend.

Business idea: Hpod – self-contained, stackable housing unit; made from polished concrete, aluminium and glass

Benefits: internal wiring and plumbing built in; simple design – no joins and sharp corners; three sizes: 1, 2 and 3 bedrooms (8 x 6 m, 8 x 9 m and 8 x 12 m); available within a month of ordering

Future benefits: order a second Hpod and plug it in; can be stacked to 30 stories high; long-lasting materials

Current stage of development: spent four years on research and design; you've lived in Hpod yourself – practical and comfortable; manufacturer interested in making Hpods; $350,000 needed to start production; target – treble investment in three years

(Source: http://www.springwise.com)

Business idea: Concrete Canvas – inflatable concrete shelter, ideal for emergency situations like earthquakes, or for military use.

Benefits: cheap to produce and buy, light, strong

Future benefits: aid organizations can buy and store the shelters cheaply; easy to transport; easy to use (no training needed); offer better protection than tents; can be made medically sterile

Current stage of development: talked to many aid organizations; prototypes built and tested; $300,000 needed to make the full-sized prototypes for field testing with an aid organization; target – double investment in three years

Business idea: Spider catcher – remove spiders from your home without harming spider

Benefits: keeps you at comfortable distance from insects while you catch and transport them outside; unbreakable nylon bristles controlled by trigger handle – surround insect and hold it securely; two sizes: compact (for travelling), standard (for home)

Future benefits: have an instant solution for family / friends afraid of spiders; no harm to spider

Current stage of development: prototypes made and design refined; patent obtained; product promoted at innovation exhibitions worldwide; $100,000 needed to produce and market product; target – double investment in three years

(Source: http://www.ideas21.the-dude.net)

File 10 | Unit 2

Case study, Task, page 17

Student B

MIDDLE MANAGEMENT COMMENTS

Generally, middle management staff are satisfied with remuneration but feel they lack support.

'Financial rewards are ok – no complaints. My team works extremely hard and I really appreciate what they do for me, but who appreciates me?'

'My team seems to compare us with other departments and there's a lot of dissatisfaction. I don't know where I'm going wrong and there are no channels for discussing this.'

'My department works very hard for me and we're lucky to have such loyal workers in this department; staff retention has been good – especially compared to other departments – but I don't get any praise or thanks for this!'

'How can we expect our staff to stay, if our department managers change every two years?'

'It would be nice to have more guidelines when allocating our budget from HR.'

File 11 | Unit 5

Language at work, Exercise 4, page 34

Student A

1 You are at a travel agency enquiring about flights to / from New York and hotel accommodation for a business trip. You want to leave a.m. 20 March and return p.m. 23 March. Find out about
- departure and arrival time of flights
- cost of flights
- recommended hotels
- hotel location and cost.

2 You work in Reception at a hotel in Prague. Use this information to answer your partner's questions about things to do in Prague.

The Grand Tour of Prague: see all the most important sights of Prague (starting in the Old Town Square)
- Includes a tram ride and 'Walks of Prague' CD
- Daily at 11.00 a.m. and 2 p.m., lasts 4 hours
- Price: CZK450

Prague Castle: largest ancient castle in the world with several museums
- Take tram no. 22 or 23
- Open 9 a.m.–4 p.m.
- Price: entry to courtyards and gardens is free; entry to all castle museums is CZK350

Trade Fair Palace: Gallery of modern art – four floors of art exhibitions
- Take tram 5, 12, 14, 15 or 17
- Open 10 a.m.–6 p.m. from Tuesday to Sunday
- Price: CZK100 to CZK250.

File 12 | Unit 7

Case study, Task, page 47

A management consultant was engaged to give advice. He suggested
- reviewing and, if necessary, rewriting their business plan to have available for potential investors
- looking for possible investors
- focusing on improving production in terms of price, speed and volume in order to be able to supply bulk orders
- actively looking for business partners – attend events, etc.
- focusing on marketing and PR activities.

James and Natalie followed all the advice and this resulted in
- generating investment capital – €348,000
- moving manufacturing to China – faster, cheaper and better quality
- increasing profit margin to 76% as a result of the previous decision
- ensuring the company can supply on demand
- winning an award for Young Entrepreneur of the Year.

File 13 | Unit 5

Case study, Task, Exercise 1, page 35

Student A

1 **Situation:** you work in Marketing and recently ordered a print advert to be placed in an international magazine. You have noticed some errors which must be corrected before the ad goes to print. Your superior is angry and wants confirmation that things can be amended asap. Call your advertising agency about the changes.
Problem: misspelled name: not *Katherine* but *Katerina* / wording – change contact information to: chocorollo@dandp.com / ad to appear twice monthly, not weekly
Deadline: by Thursday (today is Tuesday)

2 **Situation:** you work in Marketing in the Lisbon office. Your company is decentralized – departments are responsible for own office area and finances. You are holding an international meeting in the Barcelona office and need to reserve two meeting rooms and equipment. Call to discuss your needs.
Problem: two weeks ago, you were quoted €1,000 for the rooms – is this correct? / need a quote for the use of two data projectors and videoconferencing equipment / must have room rental agreement forms and confirmation for your procurement department asap
Deadline: next Wednesday (today is Thursday)

3 **Situation:** you work in Marketing in a French confectionery company. You're responsible for marketing events and ensuring the necessary promotion material is available for the region Europe West. You have a lot of events currently taking place so some of your material is out of stock. You receive a call from a colleague from PR in Denmark. Make a note of the problems and clarify any information that isn't clear.
Action: decide which course of action you can promise.
a Call back later today after checking what's in stock.
b You need time to calculate stock and see if you can get any material back from neighbouring countries. Call back next week.
c You're expecting a delivery of merchandise at the end of next week. You could send some material when it arrives – it'll reach Denmark in 10–12 days and is only merchandise.

4 **Situation:** you run a successful translation agency, working with mostly European languages. You receive a call from a client about an urgent matter. Make a note of the problems and clarify any information that isn't clear.
Action: decide which course of action you can promise.
a Accept the translation immediately before you've contacted the translator (specialist languages are big money and there's an added charge for short notice translations).
b Promise to send an offer by this afternoon and confirm if the translator has time by this evening.
c Promise to call back / email all details by lunchtime tomorrow.

File 14 | Unit 6

Working with words, Exercise 9, page 37

Company X

- Donated 100,000 trees to Nairobi, Kenya, to aid reforestation
- Provides funds for a project that gives loans to farmers and fishermen
- Established fund to promote research into conservation of drinking water
- Sponsors disabled sports in Germany
- Committed to offering equal entrance requirements and development opportunities to male and female employees

Company Y

- Failure to perform routine inspections led to corroded pipelines and oil leaks
- Oil spill has polluted large area of coastline
- Lack of attention to safety led to oil refinery explosion – injuries to employees
- Currently an investigation into whether company manipulated oil markets – staff bought large quantities of company's product
- Committed to renewable energy: invested heavily in solar and wind power; runs a project to generate electricity from petroleum coke

File 15 | Unit 6

Business communication skills, Exercise 7, page 39

Kokua Likeabike – based in Germany

Core business: selling wooden children's bikes – various models and styles

- Made from various types of wood – environmentally-friendly, sustainable product, sourced from well-managed forests
- Specially designed without pedals for young children to learn to balance before moving on to a 'real' bike
- Distributors and sales partners are worldwide

Possible open day ideas:

- Demo of new models
- Tour of the factory
- Trip to wood source for forest management presentation
- Likeabike races – challenge country against country in a race on the bikes
- Ideas exchange – distributors share marketing ideas / strategies from each country
- Gala dinner

File 16 | Unit 6

Working with words, Exercise 10, page 37

Your company would like to be seen as an ethical business, and you are presenting details of some of the initiatives you have undertaken. You can talk about your own company or use one of the companies below. Your speech should include

- brief details of what your company is and what you do
- your attitude towards corporate social responsibility
- an outline of some of the work that you have been doing
- a short conclusion outlining your hopes for the future.

Prepare your speech and then give the press conference. Be prepared to answer any difficult questions.

Vodafone

Sector: Computers and electronics

Vodafone, Europe's largest cellular telecom company, doesn't have the environmental or political challenges that a big oil company does but it does a superb job of questioning shareholders, employees, customers and outside experts about how its services and infrastructure impedes – or might be able to help – economic development. That has resulted in programs like Mpesa, a pilot project that helps Africans do banking with their mobile phones. Vodafone has also changed the way it builds networks to give emergency health-care workers better access, and helps screen mobile video content for users with children.

Carrefour

Sector: Trading and merchandise

Carrefour, the hyper- and supermarket chain, produces a comprehensive annual responsibility report, which includes simple numerical indicators for things like the quality of its food products, the percentage of local producers among suppliers, and the percentage of women among its managerial ranks. It is committed to promoting responsible fisheries that contribute to the sustainable management of resources. And it operates a waste management and water and energy consumption reduction policy.

Peugeot

Sector: Automotive

Like other carmakers, Peugeot addresses global warming. It has an overall measure of the total greenhouse gas emissions of its vehicles – unique among big automakers. But Peugeot also looks at its cars' impact on road safety and urban areas. It first talked to stakeholders – like city dwellers, drivers, and roadside communities – then developed indicators like noise emissions that its engineers could aim to reduce in new models.

(Source: http://www.money.cnn.com)

File 17 | Unit 9

Case study, Task, Exercise 2, page 59

Group A: Team Leaders

1 Look at the proposed incentives and possible consequences. Think of an alternative proposal for each incentive (based on the original idea), which could be a realistic compromise if you need it.

Proposed incentives / perks	Consequences of this	Alternative / amended idea
Overtime is paid at double time	To give incentive for extra work and show appreciation for extra work	e.g. Overtime is paid at time and a half
Costs of children's schooling at the private International School covered	To allow children to continue level of education they've been used to	e.g. 60–80% of cost is covered by company
Interest-free loan for living costs, e.g. deposit for a house or car	To ensure employee can continue to live at the same standard as when abroad	e.g. Loan at favourable interest rates (2%)
1 month assimilation time before going back to full-time work	To make employee feel more confident in fitting back into old lifestyle and job	
Job promotion on return	To show that experience gained during deployment is recognized and valued (will encourage more good workers to return to their country)	

2 Think of two extra proposals (plus the possible consequence) to suggest to the HR Manager.

3 Prioritize the three incentives you would really like to persuade your HR Manager to accept.

Points system

While you negotiate, consider this scoring system.

2 points if you get the whole incentive without an alternative

1 point if you get some of the incentive – or agree on an alternative

0 points if the incentive is refused

File 18 | Unit 7

Working with words, Exercise 5, page 43

You will have four letters: E or I, S or N, T or F, J or P. Find the corresponding four-letter combination opposite (the combinations are in alphabetical order.)

ENFJs care about people and seek peaceful relationships. They are expressive, warm and intuitive, and enjoy helping others develop their potential. They like to organize the world around them, and get things done.

ENFPs are excited by anything new – ideas, people, or activities. They have a deep concern for people, being especially interested in possibilities for people. They are energetic, enthusiastic, and lead spontaneous and adaptable lives.

ENTJs need to analyse and bring into logical order the outer world of events, people and things. They are natural leaders who like to plan. They are intuitive and can think in abstract terms.

ENTPs are excited by anything new – ideas, people or activities. They look for patterns and need to analyse, understand and know the nature of things. They are energetic, enthusiastic, and lead spontaneous and adaptable lives.

ESFJs care about people and seek peaceful relationships. They like to organize the world around them and get things done. They are pragmatic, take their work seriously and believe others should as well.

ESFPs are enthusiastic, and are excited by new activities and new relationships. They care about people and like to give practical help. They are energetic and adaptable, preferring to experience and accept life rather than judge or organize it.

ESTJs need to analyse and order the world of events, people and things. They work hard to complete tasks so they can move on to the next. They are pragmatic, take their work seriously and believe others should as well.

ESTPs are enthusiastic, and are excited by new activities and challenges. They are logical and analytical, with an innate sense of how things work. They are energetic and adaptable, preferring to experience and accept life rather than judge or organize it.

INFJs are interested in their inner world of possibilities. Insight is very important, and they care for people and relationships. They are interested in creative expression, spirituality and human development, and like to use their ideas to help people resolve things.

INFPs are caring and idealistic, both in relationships with people and in projects they see as important. They are skilled communicators, and like ideas that can develop human potential. They are adaptable and have concern for possibilities.

INTJs are interested in their inner world of possibilities. They think systemically and logically, and need to demonstrate competence in their areas of interest. They are insightful and will work hard to make their visions into realities.

INTPs want to make sense of the world and are creative. They are logical, analytical, and detached; they naturally question ideas. They don't need to control or order the outer world, and are very flexible and adaptable.

ISFJs feel responsible for doing what needs to be done. They are pragmatic. They are realistic and organized, and thorough in completing tasks. They are warm, caring and dependable; they take their work seriously and believe others should as well.

ISFPs care deeply for living things, and can be playful and adventurous. They are practical and prefer action to words. Their warmth and concern are generally not expressed openly. They are adaptable, realistic and spontaneous.

ISTJs feel responsible for doing what needs to be done. They are realistic, well-organized and thorough. Being logical pragmatists, they make decisions based on experience. They are committed to people and the organizations they work for; they take their work seriously and believe others should as well.

ISTPs are logical and realistic, and natural troubleshooters. They are quiet, analytical, and can appear detached and pragmatic. However, they like variety and excitement, and have a spontaneous, playful side.

File 19 | Unit 8

Case study, Task, page 53

- By 2007, Russia will have 5% market share of software outsourcing revenue.
- More than 250 global companies are active in Russia-based offshore software development.
- Currently Russia ranks number three in the number of scientists and engineers per capita worldwide.
- There are approximately 250,000 IT professionals in the country.
- The number of newly-graduated IT specialists has risen by 11% this year.
- Scientific talent has attracted western companies to open development centres in Russia: Intel, Sun, Motorola, Siemens.

Advantages of Russia vs Asia

- Russian business hours are in better sync with US and Europe.
- Russia is physically closer to US and Europe – more face-to-face interaction possible.
- Russia has closer cultural affinity with Europe and US.

File 20 | Unit 9

Language at work, Exercise 5, page 58

Student A

You are the manager in a small country office. Student B wants a temporary secondment for six months in a department in a large city office – to get wider experience (and to fill in for someone on maternity leave). Say 'no' to the request at first, but see if you can come to an agreement.

Student B

You work for Student A in a small country office. You have the chance of a temporary secondment for six months in a large city office. This will help you get wider experience while replacing someone on maternity leave. You are prepared to make a lot of compromises to get Student A's agreement.

Talk about:

- A: The negative effects on the day-to-day running of office
  B: The positive effects in terms of learning new skills, etc.
- A: The staffing difficulties this would cause
  B: The solutions for the staffing problems
- A: The negative effects on B's ability to do the job when B returns
  B: The positive effects of the secondment in terms of personal development and experience
- A: The impracticality of a long transfer as opposed to a two-week secondment
  B: The impracticality of a two-week secondment as opposed to a long transfer
- A: The possibility of a salary reduction after the secondment
  B: The possibility of a salary increase after the secondment
- A: Other outcomes if the secondment was approved
  B: Other outcomes if the secondment was not approved

File 21 | Unit 9

Business communication skills, Exercise 6, page 57

Pair B: Employees

Your company is finding it difficult to keep staff – its competitor has better working conditions. You have spoken to your managers about leaving to join the competition. You don't really want to change jobs but the offer is very attractive. Your managers have invited you to a meeting to discuss whether they can improve working conditions. The areas that the competitor has made attractive to you are

- flexible hours / home working
- better travel expenses
- more perks: fitness club membership, lunch vouchers, new computer
- increased salary
- less bureaucracy in the job
- more training for future promotion.

Discuss these with your managers and see if they can improve your working conditions. Decide which points are important to you and what you want the company to offer. Be ready with some proposals and be prepared to bargain.

File 22 | Unit 10

Language at work, Exercise 5, page 64

Student A

1 Use the information in the table to answer your partner's questions. Say what you have been doing this week and what tasks you have / haven't done.

Ongoing this week	Done	Not done
Telephone insurance companies to get quotes. Research possible accounting systems. Discuss website with local IT company.	Write business plan. Check availability of our proposed company name.	Contact solicitor about drawing up legal documents.

2 Use these prompts to ask questions about the progress your partner has made. What two tasks has your partner actually completed?

- contact business adviser
- think about business locations
- make list of estate agents
- find information about premises
- look into transport
- visit any locations

File 23 | Unit 11

Business communication skills, Exercise 3, page 68

Procedures for a teleconference

- Make sure room and equipment are available.
- Have a technician on hand in case you have technical problems (and can't solve them yourself).
- Make sure there's an agenda and this has been emailed to the participants ahead of time – the same applies for any documents you may want to refer to.
- Do a roll call – check who is there.
- Encourage participants to state their name before speaking.
- Speak loud and clearly – avoid background noise like rustling papers, mobile phones, coffee cups, scraping chairs.
- Stick to the agenda – keep participants' contributions short.
- Clarify and check everyone understands.
- Summarize points whenever necessary, especially before any decisions are made.
- Encourage the KISS acronym (keep it short and simple).
- Call people by name and location – *Chris (from Milan) what do you think?*
- Vary the tone of your voice, to keep people interested, and be enthusiastic.

File 24 | Unit 11

Case study, Task, Exercise 1, page 71

An international company is responsible for the check-in systems at airports. There are eight employees in the Technical Support Department and shift work has been introduced. This has been divided into four shifts, with two employees on each shift (four teams of two). In order to make the shift work fair, shifts are rotated, so that each week an employee's shift changes to the later time. This means the same two people do one shift for only one week at a time before it changes. As the team is made up of both new and existing employees, none of the clients are allocated to one particular employee – the employees work for all clients and the team leader distributes the tasks, queries and problems among them as they arise.

The problem

When clients email or call, they never know who they will deal with or if the member of staff will have knowledge of their specific problem. The emails and calls are generally to report problems or bugs, or to ask for support. It is essential that these are prioritized so the most urgent problems are dealt with immediately.

File 25 | Unit 10

Case study, Task, page 65

Student A

Favour	Name of person agreeing to favour
Lend me one person from your department for my team – temporary measure.	
Give me some contact names to add to my client mailing list.	
Share a data projector – my finances are too tight to buy one.	

Favours you must refuse to do:

- Help with next year's budget.
- Help organize an 'office warming' party.
- Substitute colleague at meeting in Brussels.

File 26 | Unit 13

Business communication skills, Exercise 6, page 81

Student A

	Facts and figures	Comments
No. people surveyed	Just over 4,500	
Type of people	1	2
Survey results		
read blogs	80%	Ads will reach a lot of people
read blogs once a week	3 % (approx. 4)	
read blogs weekly for business information	5	6
read weekly on technology topics	57%	
pass on information or content from blogs	70% (approx. 3,150)	Word-of-mouth advertising will be useful
indicate that blogs influence their purchase decisions	7	8
are thinking of starting their own blogs	32%	Growing market!

File 27 | Unit 13

Working with words, Exercise 10, page 79

Talk about your own company or one of the companies below, giving as many figures and trends as possible. If you do not know the exact figures, use some of the 'approximating' language from **4**. Give details of

- company activities
- company HQ
- number of countries it operates in
- number of employees
- annual revenue
- performance in the last ten years (turnover / profit / loss).

Name: Hengist Healthcare
Activities: Biopharmaceuticals, antivirals, hepatitis care
Company HQ: Copenhagen, Denmark
No. of countries: 16
Employees: 372
Annual revenue: €93,000,000

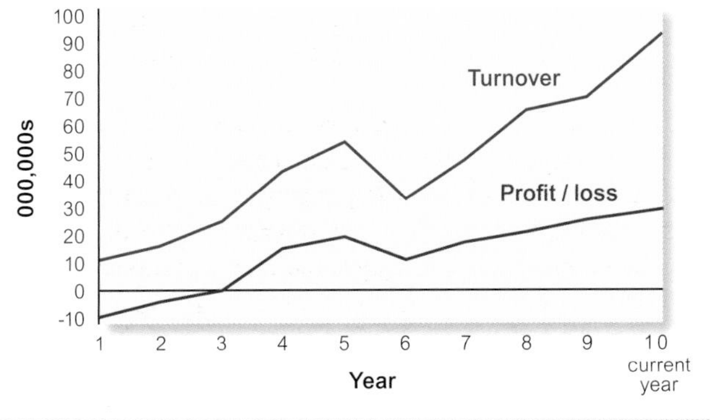

Name: Wengler
Activities: Accountancy and financial consultancy
Company HQ: New York
No. of countries: 22
Employees: 950
Annual revenue: US $28,000,000

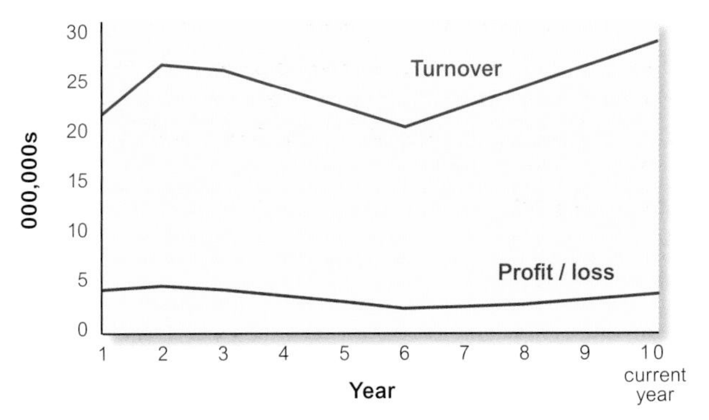

File 28 | Unit 13

Case study, Task, page 83

Student A

Craiglist.org

Founded: 1995
Users: 4bn page views per month
What is it?: Centralised network of urban communities featuring free classified ads and forums
Who started it?: Craig Newmark
Approximate statistics / facts:

- Began as an email listing events in San Francisco
- Risen to more than 30m users a month
- 2004: eBay acquired 25% share of company
- Receives 25m classified ads each month
- Up to 500,000 new job listings each month
- 80 topical forums with 40m user postings (comments)

File 29 | Unit 14

Case study, Task, page 89

Student D

PCR finds it very frustrating when cut over is postponed, especially when it needs to see what problems arise once the system is actually being used. PCR sent regular emails and made phone calls to get feedback about the project. Emails remained unanswered and PCR was frustrated by what it saw as a lack of communication. The Malaysian customer felt hurried and hassled by the constant bombardment of calls and emails.

File 30 | Unit 2

Case study, Task, page 17

Student C

COMMUNICATION

There was a mixed reaction to this subject. Positive comments were made about the emailing policies we introduced two years ago. However, overall face-to-face communication can be seriously improved upon.

'Each department seems to go their own way on many matters. We employees just do what we're told and don't bother to question it any more.'

'Sometimes I don't know what's going on. Decisions have been made and I haven't been consulted – and I'm in a more senior position and need to know these things!'

'There must be more communication between us! We work together but don't actually have time or opportunity to get to know each other.'

'It's difficult for ideas to filter through.'

'The company is quite big – so I sometimes feel I'm just a number.'

File 31 | Unit 15

Business communication skills, Exercise 5, page 93

Student A

1 You are the appraisee. Discuss your personal performance over the past year with your appraiser, using this information.

Achievements / Failures	Explanation / Comments	Requests for resources / Advice
+ Presented new office procedures at Europe-wide meeting	This was my first presentation. Very nervous.	
+ Organized a regular office meeting – brought great results: more communication and cooperation in office	If management attended regularly – been even better	Ideas for ensuring management attend
– Dropped out of company English course	Stayed if teacher spoken my language	
– Turned down PA job offer	'Better' job, but not much more pay	Other chances for promotion?

2 Change roles. You are the appraiser. Conduct the appraisal interview. Comment and ask questions as appropriate to complete this form.

Achievements / Failures	Explanation / Comments	Requests for resources / Advice
+ Organized successful kick-off meeting for international salespeople – v. happy with this		Offer: to get more work like this, possibly a transfer to international department?
+		
– Rejection of trainee mentoring scheme – extremely disappointed		Could look at budget again for next year
–		

File 32 | Unit 14

Case study, Task, page 89

Student A

The biggest problem was time-wasting. When PCR arranged teleconferences and called at the scheduled time, only half the participants had been there. PCR employees regularly had to wait 30 minutes or longer until they all turned up. Occasionally PCR employees were called and put through to teleconferences which hadn't been scheduled. They didn't want to refuse as these conferences provided an opportunity to follow up on unanswered questions, and any direct contact was very important. However, these unscheduled calls often meant the PCR employee was participating in a teleconference on the way to work and being bombarded with questions which they hadn't prepared for.

File 33 | Unit 5

Case study, Task, Exercise 1, page 35

Student B

1 **Situation:** you work in Graphics in an advertising agency. There are a lot of campaigns starting at the moment. You receive a call from a customer. Make a note of the problems and clarify any information that isn't clear.

Action: decide which course of action you can promise.

a You promise all changes can be made in time for the deadline.

b You need to check details with the magazine publishers and try to change things with them – ad has already been sent! Will get back to customer by the end of the week.

c It's too late to make any changes as the ad has been sent; the ad was sent for proofreading to your client weeks ago so it isn't really your fault.

2 **Situation:** your company is decentralized, so every department is responsible for its own office area and finances. You are the PA for Marketing and you coordinate the booking of meeting rooms, equipment, etc. and issue offers and invoices for use of the rooms by other departments. It's a busy time of year. You receive a call from a colleague in Lisbon. Make a note of the problems and clarify any information that isn't clear.

Action: decide which course of action you can promise.

a Check everything's free, but also check options from other departments and send new quote by the end of the week.

b Deny giving the original quote and ask for the information again in writing. You'll reply some time next week.

c Check all rooms and equipment are free and send a new quote by this afternoon.

3 **Situation:** you work in Denmark in the PR department of a confectionery company. You've been invited to a local school to talk about nutrition. Call Marketing in France.

Problem: none of your PR literature is suitable for children. You need

- 350 free merchandise, e.g. hats, pens, badges
- 400 free sample products – chocolate / biscuits, etc.
- 450 information folders with recipes, quizzes, etc.

Deadline: talk in two weeks' time

4 **Situation:** you work in a company PR Department. You have received a press release which needs to be translated into Urdu. Call your translation agency.

Problem: 1,000 words approx. over 5 pages – some graphs which need titles translating too / financial text – need translator who is familiar with this type of text / need an offer before work can commence

Deadline: by tomorrow

File 34 | Unit 15

Case study, Task, page 95

Maximuscle

Zef Eisenberg didn't hire an expensive PR agency to deal with the bad press. He invited journalists to the company and spoke to them – showing all the necessary certificates and documentation about his product. This led to him getting a few million pounds of free advertising through the newspaper articles and, as a result, his company took off again. The only negative effect of this was that he didn't have enough stock to cope with the demand. Maximuscle grew exponentially and Zef soon had to find a strong management team to lead the company through the fast expansion. A couple of years later, Zef decided to make his product more appealing to a wider range of consumers. He relabelled the product, making it clearer and less technical. He then did some brand advertising and finally began securing good relations with national chains.

Innocent Drinks

One holiday weekend, they loaded up a van and took the drinks round 50 delicatessens and health shops in their local area. They gave four boxes free to the companies and told them to contact them if they sold. Forty-five of these shops called to order more. The Innocent team then went back to the distributors and gave them a box, telling them how many retail outlets had requested the product. Five years on and 10 million sales later, Innocent drinks are in shops across the country and word is spreading. But despite the overwhelming growth, until last summer, Innocent hadn't spent a penny on advertising. An effective marketing ploy is to distance itself from the big corporates and provide an alternative, 'student' image.

Innocent also gives away drinks to the homeless, plants trees, encourages recycling and donates to the third world, while its entire staff are treated to a snowboarding trip every year, awarded £2,000 for the birth of each child and invited to apply for a £1,000 scholarship to achieve something they've always wanted to do.

File 35 | Unit 13

Case study, Task, page 83

Student B

Myspace.com

Founded: 2003 **Users:** 100m

What is it?: Social networking site / friend-making shop

Who started it?: Tom Anderson / Chris DeWolfe

Approximate statistics / facts:

- More page visits in UK than the BBC website
- Growing by 240,000 a day
- 4th most visited website in the world
- Many attractions: adverts, events and chance to upload music
- 2.2m new music bands have used site
- 2005: website bought by media tycoon Rupert Murdoch for $580m

File 36 | Unit 5

Business communication skills, Exercise 4, page 33

Student A

1 You work in the Communications Department and receive a call from an internal customer.
Action to promise: look into problem / call back tomorrow.

2 You work in the Customer Services Department and phone the Logistics Department.
Problem: a customer needs its goods earlier than expected.
Further information: a loyal customer has asked if their goods can be sent a week earlier – is this possible?
Deadline: need to let the customer know by tomorrow afternoon at the latest.

File 37 | Unit 3

Language at work, Exercise 4, page 22

1 **Student A:** You were unexpectedly called away from the office and left a list of tasks for your colleague to do. It is now 4 p.m. and you are back in the office. Ask your colleague about the tasks on the 'To do' list.
Student B: Decide which two tasks you have done on the 'To do' list, when they were done and what exactly you did. Decide which two tasks you haven't done and think of an explanation why.

2 **Student B:** Your colleague has asked you attend a conference in Madrid on his / her behalf. This morning you gave your PA a list of things to organize for the trip. It is now 4 p.m. Ask your PA about the tasks on the 'To do' list.
Student A: Decide which two tasks you have done on the 'To do' list, when they were done and what exactly you did. Decide which two tasks you haven't done and think of an explanation why.

File 38 | Unit 10

Case study, Task, page 65

Student B

Favour	Name of person agreeing to favour
Help me with next year's budget – I don't have much time.	
Contact the IT company to set up the internal network – I don't have time.	
Borrow your secretary until I've appointed a new one for myself.	

Favours you must refuse to do:

- Lend one person from team to move to another department – on a temporary basis.
- Give two of your offices to your colleague.
- Buy a pool of software licences.

File 39 | Unit 9

Case study, Task, Exercise 2, page 59

Group B: HR Managers

1 Look at the proposed incentives and possible consequences. Think of an alternative proposal for each incentive (based on the original idea), which could be a realistic compromise if you need it.

Proposed incentives / perks	Consequences of this	Alternative / amended idea
Overtime is paid at double time	This puts you over budget and would have to be implemented for the whole company	e.g. Overtime is taken as time in lieu
Costs of children's schooling at the private International school covered	There's not enough money to pay for school fees for all employees on the project	e.g. Help children to get a scholarship for the International School (private tutor if necessary)
Interest free loan for living costs, e.g. deposit for a house or car	This would make a divide within the workforce – not fair for those who weren't chosen for the project abroad	Assistance for rehousing and / or loan for deposit for a house / car
1 month assimilation time before going back to full-time work	May give employee time to look around for another job	
Job promotion on return	This is difficult to implement as there may not be a position available	

2 Think of two extra proposals (plus the possible consequence) to suggest to the Team Leader.

3 Prioritize the three incentives you would really like to persuade your Team Leader to accept.

Points system

While you negotiate, consider this scoring system.

2 points if you get agreement on an alternative

1 point if you agree on the whole incentive

0 points if you completely refuse the incentive

File 40 | Unit 14

Case study, Task, page 89

Student B

In theory everyone has been trained up who needs to be trained. There was no regular training as there was a lot of time between visits. PCR tried to check everyone was following in the training sessions and regularly took breaks for questions and to clarify misunderstandings – but everyone always said they understood. After the breaks PCR recapped and asked each trainee to run through a bit of the program they'd just covered. The trainees generally got it wrong or seemed confused. PCR are not sure where the problem lies but are sure there are still areas that aren't clear for the Malaysians.

File 41 | Unit 2

Case study, Task, page 17

Student D

WORKING CONDITIONS

The offices were given a good rating and the facilities are satisfactory. Improvements need to be made to working times and perks.

'I sometimes need the flexibility to work from home and look after my children.'

'One major reason my colleague left her job recently was because she needed somewhere with flexitime, to fit in with her family commitments – I agree with this.'

'Extra provisions for women returning to work after having a baby would be nice.'

'Pay is fair (but not great) but I'd like to see some more benefits, which would compensate for the salaries.'

'We must be the only subsidiary which doesn't offer its staff discounted products!'

'Our subsidiaries in other countries provide private health insurance. How can it be possible for them and not for us?'

File 42 | Unit 3

Language at work, Exercise 3, page 22

Student B

1 You are in a project team which is converting an old building to provide new company premises. Update your colleague, using these prompts and / or your own ideas. Use *already* and *yet* and appropriate time expressions.

- finish the first floor building work
- have delays caused by plumbing contractors
- not complete the second floor adaptations
- postpone date for roofing work
- find good decorating firm

2 Your colleague is involved in the building of a new warehouse and office complex. Ask how the project is going. As your colleague is speaking, comment on what he / she says and ask additional questions.

File 43 | Unit 10

Case study, Task, page 65

Student C

Favour	Name of person agreeing to favour
Help me organize 'office warming' party for new division – I'm not very interested in doing this.	
Give me two of your offices as we don't have enough space in our department.	
Give me the name of a good, reliable, financial controller.	

Favours you must refuse to do:

- Give contact names for mailing list.
- Contact IT company for internal network.
- Use / share your department's coffee machine.

File 44 | Unit 13

Case study, Task, page 83

Student C

Slashdot.org

Founded: 1997 **Users:** 5.5m per month

What is it?: Technology news website and technical forum

Who started it?: Ernst Kohl / Luciana Francolini

Approximate statistics / facts:

- Hosts discussion forums for 'techies'
- Discussions run to 10,000 comments a day
- Pioneer of 'user-generated' site
- Developed from a personal blog – was bought by current owners for $5m in 1999
- Only 10 employees maintaining the site!
- Holding company was bought for $900m in 2006
- Based in California

File 45 | Unit 14

Case study, Task, page 89

Student C

PCR employees took part in meetings and expected a round of discussion resulting in a decision. They questioned their Malaysian counterparts, asking for opinions and tried to draw conclusions from the answers. However, there were no direct answers to the questions. A result of this was that PCR became frustrated, thinking meetings were a waste of time. The Malaysian counterparts were frustrated because the decision-maker wasn't always consulted and PCR seemed to be expecting decisions to be made from any one of the participants.

File 46 | Unit 2

Case study, Task, page 17

- Set up 'sideways' moves across to different departments / job areas and promotion. Organized internal transfers with subsidiaries abroad.
- Revised pay scales in alignment with industry standards.
- Introduced compensation package which included private health scheme.
- Brought in a 24-month leave period for new mothers – although legal requirement is 15 months.
- Promoted flexible working and home working.
- Introduced training budgets per head – encouraged training and personal development. New policy: each employee is entitled to four training courses a year – two must be attended, one of which is job-related.
- Arranged a monthly managers' breakfast. This took the form of an informal meeting where a big breakfast was provided. The idea was to promote discussion / small talk amongst managers in an informal setting.
- Made gift giving at Christmas standard throughout company – same given to everyone.
- Required departments to arrange a once-a-month Friday lunch to encourage socializing and teamwork.
- Management met department heads individually, twice a year, to review job and discuss concerns, wishes, etc. and most importantly, to give them feedback, thanks and praise.

Results:

As a result of these changes, voluntary staff turnover reduced to 3.3%; absenteeism reduced to 0.3%; 20–30% of staff accepted the offer of working some of their week from home.

File 47 | Unit 16

Language at work, Exercise 5, page 100

Student A

You want to take a one-year career break but do not want to risk losing your job on your return. Answer your manager's questions (use your own situation or invent the details).

Student B

You are the HR Manager. An employee wishes to take a career break. Ask questions to find out:

- what they like about their current job
- if there is anything they dislike about the work
- what they are planning to do / where they would like to go
- how long they hope to go away for
- if they are planning to develop any new skills
- if they want to carry on working with the company when they get back / if they are expecting to get the same job back
- if they would be prepared to do a different job on their return
- if they will mind earning less than their colleagues.

When you have finished, change roles.

File 48 | Unit 5

Case study, Task, Exercise 2, page 35

1 (Student B)

a 2 points. This is very generous of you but might backfire! You are also working with the magazine which may have its own deadlines – don't promise anything until you're certain you can meet your promise.

b 6 points. Very sensible. You're giving yourself enough time to make sure everything's possible – you can always contact the client sooner if you have the information.

c 4 points. This is quite harsh but if it's not your job to deal with the problem, pass it on to someone who can deal with it more effectively.

2 (Student B)

a 6 points. You're keeping your options open – also for the client. This is a good strategy, especially if you fear your department is already booked out.

b 2 points. Stalling your client isn't going to help anyone. If you don't have any rooms available, admit it early enough to negotiate an alternative.

c 4 points. Very efficient – but are you certain you'll have enough time to look into this and also find alternatives if your rooms are fully booked?

3 (Student A)

a 4 points. Your colleague will at least have an immediate answer but if you don't have the stock, the problem hasn't been solved. You'll probably still have to look at option b after this.

b 6 points. You're winning yourself valuable time here and also going out of your way to help your colleague get the material they need. Very customer-oriented!

c 2 points. Waiting until the last minute isn't going to help you or your colleague and also means you still have the problem to deal with later rather than sooner. In the meantime, surely there is something else you can do to help as the final solution won't be satisfactory for your colleague.

4 (Student A)

a 2 points. This is risky, greedy and can easily backfire! Once you've accepted the translation you must find a translator; and your reputation could be compromised if you don't find a good one.

b 6 points. You're doing exactly what the customer wants: sending an offer first. In the meantime, you can contact your translator. The company can still turn down the offer if necessary, but will respect you for your professionalism and continue working with you in other capacities.

c 4 points. This is rather 'last minute' but will give you time to contact your most reliable translator(s). If a client wants something done by a tight deadline, they have to be willing to work to your deadlines too.

File 49 | Unit 14

Case study, Task, page 89

Doing business in Malaysia

Concept of time Predominantly Malaysia is made up of a mixture of Malays, Indians and Chinese. Which nationality you're working with determines whether deadlines and punctuality are important. Malays tend to be less strict about punctuality and deadlines than Indians and Chinese. It's important to know which nationality the decision-maker and organizer is as this will determine whether meetings are planned or just take place without prior warning, and whether appointment times are strictly kept.

'Yes' meaning 'no' Loss of face is an important issue in Malaysian culture. For example, when a trainer asks a group if they understand, the group will say 'yes', even if they don't. It may only be when the trainer is alone with a trainee that the trainee will ask about a point not understood. To do this in front of the group would be to lose face. Direct answers, particularly negative ones, are avoided in order to prevent disagreement and preserve harmony (two very important aspects of Malaysian culture). Therefore it often takes time to get feedback.

Hierarchy and decision-making process Hierarchy is extremely strong within organizations. There is normally one person at a meeting who can make the decisions and other participants are expected to give their opinions only when asked by their superior.

Relationship building This is an important aspect of doing business. Business relationships take time and one should not rush things. If a business partner needs longer to work through a contract or try out a product, so be it. If a contract has been signed, one shouldn't expect that to be the business finalized. There will probably be a lot of discussions and decision-making behind the scenes, which will eventually be discussed together with the new business partner.

File 50 | Unit 10

Case study, Task, page 65

Student D

Favour	Name of person agreeing to favour
Fly to Brussels and take part in kick-off meeting instead of me.	
Buy a pool of software licences – to save money.	
Share your department's coffee machine – budget is empty.	

Favours you must refuse to do:

- Share your department's data projector.
- Lend your secretary to your colleague.
- Give a name of a financial controller.

CD 1

Unit 1

01

Presenter So is most of your work to do with translating websites from English?

Zhifu No, not really, although we do get a lot of Western companies who want to break into Asian markets. The problem is ... they think they can just come along and translate their website, just like that ... But really that's a very expensive and ineffective way of doing things.

Presenter There's more to it than that?

Zhifu Yes. And to be honest, it's quite arrogant to think you can create a favourable impression and attract a lot of customers without really trying. To start with, customers are still wary ...

Presenter What ... of newcomers? Or of the technology?

Zhifu Both. You have to work hard to show that you are trustworthy and to make customers feel confident in your company.

Presenter Yes, but that's not a particularly Asian phenomenon, is it? I mean, if you have a website with spelling mistakes, people are bound to be suspicious, aren't they?

Zhifu That's right, but just like in traditional advertising, some things are more effective in some cultures than others.

Presenter So you're saying a localized website would need to be genuinely different in some way?

Zhifu Yes. In the West, the websites have a lot of words – lots of facts and figures, they're often quite complex. But here, the websites that work best are simple and functional ... in the same way that many Asian cultures prefer offices that are modest rather than ostentatious.

Presenter A case of less is more?

Zhifu Yes, exactly. And you have to understand the local culture. For example, here in China, when people go shopping online, they like sites where they can bargain and make a deal, because that's what they like to do in real life.

Presenter So a website like that would need a lot more than just translating. You might have to rebuild the whole site.

Zhifu That's right. For really successful website localization, you have to start the process from the beginning, taking all these cultural things into account ... not just translate the words and hope for the best.

02

Ivan Ivan Formanek. How can I help you?

Sean Hello, Ivan. This is Sean McFee. I'm calling about the email I sent you regarding your new website.

Ivan Oh, hello. Yes, I remember. Thanks for responding so quickly.

Sean No problem. I wondered if you'd had time to look through the portfolio I sent.

Ivan Yes, I have. Your work looks very interesting.

Sean What exactly do you want to do? Do you want to change the whole site or just update parts of it?

Ivan Well, we're currently updating our corporate image, which means redesigning the logo, the brochures and the website. We've already done some of this in-house, but we need help with the website in particular.

Sean Well, I could certainly help you with that.

Ivan Great. I suggest we meet to discuss things further. I have to be honest, though. You aren't the only designer we're talking to.

Sean I understand. When would you like to meet?

Ivan Well ... I go to Berlin once a month to interpret for a client of ours – I'm covering for a colleague who's on maternity leave. In fact, I'm leaving the day after tomorrow, but we can meet when I get back.

Sean Fine, whatever's best for you.

Ivan Let's say, provisionally, Tuesday the 13th at 11 o'clock and I'll get my assistant to call you later today to confirm. You'll be travelling in from Krakow, won't you?

Sean That's right.

Ivan It might be best to discuss travel arrangements with my assistant then. Her name is Catherine, by the way.

Sean Fine. Well, thanks for your time.

Ivan You're welcome. See you in a couple of weeks.

03

Sean Hello, Sean McFee.

Catherine Hello, this is Catherine, Ivan Formanek's assistant. I'm calling about the meeting on Tuesday the 13th.

Sean Oh, right. Thanks. I wanted to speak to you about that. I'm actually going to be in Prague already as I've arranged to meet some other clients on the Monday.

Catherine OK.

Sean Can you tell me how I get to Simply Speaking? Is it best by taxi or public transport?

Catherine Public transport's fine. Let me know where you're staying and I'll email you a map and directions from your hotel.

Sean Thanks. Another thing I wanted to check ... How long are you scheduling the meeting for? There's a train that leaves at 3 o'clock. Will I have time to catch that one or should I take a later one?

Catherine We'll be finished by 2.00 at the latest ... It only takes 20 minutes to get to the station, so you'll have plenty of time.

Sean Thanks. I'll probably take a taxi to the station to be sure.

Catherine OK. When you arrive at the company, give your name to Reception and they'll send you up to us on the fifth floor. And let me know if you need a taxi and I'll book one for you.

Sean That's very kind. Thanks a lot.

04

1

A Let me take your name and number and I'll let you know when we're having another exhibition.

B That's great. Thanks. Here's my card.

2

A Can I have Suzy's number and email address? I want to invite her to the next exhibition we host.

B Sure, they're in my phone, so I'll send you her contact details by text. Is that OK?

A Yeah, fine. That way I'll have your new mobile number too.

3

A It was great meeting you again. I have an email address for you but I'm not sure if it's current.

B No, you've probably got my old one. Here's my new card with my email address ... Er ... The one above is my business email. I check it regularly so please use that one.

A OK. I'll use the business one then if that's OK?

B Sure.

Unit 2

05

1

Claudia My job involves visiting different hotels to sell various ranges of soap, shampoo and other toiletries for their guests. My sales territory covers the whole of Germany and Austria. I love my job. I get a lot of fulfilment from meeting new people, and from the travel – I can't imagine being stuck in the same place all the time. I also value the autonomy the job gives me – I have to report to my manager once a week but apart from that, I'm responsible for all day-to-day decisions and organization. Because I'm on the road so much of the time, I'm provided with the essential benefits like a BlackBerry® and a laptop, and a company car, of course. I get quite a good basic salary, but what is also very important for me is the amount I can earn in commission – I get 15% of everything I sell and there's no upper limit – and that's a big incentive for me because I'm one of the top-selling sales people. My company are very generous with rewards, too ... you know, merchandise, vouchers, social events. I do think these help me to do my job better – it's nice to be acknowledged and recognized for my achievements.

2

Peter Every month, we have a sales competition with lots of prizes, and each dealership has to send in figures for the month to Head Office – you know, to show them how well we're doing – and then, if you've met your targets, you get reward vouchers for things like … I don't know, a hot-air balloon trip or a spa treatment, or something … and I usually give these to someone on my sales team, whoever deserves them. I think it works well – it motivates them – but the real value of prizes is that it helps to make people feel appreciated. Positive feedback and praise are very important, they do a lot for job satisfaction. Managers like myself don't get monthly prizes. The real incentive for us is that, if we make the grade, we get invited on a special trip once a year. It really makes you feel positive about working for the company, you feel valued … like an important member of the team. Last year, it was a week in Africa and a chance to climb Mount Kilimanjaro, and that's something I'll never forget. The company also thinks that development is important for staff morale, so there are lots of opportunities for training, not just staff development but non-professional training like horticulture or painting. That's a popular benefit of the job, but one of the biggest perks is the very generous staff discount we get on all our models – and when you're talking about a new car, you're talking about a lot of money.

3

Macie There are a lot of popular misconceptions about this job … you know? I mean, people seem to think you get to travel all over the place and see different countries every week. But that's only true on long-haul flights … most of the time it's a fast turnaround, and back to checking seat belts and serving drinks. So, on a regular basis, the travel really isn't that exciting. But one of the main benefits is the staff discount. Me, my husband, my kids … even my parents … we get hugely reduced fares when we use the airline – and that's when we can really travel and … see the world. The salary's OK, a little below average maybe, but the compensation plan is good. Let's see … it includes a profit-sharing scheme, a non-contributory pension plan … we have private medical insurance and there are incentives like attendance rewards and on-time bonuses – so, all in all, yeah, it's a pretty good deal. One of the good things about the company is that we do get appreciation when we do our jobs well. Senior management actually comes round and thanks us personally when we've met our targets … and that certainly gives me a sense of achievement.

06

Conversation 1

Harry Hello, I saw you sitting on my table at dinner but I didn't have a chance to speak to you. I'm Harry.
Alessandro Hi. I'm Alessandro.
Harry Who did you come with? Is this your first company event?
Alessandro Yes.
Harry Well, I'm sure you'll have a great weekend. Have you seen the programme?
Alessandro No, not yet.
Harry Oh. Well, it looks very entertaining. I think there are some left at the information desk. Are you, um, here with colleagues?
Alessandro No.
Harry Well, you'll soon get to know people. So, um, would you like another drink?
Alessandro No, I'm fine, thanks.
Harry Well, it's been nice talking to you … erm ... Alessandro. You don't mind if I go and get myself a coffee? See you later.

Conversation 2

Paolo Hi, I don't think we've met. I'm Paolo from Napoli – I work for one of the company's suppliers.
Sonia Hi, nice to meet you. I'm Sonia … from France.
Paolo Nice to meet you.
Sonia So … I've heard that Naples is becoming very popular for foreign investors – is that true?
Paolo Well, Sonia, it's interesting that you say that because …

Conversation 3

Sumitra Hi, I'm Sumitra, based in the UK.
Krishnan Hello, I'm Krishnan. Sorry, where are you from originally?
Sumitra Well, my parents live in Calcutta. I was born there, but I've moved around a lot.
Krishnan You are from Calcutta? No! That's amazing! My parents are from India – in fact, they are there now visiting relatives.
Sumitra What a coincidence! Where do they come from?
Krishnan From Bhiwandi – near Mumbai.
Sumitra Bhiwandi … Isn't it famous for its textile industry?
Krishnan That's right, yes … So have you spent much time in India recently …?

Conversation 4

Adam Good evening, Adriana. I thought I might see you. Back for another company event?
Adriana Oh, Adam – how lovely to see you here. I heard you weren't coming.
Adam Really? Who told you?
Adriana Um, I can't remember – but anyway, how are things?
Adam Oh, Adriana – where should I begin? I injured my leg in January in a skiing accident. The doctor told me to take it easy. But how could I rest, with my job? Then I got flu, but we were organizing a huge trade fair at the time so I had to keep going …
Adriana Oh, oh dear …
Adam … then I had problems at home with my daughter, she's fifteen, you know, and she …
Adriana Oh, I'm so sorry to hear that. Look, I have to go, Adam. Catch you later.

07

Harry Hello. It's Adriana, isn't it? We met before dinner.
Adriana That's right. You're Harry. Dinner was fantastic, wasn't it? (**Harry** Yeah, it was, yeah.)
How are you enjoying the event?
Harry Very much. It, you know, it's good to meet people from different parts of the group. Have you been before?
Adriana Yes, I have. About three years ago, in Egypt. Were you there?
Harry No, I wasn't, unfortunately. I heard it was good fun. Where are you from, by the way?
Adriana I'm from Spain originally, but I'm working in Switzerland. I have a two-year posting in Head Office in Geneva.
Harry I see. Who are you working with?
Adriana With the European HR team. I work with Ulrika Thomson.
Harry No! What a coincidence! I know her very well. We joined the company on the same day. It's a shame she couldn't be here. Say hello to her for me, won't you?
Adriana Of course I will.
Harry So … um … what are you working on?
Adriana Er … right now, we're trying to harmonize remuneration packages across the group. I'm working on pension plans and other savings schemes. What about you? Don't you live in Italy?
Harry Yes, I do. In Milan. I work in R&D, but I'm thinking of moving.
Adriana Really? Can I ask where?
Harry Well, I'd like to stay in Italy but maybe move within the group. I'm thinking of talking to HR, actually. Apparently they're interested in people who've worked in different divisions …
Adriana That sounds interesting. In fact, I'm coming to Milan in a couple of weeks. Would you like to meet up and talk some more …
Harry Yes, I would. Thanks very much. Do you know Milan?
Adriana No, not really. I've just been there for meetings.
Harry Well, I'd be delighted to show you around.
Adriana Thank you. That would be very nice.
Harry Good. So do you actually live in Geneva …?

08

1 Is that the time? My parking ticket runs out in five minutes.

2 I promised to meet someone else. But I'll come back when I've seen them.
3 I'm going to get some food. I missed lunch because of the conference call.
4 Is that James over there? Excuse me, I really must go and speak to him.
5 Look, I really don't have time to chat at the moment. I'll call you tomorrow though.

Unit 3

09

Part 1

Sarah ... OK, I sent you a proposed agenda yesterday. Have you had a chance to look at it?
Ian Yes, it looks fine.
Sarah So, the purpose of today is to update each other on progress and consider anything that might affect our schedule.
Ian OK.
Sarah So, Michelle, why don't you start? How are things with the marketing department?
Michelle Up to now, the launch date has been set for the 15th of November, to capture the Christmas trade – this means we must meet our deadlines.
Sarah Good point. So how's the advertising campaign coming along?
Michelle That's fine. We've set a realistic schedule and planned in a bit of extra time in case the printing takes longer than expected.
Sarah Great. And how far are you with preparations for the launch party?
Michelle Our events manager says we're on track. He booked the venue two weeks ago and I've already received offers from various catering companies. I haven't made a final choice yet, but most of them are well within our budget.
Sarah That sounds good, Michelle, thanks. So, how does your side of things look, Ian?
Ian Well, actually, things aren't running as smoothly as I'd hoped. We've hit a problem with the handset battery life.
Sarah OK ... so what do you mean exactly?
Ian Well, in some cases, the battery can run out in six hours if its key features are in permanent use.
Michelle So what you're saying is we're about to launch a new revolutionary low-cost mobile phone and its battery only lasts six hours!?
Ian Well, obviously, that's an extreme case, but the engineers *have* identified that there is a basic design problem with the battery.
Sarah So the *real* problem lies with the battery manufacturers?
Ian Yes.
Michelle But, Ian, what about our deadlines? Can this problem be resolved?
Ian Well, our engineers are looking into it and if it's fixable, they'll do it, but they'll need time. We may have to reschedule.
Michelle But we can't postpone the launch at this stage! There must be something you can do.
Sarah Are there any alternatives?
Ian Well, I've got some suggestions but you may not like them.
Sarah Ian, you've put us in a difficult position – why don't we get another coffee and then we'll look at our options.

10

Part 2

Sarah The battery problem has to be resolved; otherwise the whole project is in trouble – that's how I see it.
Michelle Is that really the case? How about finding another battery supplier?
Ian I don't think that would help us meet our current deadlines. We could keep the same battery but not mention its lifespan.
Sarah That's possible, but our reputation is at stake here.
Michelle Yes, and if the project fails we have no chance of becoming market leader!
Ian OK. Why don't we wait and see what the technicians suggest and in the meantime move the launch date?
Michelle That's not an ideal solution. It means cancelling the printers, the caterers, the advertising ...
Sarah Do we have any other options?
Ian Well, using a different phone for the launch would be my proposal. We could use the VP20: it's new, cheap but not as hi-tech.
Michelle I'm not convinced. The whole idea of this project was to offer a hi-tech phone and services at an attractive price.
Sarah Yes. If you ask me, we should look at what we can reschedule.
Michelle Oh, I suppose so.

11

1

A What are you doing at the moment?
B I'm learning Mandarin at an evening class.
A Good for you. That must be quite ... um, challenging.
B Yes, but it's a lot of fun too. We have a very good teacher. What about you? Are you still playing golf?
A Yes, I am. But I don't play as much as I used to.

2

A ... So how's the new job going?
B It's going well, thanks. I'm really enjoying it.
A That's great. I'm glad it's working out.
B Yes, it's good. Anyway, how are things with you?
A Oh, fine. You know ... working hard.

3

A ... Have you been away recently?
B I've just come back from a long weekend in London. That's all, really. How about you?
A No, I haven't been on holiday for ages. I really need a break.
B Have you booked any holiday?
A Not yet. It's difficult to find the time. I'm always so busy.

4

A ... Do you still work for the same company?
B Yes, and we're really busy – as usual.
A And are you still enjoying it?
B Yeah, definitely. It's always different. And it keeps me on my toes.
A I'm sure it does.
B So, how about you? Are you still ...?
A No, I changed jobs about three months ago. It was a good opportunity, so ...

Unit 4

12

We run a project in the Rathnambhore National Park in India, which is home to a large tiger population. The villagers living near the park had been cutting down trees in the park for firewood. This was causing a serious problem, and we were asked to come up with a practical solution.

We set up a project to build a lot of small biogas systems. It's not cutting-edge technology, but it's very reliable and cheap. Basically, you mix cow dung and water in an underground tank. From this, you get biogas which you use for fuel, and the rest can be used for fertilizer. We based the idea on an earlier model at Deenpandu, with a few small developments.

It's an innovative concept – we give the families the specifications and some training, and they build the system themselves. You need at least four cows – it's not feasible with fewer than four animals. Projects like this bring about real improvements for everyone. The villagers get clean fuel and excellent fertilizer ... and another major advantage is they don't need to cut down so many trees. So, it's good news for the tigers too – a real success.

13

We came up with this revolutionary idea just a couple of years ago, and we moved very quickly from an idea in R&D to the prototype, and then to the first production models. Our wind turbines make the production of electricity from wind power very efficient. They're small enough to fit on the roof of a building, and they can generate a significant fraction of a household's electricity so the initial investment will pay off in the long term. So, the key features of the turbine are its size, obviously, and its state-of-the-art design. As you know, conventional wind turbines are often very large – this causes concerns about where to locate them, about their environmental impact. But the

technological breakthroughs we've made in the design have allowed us to get round this problem – and our turbine is vibration-free and almost completely silent.
At the moment it is still quite expensive to buy and install, but with mass production we're hoping to bring the costs right down, and make installing a turbine a commercially-viable proposition for many people.

14

Part 1

Shireen Firstly, I'd like to thank you for inviting me here today. We really appreciate this opportunity to work with PharmaLab again.
David Thank you for coming, Shireen. We're looking forward to hearing what you can offer.
Shireen Good. OK, what I'd like to do in this presentation is basically three things. First, I'll give you a brief overview of the product. Then I'll talk about some of the advantages for your company. After that I'd like to show you a short demo film so that you can see the system in operation. And after that, you can ask me any questions. Does that sound OK?
... OK. We call the system DiScan. Basically, DiScan is a state-of-the-art security system based on fingerprint scanning. It's the result of two years of intensive R&D, and it has only been on the market for three months. However, it's already being used by five major organizations and our order book is filling up fast!
How does it work? Well, it's a pretty simple concept – employees are identified by their fingerprints. When they enter and leave a building or secure area, they touch a glass plate. The system scans their fingerprints and compares them with a central database set up by you.

15

Part 2

David So what are the advantages of DiScan compared to our existing system?
Shireen OK, let's look at what DiScan has to offer. There are two main benefits of using DiScan – enhanced security, and increased flexibility.
Why enhanced security? Well, the biggest potential benefit of fingerprint scanning is that no two people have the same fingerprints – every one is unique. This means that DiScan is extremely secure in comparison to systems where a code is needed. You can learn someone else's code, whereas you can't copy their fingerprints. Another advantage is that you can't lose or forget your fingerprints – they're always with you.
With your current system, if someone gets hold of a security code, they can go anywhere they want in your company. However, with DiScan, they won't be able to do that. And another thing ... At the moment, you can only tell that someone is in a secure area, whereas in the future, you'll be able to tell exactly who that person is as well.
David And the second benefit?
Shireen The other major advantage of DiScan is its flexibility. Although it may sound radical, it's up to you how far-reaching you want the security to be. You can decide exactly which employees have access to which parts of the building – so you have complete control over who goes where. And this is another great thing about DiScan – you can not only restrict entry to all parts of the building, but also access to your computer system.
David It sounds impressive.
Shireen So, is everything clear so far? OK, now I'd like to move on to some other advantages of the system, and after that we'll watch a demo ...

16

1
A Thank you for having me – it was a really interesting visit.
B It's a pleasure – it was good to see you.

2
A Here's that document you wanted copied.
B Thanks a lot – I appreciate it.
A No problem – any time.

3
A Thank you very much for lunch – it was delicious.
B You're welcome – I really enjoyed it.

4
A Thanks for your time this morning – it was good of you to come in.
B No problem – thanks for your help.

5
A I'd like to thank you for inviting me here today.
B Thank you for coming – we're glad you could be here.

6
A After you.
B Thanks.
A That's OK.

17

Richard So to sum up, Boatnet is a specialist Internet service provider that provides wireless Internet access at all the major marinas in the country. From the start, I could see that there was definitely a market. Boat owners want to be able to access the Internet to get information about the weather and sea conditions, as well as sending and receiving email. In the past, they could only do this on land because the technology wasn't in place. At the moment, in most parts of the world, you still can't access the Internet from your boat without the right technology. From now on, our subscribers will be able to access the Internet from their boats for a basic monthly fee. We set up a very successful pilot project in three marinas last year, so we were able to test the system extensively and we know it works. We've done a lot of research and we can offer the service for £25 a month – that's less than 40 euros. We'd like to be able to increase this in the future.
Jason My name's Jason Black. It's an interesting idea. Have you been able to get any sort of protection for it?
Richard Well, of course, we couldn't get a patent or anything like that because it's not new technology, but we have been able to get exclusive contracts in all the major marinas in the country.
Jason And how long are these contracts?
Richard Seven years.
Jason So other companies won't be able to compete with you for the next seven years?
Richard That's right.

Unit 5

18

Interviewer ... Thanks for your call, Deepak ... So that's a good experience of customer service. I'd now like to turn to Maria who has a very different story. Maria ...
Maria Yes, well, this was something that happened quite recently. I wanted to get a Christmas present for a friend. Some time ago, she took me to a fantastic chocolate shop in Bond Street, I won't say the name, where we had the most amazing hot chocolate. Anyway, she's been very kind to me over the last year and I wanted to get her some of their handmade chocolates ... they're really special. I work in South London, so it's quite a long journey into the centre of town. I left work early – along with my laptop and stuff from work because there was going to be a tube strike the next day. It took quite a while – and I finally arrived at the shop at literally two minutes past five, only to discover that they'd closed at five. I could see there were still two assistants inside.
Interviewer So there were still people in the shop? (**Maria** Yes.) So what did you do?
Maria Well, I banged on the door and nobody took any notice. So I carried on and eventually one of the assistants opened the door and said they were closed and I should come back tomorrow. I explained that I wouldn't be able to get back if there was a tube strike the next day. I said, 'Look, it's the Monday before Christmas, and this is a present for a friend'. Basically she just said that was tough, they were closed. I

said, 'I'll pay cash, ring it up tomorrow, don't worry about a bag'. No luck. They just weren't interested.

Interviewer So you didn't get your chocolates …?

Maria I didn't get my chocolates. And my question is this: When it comes to customer service, where should companies draw the line? I'm not someone who thinks the customer is always right. But I do know that if they had tried to help me, I would have been a customer for life. This shop does many things right. It has wonderful packaging, a superb product, a great café. But all that investment counts for nothing if a loyal customer who's made a special effort to buy their product is turned away at the door.

Interviewer OK, thanks Maria. Don't forget, you can call us on 0207 …

19

Conversation 1

Borys Hello, Procurement, Borys speaking.

Paola Hi, Borys. This is Paola, from Sales in the Milan office. I have a question about an order we placed.

Borys What seems to be the problem?

Paola It's the approval for our training course – the course should begin next week but the training company hasn't received the signed contract from us.

Borys OK. Could you give me the order number and I'll look into it?

Paola It's 02/584.

Borys Can you tell me when you sent it to us?

Paola At least a month ago. Training Direct need the contract before the course can begin. That's by Friday at the latest.

Borys Let me get this straight. What you're saying is we still have the contract and you need it back, signed by us?

Paola Well, yes.

Borys OK. These things do take time, I'm afraid. Oh … I have the contract here. What I'll do is check the figures and see if Angela can sign it by tomorrow. If you give me the fax number of Training Direct, I'll fax it straight to them and post you a copy.

Paola Will it be ready in time for the deadline?

Borys I'll do my best.

Conversation 2

Chris IT Help desk. Chris speaking. How can I help you?

Johann Hi, Chris. It's Johann here from Copenhagen.

Chris Ah, hello, Johann. I haven't heard from you for a few days! Have you worked out our new customer database yet?

Johann Very funny. This isn't a problem about that. My computer keeps going black.

Chris You mean the screen goes blank?

Johann Um, yeah – but the hard drive light is still on.

Chris If I understand you correctly, this is a hardware problem, so I'm afraid I can't help. Ask one of your IT guys in-house.

Johann I tried. They told me to call you.

Chris OK. Could you explain exactly what the problem is? Talk me through it.

Johann Well, firstly, when I open the customer transaction program …

Chris … OK. Good. Yeah, I've noted all that down. Um, I'm going to have to look into this, OK. I'll get back to you shortly.

Johann Do you know why it's doing this?

Chris Well, give me time to check the system, hey? Say, by lunchtime? Don't open the program for the next couple of hours and I might be able to sort out the problem.

Conversation 3

Marcel Hello, Marcel LeGrand speaking.

Donna Hello. This is Donna Fitzpatrick from AS Consulting.

Marcel Good morning. What can I do for you today?

Donna Well, we received a delivery from your company … but it arrived out of office hours and was just left in front of our door.

Marcel Could you tell me when this happened?

Donna A couple of hours ago.

Marcel OK … And can you tell me if you've got an order number?

Donna Umm … 560H. We specifically requested that our paper delivery arrive between 9.30 a.m. and 4 p.m. We now have twenty heavy boxes that need carrying up to the third floor. You're normally so reliable.

Marcel Right … Could I just clarify what you're saying? You ordered paper and informed us of the required delivery date and time?

Donna Yes. I have it here in black and white. Oh, and even more importantly – the order was wrong too! There's too much paper and no printed envelopes.

Marcel OK. Once I've checked the details, I'll call you back.

Donna Could you let me know how long it will take? We need everything for a mailing tomorrow.

Marcel As soon as I've looked into it, I'll call you back.

20/21

1

A How's the new job going?

B Today was terrible! I couldn't remember any of the training we did last week.

A I know it's hard at first, but you'll soon find your feet.

2

A How did the call with that difficult client go?

B Um … the client asked to speak to my boss. But I know I followed procedures exactly.

A Yes. I'm sure you did the best you could.

3

A What's the matter?

B I've just been on the phone for an hour with the most difficult customer!

A How awful!

4

A You seem a bit unhappy.

B Yes … I've broken the bulb in the data projector and they cost €200 to replace!

A Oh no!

22

José It was one of those unfortunate situations that occasionally occurs with online ordering. My customer services team reacted appropriately and did their best to satisfy the customer. It's regrettable that the money for the goods was deducted from the customer's account without any documentation to the order. We decided to refund the complete amount of the order, not only the goods that were missing – though without any record of the order being made, this wasn't an easy decision. Obviously we couldn't offer this to the company immediately as the situation needed investigating before compensation was given. I feel we did the right thing and the main thing is, we have a satisfied customer who will continue doing business with us.

Unit 6

23

Interviewer … and now on to business. And we have with us in the studio Shamsul Aziz from Carno Oil and Gas Exploration who will be telling us about their latest initiatives in social responsibility. Mr Aziz, isn't it dishonest to pretend that you're anything other than a big multinational, motivated by greed, with a reputation for ruining the environment and exploiting local people?

Shamsul Not at all. We take corporate social responsibility very seriously, because as a leading gas and oil exploration company, we know that we can have a dramatic effect on people's lives …

Interviewer Not necessarily a good one.

Shamsul If I may answer the question … We are proud of our business ethics. Looking after our staff isn't just something we have suddenly discovered – it's one of our core values. We've always had a strong commitment to our workforce and an ethical approach to the environment … and the communities we work in. We have a reputation for fairness, we work hard to combat discrimination and prejudice within our organization, and we are constantly improving working conditions for our staff. Safety has always been at the

top of our agenda, but we have schemes in place for education, health and training. We do take care of our people.

Interviewer Leaving that aside for a minute … How can an oil company have any credibility when it claims to be environmentally friendly? Surely that's deception … Your industry is probably the greatest contributor to pollution that there is.

Shamsul No. Not at all. As regards the environment, we can't say how people should or shouldn't use oil, but what we can do – and what we have done – is to reduce our own methane and hydrocarbon emissions … and we've made good progress. We also support a range of local projects – to take just one example, we provide financial support for turtle conservation in Bangladesh, and have done for several years.

Interviewer Apart from a few turtles, what do you actually do to help the people who are affected by your operations?

Shamsul One of our guiding principles is to give back to the communities where we are carrying out our operations. So, in Sangu, for example, we have established a community project to provide skills training for unemployed youths, and in Rajasthan we have undertaken health initiatives and other schemes to encourage sustainable livelihoods.

Interviewer Some people might see that as a form of bribery rather than generosity.

Shamsul I don't agree. It could be seen as corruption if all the money went to just one individual. But the support we provide, the health clinics, assistance to the air ambulance and so on, now these are things that benefit everyone, not just the people who work for us directly.

Interviewer OK, well, if I can now turn to the question of …

24

Part 1

Reporter 1 … Will we get our itinerary in writing after this meeting or should we take notes?

Clare We'll email you the final itinerary once you've decided what you'd like to see. And if you have any other questions, you can ask our Travel Coordinator, Janet Lawson – she's coming in later on this morning to speak with you.

Reporter 1 Thanks.

Clare So, we're planning to show you how Hummingbird's operation works in China and some of the projects it's involved in.

Reporter 2 That sounds good.

Clare The idea is to spend four days at one of the sites where the tea is grown. This will give you the opportunity to talk to the locals who supply the company.

Reporter 2 So, can we interview them?

Clare Yes, but we advise you to set this up directly with them and ask their permission first. And of course, do be discreet and respect their privacy.

Reporter 2 Of course.

Clare While you're there, you'll get the opportunity to accompany the workers in their daily work. This will give you a real insight into their lives and how Hummingbird's teas are produced.

Reporter 1 That sounds really interesting.

Clare OK, now, the schedules. We've looked at all the options, and we're going to arrange two dates – one in February and one in May. The February flight leaves on the 15th so we need fixed bookings from you by January the 10th.

Reporter 3 Can I just ask – are we returning on the 19th or 20th of February?

Clare The 20th. The trip will involve a lot of road travel and one internal flight …

25

Part 2

Clare … So that was the timetable. Now, I'd like to tell you a bit about your stay. Feel free to ask any questions you may have. We'd like to invite you to watch the tea being prepared and spend a day sampling the local specialities which are produced by the cooperative in the village.

Reporter 1 That would be great. Er … Does anyone there speak English?

Clare On the whole, English isn't spoken so we strongly recommend you stay with our guide who can interpret for you.

Reporter 1 Good idea.

Clare On the subject of language – you're also welcome to visit a project set up to promote schooling in the Tibetan language.

Reporter 2 That sounds really interesting. I'd like to take you up on that.

Clare Good … but I should warn you it's quite a long trip. Let me know how many of you would like to do this as it would be a good idea to travel with our interpreter.

Reporter 2 That makes sense. We'll speak to our colleagues and let you know.

Reporter 3 What about environmental projects?

Clare The company is supporting a charity called Tree 2000 Foundation and there's a reforestation scheme in one of the regions where it does business. As Hummingbird Teas is just a financial backer, it doesn't actively work in this field but a visit to the site is highly recommended.

Reporter 3 What will we see?

Clare The project managers who work on site are all professional environmentalists. They'll explain what's happening to the area and show you what the charity is doing to improve the management of the forests. I was there for the first time last month and found it fascinating. It's well worth a visit.

Reporter 2 Mmm … That's not really what I'm looking for. The feature I want to write should focus more on the people.

Clare Well, alternatively, we'd be delighted to introduce you to the team who work for Hummingbird in China. They aren't tea-makers – they're employed to coordinate the business. I'm sure they have some interesting experiences they'd like to share.

Reporter 2 That would be great – it's just the kind of thing I need.

Clare OK, so let's just run through …

26

1

A How about joining us for a coffee after work?

B Maybe … Can I let you know later?

2

A Do you feel like coming to the cinema with us?

B Sorry – I'm heading straight home tonight, it's my partner's birthday.

3

A Would you like to go to that new pizzeria for lunch?

B Why not?

Unit 7

27

1

The most important factor in making and implementing decisions is listening. I like to ask everybody I know to give me an opinion. I get different perspectives – and I listen to them. I also listen to my own intuition. I really do believe that using your intuition is the best way of processing and weighing up information. If I have to make a big decision, I'm never impulsive. I think about it, and I listen to what other people think. But ultimately, I listen to my intuition. I delay my decision until I wake up one morning and know what I'm going to do.

2

I used to think that decision-making was something you could do logically … but for me, this didn't always work and I made some bad decisions. So I thought I'd try a new approach – one that takes feelings more into account. So now … particularly for the big decisions in life – what job to take, where to live – I let my inner wisdom emerge and trust my instincts. We don't always make strictly logical deductions. Instead, we rely on patterns – and on feelings associated with those patterns. So for those big decisions, you need to let patterns develop in your mind. Once you realize that your intuition is reliable, making a decision is quite easy.

3

If you have to make a decision, don't listen to your intuition. Intuition is for people who don't want to think. OK ... it's fine for the small decisions in life, like what kind of ice cream to buy. But for the big decisions, you need a more systematic way of thinking. Let's say you have to decide between two things – two applicants for a key position, two properties you're thinking about buying. You check the facts, check the figures, and your analysis says to pick A over B. But your intuition says to choose B. What do you do? Most people stick with their intuition – which is wrong. You need to delay your decision until you can work out why your intuition is telling you something different. That's the whole point of analysis: to make you consider all the options – so you don't make the wrong decision.

4

To make good decisions, you need to have confidence in your own judgement. We all make bad decisions, but the important thing is not to worry about them. As a judge, I often have to decide between the evidence of two people standing in front of me. I don't know which one is being honest but I know one of them is lying. That's when making decisions becomes very difficult. Even so, I never base my courtroom decisions on my feelings or my instinct. I do it by the evidence, and by what the law tells me.

28

Sinead Today, I'd like to establish where we think we can cut costs. We can discuss actual figures when we've considered what's possible. Jens, could you start us off, please?

Jens Yes, well, if we look at the facts, we'll see that our costs for personnel are very high ...

Anna Yes, but we've discussed lay-offs before.

Sinead Hang on, let's hear what Jens has to say about personnel before we reject the topic.

Jens You're right, Anna, but I'm not talking about reducing the number of employees. Look at the overtime figures. They're here in black and white, and they're costing us a lot of money. The fact is we need to keep these to a minimum to save money.

Sinead Matt, what's your position on this?

Matt What Jens says is right. The thing is, we need to look at why we have so much overtime and if it's realistic to try to reduce it.

Anna If we do reduce it, it'll mean dramatic savings. We could set up a ...

Sinead ... That all sounds pretty positive. Let's look into it at a country level and discuss it again at our next meeting. Can we move on to office resources? Anna, this was your point. Could you give us some detail, please?

Anna Yes, what I mean is paper, office supplies, that sort of thing. I think if we look closely at what we actually use, we'll find there's a lot of waste. A classic example is printing emails out on expensive copy paper.

Matt So what you're getting at is monitoring the office supplies and making sure we're not using too many or wasting too much?

Anna Exactly.

Jens I'm not convinced. As far as I'm concerned, we'd make hardly any savings compared to the personnel costs.

Matt The drawback is, it's quite labour intensive to keep a check on this. ... But it could be a project for one of our work experience students.

Anna Yes, we're ...

Sinead ... I don't want to spend too long on this point. We should set up the project Matt mentioned with the student – and see how it goes. There are plenty of other areas we could consider. Let's turn to the next item, customer expenditure.

Matt If you ask me, we should look carefully at client travel expenses and entertainment costs.

Jens Absolutely. We spend far too much money on clients. The expense accounts aren't taken seriously enough ... that's my view.

Sinead Anna, you've been very quiet.

Anna Yes, I was just doing some calculations ... Matt is right. But I think it would be crazy to cut expense accounts. In my opinion, we should introduce tighter guidelines.

Sinead Good, we seem to be getting somewhere. Let's draw up some action points on what we've discussed so far.

29

1

A What've you got on this weekend, Alex?
B Well, I'm supposed to be helping a friend move house.
A Oh, poor you.

2

A What are you up to tonight?
B We'll probably catch a movie.
A Sounds good.

3

A Are you taking any time off in the summer?
B Mmm – it depends on my colleagues and their vacations.
A I see.

4

A What are you doing this weekend?
B We're off to Paris!
A Lucky you!

5

A Anything nice planned for the weekend?
B Nothing special. What about you?

Unit 8

30

1

Paula Every day, EU companies are outsourcing business process tasks to emerging economies where labour costs are lower – in areas like call centres, airlines, legal processing, finance, and IT of course. The UK jobs are going to India, French jobs to North Africa, Spanish jobs are going to Latin America. Germany is outsourcing to Central European countries like Poland and Hungary, and Scandinavia is outsourcing to the Baltic States and India. Of course outsourcing benefits these countries – by injecting money into their economies and driving the development of a modern communications infrastructure. But it also leads to significant job losses in the home countries. I believe that member states of the EU need to do much more to respond to such losses, which can have a big impact on communities. This is not about protectionism. But we need to develop strategies to cope with serious job losses, and to create more high-quality jobs in the EU.

2

Christian I work for a Swiss financial services company. We first started outsourcing some of our back-office work to India a couple of years ago – at a time when we were considering what cost-cutting measures we could take. Labour costs out there were actually 70% lower than in Switzerland. It's been very successful. We've been able to streamline our operation and free up resources for our core activities. We've now moved two-thirds of our IT work to India. We have an IP-based VPN, a Virtual Private Network, which simplifies the operation and improves efficiency. But it's not just about savings, or gaining a competitive edge. If you look at countries like Brazil, Russia, India and China – they're obviously very important for outsourcing, but they are also important potential markets in their own right. They're growing very very fast, and with hundreds of millions of customers, you can't afford to ignore them.

3

Chitra I am working in Bangalore as a customer adviser for a UK company. There are many companies coming over here nowadays, and it's not just because they can achieve lower overheads. There are a

lot of advantages for the companies – they have 24/7 productivity, and with the extra staff, they can be much more flexible and responsive, and they can get through a higher volume of work. Personally, there are a lot of benefits for me. It's a dream job and it has certainly improved my quality of life. In the past, it was really difficult to get a well-paid job here in southern India, especially for a woman. It's not a rich part of the world. But the pay I get now is absolutely fantastic. Call centres are a growth industry in India – and working for a western company is a high-status job for Indian people. So if you perform well, you stand to make a lot of money, about the same as a junior doctor.

31

Part 1

Director Thank you all for coming this morning. As you know, we are looking into the possibility of outsourcing our IT department overseas. This is being done in order to cut costs and improve efficiency. I'd like to introduce you to Sanjit Kundu, from Business Initiatives Bangalore, who is here to tell us about Bangalore as a possible location for outsourcing. Sanjit …

Sanjit Good morning, and thank you for inviting me to your headquarters. Today, I'd like to give you an overview of the business potential and possibilities of Bangalore as a location for outsourcing. As you probably know, Bangalore is situated in central southern India – it's the capital of the state of Karnataka.

So, to begin with, let's look at some general facts about the area. What does Bangalore have to offer in business terms? Well, statistics show that 10,000 companies are based in the region, and a population of nearly seven million people ensures that there is a buoyant labour market. How well qualified is the workforce? Recent data illustrates the fact that Bangalore's educational institutions have been awarded international recognition as a result of the quality of graduates being produced – from the Indian Institute of Science, for example. In fact, due to the dominance of a highly-educated workforce, Bangalore is becoming the fastest growing city in Asia and has earned the nickname 'India's Silicon Valley' …

32

Part 2

Sanjit … I've briefly looked at the background, so let's move on to some business facts. You will notice on this chart the breakdown of traditional industries, such as engineering, in relation to the emergence of IT companies. Bangalore has a strong tradition of attracting engineering companies to the region as a result of its engineering colleges. A knock-on effect of this has been the establishment not only of government-run companies such as Hindustan Machine Tools, but also companies from the private sector. A subsidiary of the German Robert Bosch group has been present in this region for several years. What's more important and exciting for our potential investors is the new emerging economy focusing on IT. As I mentioned earlier, this has earned us the name 'India's Silicon Valley' and it is easy to see why. IT is booming.

Let's turn our attention to some specific facts on the IT sector. Looking at this slide, we can see it is expected that Indian IT services will continue to grow by 25–28% annually, and Bangalore accounts for about one-third of India's software exports. And have a look at these figures: more than 1,500 software and outsourcing companies – 512 of them multinationals – have offices in Bangalore, employing over 170,000 workers. In the first four months of this year alone, 64 new offices were opened in the city. Subsequently, nearly 1,000 new staff are being taken on every month. The job market is being fuelled by the tens of thousands of students in the area, many of them graduating from the Institute of Science, which I referred to earlier – and many of them specializing in IT-related subjects. A further point to mention is that a new sector of the job market is being opened up, offering opportunities for women employees – 25% of the workforce in software companies here is now female. The effect of this is more financial independence and greater freedom for them to pursue a career …

… Before I go today, I'd like to leave you with some … er … some food for thought. Investment in Bangalore has resulted in dramatic, positive lifestyle changes for its people. Their futures are being secured and their quality of life has been improved threefold. By investing in our region, you will not only have the advantage of obtaining highly-skilled employees with a strong work ethic, but you will also ensure that our skilled workforce remains within India. Surely a win-win situation for us all.

33

1

A Sorry I'm late, I got held up in traffic.
B It doesn't matter. We've only just started.

2

A I do apologize for the mix-up with your order – our ordering system crashed.
B That's all right. I understand the problem.

3

A I'm afraid I haven't prepared for this meeting – I've been really busy today.
B Don't worry about it. It's the same for me.

4

A We've finished all the coffee. Sorry about that.
B That's OK – I'll have some water. Don't worry about it.

5

A I'm really sorry about the mistake. I don't know how it happened, but it's my responsibility.
B Never mind. These things happen.

6

A I'm sorry that I wasn't here when you called earlier.
B No problem. I spoke to your colleague, Anna – she was able to help me.

Unit 9

34

1

Tyler I left high school at 16 … with no qualifications … so my career prospects were not good … but I got a job at the local automobile factory, working shifts on a production line. Work was kind of monotonous – but I had job security and the money was good. I'd worked there for almost thirty years when I was **made redundant** … the company got taken over, and just like that they decided to downsize and shut the factory down. You can imagine … in a small town like ours, when you get that many men **laid off** all at once because there's no work for them, there's no chance of finding another job. I'd lived there all my life so **relocation** to a new place was not an option. I had some redundancy money, and I went for retraining, first on a short computer course to **update my skills** and increase my employability, then a two-year course in programming. And because of my background, I ended up as an IT consultant to manufacturing companies. So it was a complete career change, but I don't regret it. It was a whole lot better than **being unemployed**, and having no job to go to, or just **taking early retirement**.

2

Fabia I worked for a multinational insurance company in Lausanne for six or seven years. The salary was good but there wasn't a lot of **opportunity for advancement** … I was beginning to feel dissatisfied. And I … I didn't feel particularly valued by the management … I felt expendable … like a commodity really … I was working really long hours for little recognition. I could have made **a sideways move**, I suppose, but I decided to opt for self-employment. We moved to Geneva, where I set up my own recruitment agency – finding staff for insurance

companies. I've come to understand why people really want to change jobs – and it's hardly ever about money. Usually it's for personal reasons, like my own experience. A lot of my clients have some sort of issue with their boss – see them as incompetent, maybe. Sometimes we have very successful women who feel there's **a glass ceiling** where they work, and know they can only get on if they move elsewhere. For others, it's all about growth opportunities – they're looking for **training** and **personal development** but it's just not on offer in their company.

3

Karl I worked for Ericsson in Sweden until a couple of years ago – I was production manager – and I was a bit restless … I had a good standard of living, my youngest child had just gone to university, and I suppose I was looking for a new challenge … **a change of direction**. And to be honest, I didn't feel particularly comfortable with the **corporate culture** any more … and I was getting frustrated by too many **rules and red tape**. I was considering applying for a **temporary secondment** to a production plant in the UK, when I came across a charity who were looking for an administrator to work in a specialist hospital in Addis Ababa in Ethiopia, and I suddenly realized that what I was looking for was a complete career change. So I discussed it with the family … I got the job and I've been here ever since … I actually found that a lot of the skills I had were **transferable skills** – like leadership and planning. I don't regret it at all. Of course there are a few things I miss, and my salary is much lower … but personally I feel much happier, it's very challenging here, but my quality of life is much better.

35

Johanna Right, Dermot, this is quite a challenge! What we need to decide on today is how to put together this new team.

Dermot Yeah – it's not going to be easy. The areas we need to discuss are: the make-up of the new team, who would be most suitable for it, and how our current teams can manage without them.

Johanna OK. So, let's look at what our options are. What I propose is we simply identify who our most capable workers are and send them.

Dermot Yeah … If we did that, we'd end up with two weaker teams back here doing all the work, and I'm not sure they'd cope.

Johanna It wouldn't be for very long, but maybe you're right. We can't send all our best people in case we need them here.

Dermot How about we look at our team members' individual strengths and then each select three people based on this?

Johanna You mean we build a team from the good workers who have other skills we need as well?

Dermot Exactly. They're going to be working together for six months so they've got to be team players.

Johanna Right. I can see we'd at least have a strong team if we did that. But I've got another idea. Supposing we stretch the budget a little, why don't we take on two contract workers and use just four internals? That'll solve the problem – if we only have four experienced staff in the new team, we won't lose our best workers.

Dermot No way! It just wouldn't work if we took on contract workers. We all know they get paid more, and that would be bad for team spirit. No. Let's try my idea of choosing our team from our existing staff – based on their strengths.

Johanna OK, I'm happy with that …

36

Dermot … So let's just summarize the situation. Taking on contract workers is a no-no. And if we chose our best workers and sent them, it would be damaging to our departments because the knowledge base would be gone. So, what we've decided to do is propose staff based on their personal strengths as well as their professional capabilities.

Johanna Exactly.

Dermot Now I've identified four possible candidates from your team who look ideal.

Johanna Wait a minute, four from my team? We can't do that. If I transferred four people, I'd only have three left! I could offer you three, but I'd expect three from your team too.

Dermot Well, yeah, I suppose that's only fair. If you guaranteed Brett, I'd let you have Jamie, Pascale and Timo from my team.

Johanna But both Jamie and Timo are straight out of school! You can't expect Brett to work with two trainees on something as important as this. He'd end up doing the work of three people.

Dermot But it'd be a great experience for them.

Johanna I don't care. It's not fair. I'll be happy for Brett to be on the team, provided you replace one of the trainees with someone experienced.

Dermot OK. I didn't think you'd agree. I'll send Sabrina instead of Timo. She's had international experience and she's good with people too.

Johanna Good. So who have we got so far? Brett, Sabrina, Jamie and Pascale. That just leaves two more from my team. How long do I have?

Dermot Unless we get this list to HR before Friday, we won't be sending anyone – it all needs discussing again with them before contracts are drawn up.

Johanna Right. Let's get this done now. I need to find two more people.

Dermot Provided one of them has got some experience, the other one could be a trainee.

Johanna Well, in that case, I'd like to send Lena and Marlon.

Dermot Great. I know them both – good choice!

Johanna So, a quick recap: if I send Brett, Lena and Marlon, you'll send Sabrina, Jamie and Pascale.

Dermot Yeah, I can live with that.

Johanna Great. That sounds like a plan!

37

1

A Do you have a minute? I'm doing a survey about the use of our Intranet.

B Yeah, sure … I never use it!

A Oh … thanks a lot.

2

A Could you just have a quick look at my computer? The screen's gone blank.

B Sorry, I'm a bit busy right now.

A Oh, well, never mind.

3

A Would you mind checking my English in this email before I send it?

B Sorry, I'm just on my way to a client's. I'll be back around three.

A OK, it's not that urgent.

4

A Excuse me, am I disturbing you? I need some help with the photocopier.

B Give me two minutes and I'll be right with you.

A Thanks.

5

A Excuse me, could you spare a few minutes?

B Certainly. Take a seat.

A Thanks. Er, I'm not sure about these figures and I was hoping you could tell me …

6

A Can you give me a hand with the holiday roster?

B Sorry, no time! Email it to me and I'll look at it later.

A OK.

38

Maria … A great deal of thought and investment goes into incentives and remuneration packages for sending employees to other countries to work. However, over the last few years, we've had to consider how to deal with returning employees and what their requirements will be.

Interviewer When does this occur? Can you give us an example?

Maria Sure. Well ... one particular company comes to mind, a large multinational, which had sent a group of highly-specialized IT experts from India to work in Scandinavia on a big expansion project. Obviously we were involved with the initial relocation and advising on the benefits package, but the real challenge came when the project was coming to an end.

Interviewer So what happened?

Maria Well, for the employees who were returning from their deployment, a sense of 'reverse' culture shock occurred. The employees had got used to a very different lifestyle – a Scandinavian standard of living and other luxuries as part of their relocation package. Adapting to life back in their own country became a problem. Even familiar things like poor road conditions or regular power failures suddenly made life very uncomfortable.

Interviewer I see. So ... what did this company do for their returning personnel?

Maria In this case, they drew up a compensation package and negotiated this with the employees. It's not an easy thing to do, I mean, relocation is a standard procedure but a repatriation package has to be made on a case-by-case basis. It depends where the employees have been working, what their lifestyle was like in that country ... how high their salary was.

Interviewer Can you give me some examples of what was offered?

Maria Well, this particular company offered its employees a returning salary that was significantly higher than the local going rate. It also offered help in financing the children's education in private or international schools, support for the employee's wife or husband to find work, and in some cases interest-free loans to buy a house, car and for other living expenses.

Interviewer That doesn't sound bad!

Maria No, but the company needed to hold on to these people so the package had to be attractive.

Interviewer I see.

Maria Other companies I've worked with have offered things such as free breakfast and dinner in the company restaurant, time in lieu or paid overtime – which sounds standard but it isn't often the case. Another thing would be a structured career path for the employee. This means their future is planned in terms of personal development and promotion possibilities, so their experience abroad isn't wasted.

Interviewer It all sounds rather expensive.

Maria It is, and companies really have to think carefully about the costs involved before sending their personnel abroad.

CD 2

Unit 10

39

James I run Glasses Direct. We sell glasses and contact lenses online, at a fraction of the price you pay if you go to a high street optician. I got the idea when I discovered the size of the markup on glasses. Did you know that a pair of glasses that costs, say, ten euros to make can sell for as much as 200 euros? So I researched the optical market – good market research is hugely important when you're starting out. I learnt about optometric testing, how the frames are made and the lenses are cut ... and it was clear that there was a gap in the market. I worked out a business plan for selling discounted glasses online ... it seemed like a viable idea that I could turn into a profitable business.

My father was incredibly generous ... he gave me a loan to get started, which meant I didn't have to raise finance by going to venture capitalists – they probably would have turned me down anyway because they don't generally take start-ups run by young people seriously ... and of course they want a big stake in the business and a high return on investment. The other people who were extremely helpful were some of my fellow students who designed and set up the website for me – I couldn't have done it without them.

The only real problem we had was getting the manufacturers to work with us – they didn't want to damage their relationship with the big retailers. It was really difficult to persuade them, but in the end we managed to get them on board.

My advice to anyone starting out would be, if you've got a sound business plan and you see a gap in the market, go for it.

Jurga I come from Lithuania, and I run Today Translations, one of the top translation companies in the UK. I set up the company six years ago ... We now have over 700 clients – and a fantastic team of linguists who interpret, translate and culturally adapt documents and websites in over 160 languages. They're totally brilliant at sharing their local market expertise with our clients. We hope to make one million euros this year, and my aim is to double turnover every year.

My background isn't actually in translation. When I was at school in Kaunas, I had my own shop and later I traded clothes in the United Arab Emirates, so I learned the importance of understanding local cultures and creating the right network of contacts. I moved to the UK to set up the translation business in 2001, and I suppose I'm completely different from most business-people because I don't like borrowing from banks or asking people like business angels for start-up capital, despite the business experience they can offer. I believe in natural business growth. The investment I made in the business was gradual, and for me that is an absolutely perfect arrangement. It was my own money – from the profit I had made and saved from previous ventures. There were a few drawbacks ... lack of financial backing meant I couldn't expand as fast as I would have liked, but sometimes you just have to be patient. The fact that I'm a foreigner is actually an advantage rather than a problem – a lot of my clients feel I'm more sensitive to their needs, and I have a really excellent relationship with all of them.

If I was going to give advice to someone starting out, I think I'd say you need to be prepared to take risks and be self-disciplined. But if you do your homework and have a clear and effective business model, you're halfway there.

40

1 ... good market research is hugely important when you're starting out.

2 My father was incredibly generous ... he gave me a loan to get started ...

3 The other people who were extremely helpful were some of my fellow students ...

4 It was really difficult to persuade them, but in the end we managed to get them on board.

5 ... and a fantastic team of linguists who interpret, translate and culturally adapt documents and websites in over 160 languages. They're totally brilliant ...

6 I suppose I'm completely different from most businesspeople because I don't like borrowing from banks ...

7 The investment I made in the business was gradual, and for me that is an absolutely perfect arrangement.

8 ... a lot of my clients feel I'm more sensitive to their needs, and I have a really excellent relationship with all of them.

41

Conversation 1

Erik ... Hello.

Nicole Is that Erik Lundberg?

Erik Yes, speaking.

Nicole Erik, this is Nicole Dupont from GBF Electronics – I'm not sure if you remember me.

Erik Nicole! Hello – of course I remember you. I haven't seen you for ages, though.

Nicole That's right – about three years, I think. Since you left GBF, life's been extremely hectic.

Erik So ... What have you been doing? How's work? It's good to hear from you.

Nicole Well, GBF have been keeping me very busy – I was promoted shortly after you left and for the last three months I've been commuting between France and Belgium.

Erik Congratulations – that sounds a bit tough, though.

Nicole Yes, it is and, er, that's actually the reason why I'm calling. The thing is, I'm looking for someone to work with us in our business in Belgium – someone local so I don't have to commute. Have you made any contacts in that region?

Erik Well, no names come immediately to mind, but I'll certainly think about it. Ah, just a minute. What about Natalie Hemery? She's lived in Brussels for years – I'm sure she'd be able to help …

Conversation 2

Xavier José? Hey, what are you doing here?

José Xavier! I don't believe it! Are you getting the flight to Lisbon, too?

Xavier Yeah, I've got a meeting there. What about you?

José I live there now – with my wife and kids.

Xavier I didn't know you were married! When was the last time we saw each other?

José I'm not sure … it must have been at that college reunion … but that was seven years ago.

Xavier Really? Yes, I suppose so … Anyway, what have you been up to? Are you still working in the car industry?

José Where should I start!? So much has happened. After the exchange programme at Birmingham University, I stayed another year and worked for Nissan, in their finance department. That job took me all over Europe and on one of my trips I met my wife, Isabella, in Lisbon. After that, I got a transfer and, well, I've never looked back since! What about you?

Xavier Nothing much has changed for me, but I've worked my way up in my present company. Things are going well, but I'm looking to … you know, branch out, maybe move on. Actually, I've been doing some freelance consulting recently, which is partly why I'm going to Lisbon.

José That sounds interesting …

Xavier Well, it's all about making contacts. Hey, by the way, could you do me a favour? Could you put me in touch with a reputable consultancy, since you live in Lisbon now? I'm looking to collaborate with an established firm.

José Let's chat about that over dinner. How long are you staying?

Conversation 3

Stanislav Good morning, Nadia. Thank you for finding the time to meet.

Nadia No problem. It's been a long time since we've been in contact, Stanislav. How's life treating you?

Stanislav Well, there have been a lot of changes in the company since we last met, but I'm fine. How's business with you?

Nadia Well, pretty good, actually. Our company has secured a huge contract with Mobelitec. We've also been talking to Strauz & Co. They've just gone public, so there should be money in that one. Anyway, you mentioned changes. What's been happening?

Stanislav Oh, things have been tough in the insurance field. We've been directing our attention to the online market recently … they've taken a serious number of our customers.

Nadia Oh, dear, I'm afraid that's the way things are going.

Stanislav Exactly. And with that in mind, maybe I could ask you for a favour. We are looking for a collaboration with some direct insurers – you have a lot of contacts and I wondered if …

Nadia Oh … I'm not sure.

Stanislav I'd really appreciate your help.

Nadia Well, it sounds an interesting proposal. Send me the details – here's my card – and I'll see who I know in the field. I can't promise anything, though!

Stanislav No, I understand that, but thank you anyway.

42

Miho Some people say I'm lucky and that I managed to hit the market with my product at a time when Tokyo was having a 'bagel boom'. But I think it was more than just luck.

Interviewer So how did you go from being a computer programmer at Hitachi to Japan's first bagel baker!

Miho OK, well I was visiting New York with some friends from college, back in 1998. We went on a trip after we finished our studies. I loved the city, but best of all I got a taste for bagels. The first one I ate … it had such an unexpected taste – I expected something like bread, but they are actually quite hard and crunchy … yeah, surprising. Anyway, at that moment, I thought there must be a market for these back home in Japan.

Interviewer How did you learn to bake them?

Miho OK … one year later, I went back to New York and I simply asked – in very bad English – could I work at the bagel shop where I ate my first bagel. Mrs Wilpon, the owner, she didn't really need anyone but she said I could spend a week with her, sweeping the floor, you know … and just seeing how the business worked. And it was good experience. Then in 2001 I went back again, I shared an apartment with some other Japanese girls and I worked for six months with Mrs Wilpon. She helped me a lot. On the one hand, I didn't get paid for the work I did … she didn't need another employee … but on the other hand I learned so much from her, how to make the bagels and the toppings. This experience was so important.

Interviewer So then you went back to Tokyo and opened your own shop?

Miho Er …, not quite. I'd been working in New York for free, so I didn't have any money when I came home. I persuaded a contact of mine to let me help him out working on an IT database project … so I could earn some money. But the reason I was able to start up my own company was I got some help from my parents.

Interviewer They lent you some money?

Miho Yes. To begin with, they weren't very sure about my plan, not really convinced … but I was so enthusiastic about it and so sure it would work … We drew up a proper contract – so I pay them back the money over time – but that was the financial support I needed to get started.

Interviewer And how's the business now?

Miho Oh, it's very good. I have some very loyal customers … and the recent publicity has been great for my business. Some mornings I arrive at work and already there's a line of customers …

Interviewer There are people outside?

Miho Yes … waiting for me to open!

Unit 11

43

Speaker 1 I think what we'll see is that communications systems will become more integrated … For example, I was involved in the development of the software for Operation Lazarus – the first telesurgery back in 2005. An American doctor in New York actually carried out an operation on a patient in France using remote cameras and a robot surgeon … Well that shows what can be done when communication is integrated with other systems. Now, as long as you can connect to the Internet, the potential of these integrated systems is almost limitless; whatever you do and wherever you are, you'll be able to collaborate with colleagues anywhere in the world … I mean the implications for, er, health, education, training, business, manufacturing, … are enormous.

Speaker 2 … What you're saying is very interesting, and to some extent I agree, but the way I see it, there are three stages to the development of communication … the first is when people use machines to communicate with people, OK – so we're talking about telephone, email, chat rooms – and we've reached that stage now. The second is when people interact with machines – digital TV, using the Internet as an information resource, playing games, voice recognition … where the machine responds to the person. We're just in the early stages of that, there's a long way to go, OK. But the last stage is when

machines start talking to machines – we saw it first in the Wall Street crash in '87 when program trading caused complete chaos – computers were cutting prices, selling stock to other computers, and people didn't know how to stop it. It's a scary scenario because it takes us into a whole new area of experience … and when that comes it's going to have a big impact on all of us.

Speaker 3 … Yeah, I think maybe we're getting ahead of ourselves here … this kind of speculation's all very interesting, but communication systems are no good if people can't use them. Now … at the moment … everyone you know may well have access to the Internet, subscribe to satellite TV and use a mobile phone, but that's just not the case for most people in the world. We need to focus on spreading around the basic technology we have now more fairly. As it is, more than half the population of the world has never even made a telephone call. Think about it – how good is a communication system if half the world is excluded from it?

44

Jimmy … So this tool and service is offered to large-sized companies only. Are you with me?
Angelika OK … Yes, I've got that.
Jimmy Mirela?
Mirela OK. I'm with you.
Jimmy Good. When you acquire your key account customer you must set up regular meetings. It's a good idea to plan these for once a quarter, every three months.
Angelika This is Angelika. What exactly do you mean by meetings? Do we still need to meet them face to face?
Jimmy Yes. We regularly bring out offers for key accounts. For example, at the moment, we're offering a special price for three job postings, one-month resumé access and logos on job ads … so there's always something new to discuss.
Mirela Jimmy, you're very faint. Oh, this is Mirela by the way.
Jimmy Hang on … Is that better?
Mirela Yes, it's fine again now.
Jimmy Can we speed up a little and discuss first meetings with the key accounts? There's another conference call booked for this room in ten minutes, so we can't run over.
All Yeah, no problem. / Fine. No problem.
Jimmy In your initial meeting, you need to make sure they've seen the demo for posting ads. What's useful is to send it to them on a CD a few days before the meeting.
Angelika So you're saying we don't have to go through the demo in the meeting?
Jimmy Normally not … no. A few years ago, we always had to train them on the software, but now it's much more user-friendly and people are more familiar with form-filling and making payments online.
Mirela This is Mirela again. What do we do about price?
Jimmy OK. What happens is … an offer is made according to the approximate number of postings the client will make in a month. Is that clear?
Mirela Yeah, that's clear. We've already started putting offers together but I just wanted to check … And how is all this packaged?
Angelika Hello? … I can't hear Mirela!
Mirela … Is that better?
Angelika Yes, you're back again now.
Jimmy Well, to answer Mirela's question … Basically, it's essential to tell them about our advantages over newspaper ads, the resumé and candidate filtering tool, the fact that responses received to ads can either be accessed online or directly sent to their email address – that's to name just a few.
Angelika Jimmy, could you slow down a bit? We're having problems following you.
Jimmy No problem. I'll email you our key account marketing information. You should read this through thoroughly and contact me if anything's still unclear.
Mirela OK. There's one last thing I wanted to ask …

45

1

A … So as I was saying, any chance of getting it to me by tomorrow?
B I'm afraid I didn't catch that last bit.
A I said, any chance of getting it to me by tomorrow?
B Sorry Veronica, this is hopeless. It's a really bad line.
A OK. I'll hang up and call you on the landline in five minutes.

2

A … So can we discuss the transport arrangements for the Japanese visitors?
B Sorry, but this'll have to be quick, Renée, I'm about to board a plane!
A So now's not a good time to call?
B Not really, no. I'll be there in two hours. Can you call me again then?
A Sure, no problem.

3

A Beatriz? Is that you?
B Yes, how did you …?
A I recognized your number on the display. Look, I'm sorry, but I have someone on the other line. Can I call you back?
B Yes, I'm around for another hour, then I have a meeting.
A OK, speak to you in a few minutes then.

46

Visitor … So, Robert, what measures have been taken to improve your communication procedure with your clients, now that you've expanded and introduced shift work?
Robert Well, one long-term measure has been to invest in some help-desk software. But until that arrives we're working with quite a new, but … er … basic idea.
Visitor Can you tell me something about that?
Robert OK. Each day we have a 'man of the day'. This is always one person from the early shift and one from the late shift, one on each, yeah? These two employees check the emails and prioritize them. They also handle all the phone calls from the clients.
Visitor So how do they prioritize them?
Robert Well, at the moment, the emails are simply prioritized by being flagged. This does have its disadvantages, though. When more employees have access to the inbox, some emails get filed away and overlooked! Then we're in trouble …
Visitor Oh … yes, I see your point.
Robert … Right. So our 'man of the day' has to prioritize the emails by content. If an email is connected to our auto warning system – that's a system that monitors our interfaces and feeds our clients with critical information – erm, that email has to be dealt with immediately. Then the employee checks and works on emails that the client has flagged as high priority … and finally … emails which are so-called 'show-stoppers' are highlighted.
Visitor Show-stoppers?
Robert Yeah, those problems that are going to affect our client's daily work and could cause delays, which obviously costs a great deal of money in the airline industry.
Visitor And how do you know what's been worked on and what's still outstanding?
Robert At the moment I speak directly to the 'man of the day'.
Visitor I see. What sort of difference will this new help-desk software make?
Robert Well, it should make a tremendous difference. It will assign a so-called 'trouble ticket' to each task or open item. As the item is being worked on, the status is updated and we can track what's being worked on, how it's being worked on, and what's already been done to it. So, for example, if a similar problem occurs, we can look back to see how we solved it last time.
Visitor It sounds as if this software will be very helpful for you.
Robert That's right. Not only for us, but in time it should be possible for our clients to receive the trouble tickets too, so they can follow the progress of the problem and not constantly have to call us to see how we're doing …

Unit 12

47

1

I'm in charge of a sales team based in Lille. Most of them are French speakers, of course ... you might think I'd prefer it if everyone spoke in English, but in fact I've been anti the whole idea ever since they brought the policy in. I told them why we were worried about it, but they don't listen, they refused to modify the policy in any way ... and now that it's been implemented, we've got real problems ... just as I predicted. They know I've always been hostile to this policy ... and I'm very critical, I admit it ... but one of the reasons is that I'm genuinely concerned about misunderstandings ... and I told my manager that my team weren't sure about trying out their language skills and doing everything in English, but she was all for it ... so what can you do? But things do go wrong ... last week we had to order up 15,000 new catalogues from the Paris office, one of my salespeople phoned them and we ended up with 50,000 – a complete waste of time and money. OK, in that example, it wasn't the end of the world, but it shows the kind of thing that can happen. I say, if two people speak French, let them speak French, otherwise, you know ...

2

When they introduced the language programme a couple of years ago, I think most people were quite positive about learning English though I personally had a few concerns. Anyway, they put on lots of courses for people who needed to develop their English, but in my department – technical support – we ran into a few problems, especially just after it was introduced. Most of my team are not really natural language learners ... basically they are techies, and they weren't very keen on having to speak English all the time. They were very resistant to the idea of using English in meetings and especially on the phone. But in fact, it's OK. They found it pretty hard to start with – some of them were quite anxious about it, especially the older ones – but now they've been speaking English for a while, it's getting easier, and they've actually improved quite a lot. We can now deal with support calls from Spain, Italy and Finland, too, and I'm optimistic that we'll be able to take on more work in the near future.

3

Well, as head of the training department, I was asked to carry out a review of language use in the company, and when it was completed, we came up with the idea of a single language policy. There was a real problem ... we had three different company languages ... in meetings, you would get a mix of languages, or the majority language would dominate, and all the documentation had to be translated, so we had an army of translators and interpreters, and there was just so much paperwork, so much waste. So that was basically why we were in favour of the new policy. At the start, people were naturally apprehensive and a few people were against it – but it was nothing serious. I think most of the staff appreciated it was the right thing to do and they were very receptive to the whole idea. Now ... I think it's all working out very well. Very few people have dropped out of the courses. We've already achieved a lot, and our different offices are communicating much better as far as I can tell ... Ask me again in a year.

48

Rachel ... OK. I've spoken about our consultants' findings and we're well aware of your concerns regarding how the changes will affect our staff. As you all know, it is likely there will be some job losses but we'd like to assure you that we will keep these to an absolute minimum and try to reduce headcount through natural wastage. Decisions will definitely have been made by March as to how big the cutbacks will be. Many of you have asked about a rumoured pay freeze ... We aren't counting this out, but this is something we'd like to avoid. Over the next few weeks, we'll be hosting departmental meetings to give more specific information ... and we plan to keep you informed about any other changes so you can answer your staff's queries with well-informed answers. Starting from next month, we'll be putting regular updates on our Intranet regarding potential changes ... but more about that later.
I'd like to pass the next point over to Imran, who has been working closely with the consultants on the subject of bottom-up management.

Imran Thanks, Rachel. Yes, bottom-up management has proven to be very successful in a number of companies and we've been working on a similar concept to implement here at FGR. Hopefully, the new model will be in place by the end of the month. Bottom-up management is quite a simple idea ...

... Normally when change takes place, this is decided and implemented by senior management. However, to make the changes work we need the enthusiasm, motivation and energy from everyone who will be affected by those changes.
Let's digress for a moment and look at this in more detail. Our idea is to give everyone the opportunity to propose changes which will benefit themselves and the company. We're proposing a Friday afternoon ideas forum where employees can put forward their suggestions for change. Each department nominates someone to present the most popular ideas to senior management, along with a business plan or some sort of proof that benefits can be gained. The first forum will be on Friday the 24th at 3.30. I'll be visiting our suppliers in Bradford on that day, so Rachel will be here to lead the session.
You may be wondering if this will work – Friday afternoons are free for most of our employees. We're convinced the opportunities outweigh the disadvantages of staying at work longer. We must see this as a step towards becoming a more effective company. It's crucial to get the employees on our side ... and we need to emphasize that there will be money available for remuneration ... which could be paid if we see real results after the changes are implemented. This last point is probably going to be difficult to administer at the beginning but the consultants had an example of remuneration scales for us to consider.
I'm sure some of you are sceptical of the consultants' proposals, but we're calling on you to be positive – pass this information on and create enthusiasm ... sell the idea of empowerment to our staff and highlight the rewards this could bring us all. Later this year we'll be reassessed to see how effective the changes are ...

49

1

A What do you think about changing the team meeting to Friday afternoons?
B I have some reservations about it. People on flexitime often choose to leave early on Fridays. And concentration probably won't be as good at the end of the week.

2

A If you ask me, this is just a way of getting rid of staff.
B I can see both sides of the argument. Management want to streamline the company's operation but employees are naturally worried about possible job cuts.

3

A I can't believe they're going to make us all learn Spanish.
B It sounds interesting – I like the idea of having a common language for the company – but people who aren't confident in their language skills might find it difficult.

4

A Do you think this latest proposal is a good thing?
B Mm. I'm not sure about it. Is management confident that extending our office hours will actually improve the service?

5

A How do you feel about relocating to Vienna?

B I need to think about it. It's a very important decision to make.

50

1

A Your project is finishing at the end of this week, isn't it?

B In theory, yes, but I might have to spend a bit more time on it – there are bound to be a few loose ends to tie up, there always are. But there probably won't be that much to do, so there's a good chance I'll be free in ten days or so.

2

Newsreader The problems for the government are getting worse, and it is doubtful whether it will be able to hold on to power for much longer. There is certain to be more bad news in the coming week – the latest inflation figures, due out on Tuesday, are likely to show an economic situation that is steadily getting worse.

3

A Cristina, I'm still in Ecuador. I'm just calling to say I definitely won't be able to speak at the conference on Friday.

B Things are still bad, are they?

A Yes, and it'll probably take a few more days at least to sort everything out. Perhaps I'll be able to get back next week sometime, I don't really know.

B OK. Then I'll get Bill to stand in for you – obviously I need someone who will definitely be there. Is that OK with you?

A Yes, that's fine.

Unit 13

51

Interviewer So what difference will the Internet have on the way people buy music?

Producer Well, like everywhere else, downloads of singles are growing rapidly in Ireland. They accounted for about 45% of singles sold last year – and that was from legal sites like iTunes. The real figure for downloads is probably a lot higher when you think of filesharing, P2P and so on. So, it is a problem for the music stores, but they aren't too worried. Sales of singles in-store have dropped slightly, but album sales haven't crashed like they have in the UK … And overall, turnover has stayed more or less the same.

Interviewer So why is that … if music sales in the rest of Europe have fallen substantially, why hasn't there been a significant drop here?

Producer I think it's the way we think of our music … and we think in terms of albums, not singles. It could all change, of course, but for the moment, it's albums that people want. The number of people with broadband is growing gradually, but there are still lots of places where broadband isn't available, so it's a lot quicker just to drive to the local music store.

Interviewer As a music producer, do you see the Internet as a threat?

Producer Yes and no. P2P and filesharing will always be a problem for the big music retailers … But I think the Internet is a fantastic tool … not just for letting people hear your music … think of artists like Gnarls Barkley and Arctic Monkeys. If you want to make a single yourself and get yourself heard, broadband and digital technology make it a lot easier. And it means that the number of artists has risen substantially – people are listening to different sounds and that can only be a good thing.

52

Renata … Could you fill us in on the most relevant information from the seminar?

Caroline Sure. It was extremely informative and, basically, it gave us an overview of figures regarding advertising via blogs and podcasts.

Yari Interesting … What did you find out?

Caroline Well, in general, traditional forms of advertising to our 18–30s market are becoming less effective. They're saying that the way ahead, is to advertise where our target audience are 'hanging out' – which is on blogs and podcasts.

Renata OK … So what are the facts and figures?

Caroline Apparently, a recent study shows a huge increase in advertising investment via this media just in the last year. In fact, spending went up to $20.4 million.

Yari What's that in terms of growth?

Caroline It's 198.4% … in one year. Which is pretty incredible.

Renata That sounds very promising …

Caroline Yes. One of the presenters, Simon Darby, said companies were investing fast and that we should take this opportunity before our competitors do.

Yari OK. How do these figures compare within the different user-generated media?

Renata 'User-generated media' … meaning …?

Yari Oh, I mean things like blogs, podcasts, RSS feeds …

Renata Ah, OK … thanks.

Caroline Yes. Simon claimed that last year blog advertising accounted for … 81.4% of collective spending on user-generated media, but, roughly speaking, by 2010 it'll only be 39.7%.

Renata So how should we interpret this drop?

Caroline Well, supposedly, podcast advertising will be the front runner over the next four years, overtaking spending on blog ads.

Yari Can we look at the figures?

Caroline Yes, I have them here on this graph. According to a recent survey, total projected expenditure on blog advertising will reach $300.4 million in four years, whereas expenditure on podcast advertising will have grown at an annual compound rate of 154.4% to $327 million.

Renata So the bottom line is that user-generated media will be our new advertising platform, whether we like it or not.

Caroline That's right. Simon assured us that this form of advertising more or less guarantees we reach our target audience.

Yari Can you give us the low-down on the types of companies advertising through this media?

Caroline Sure. The overriding trend is for technology, car and media brands to use this form of advertising. I've got examples of some of these companies here …

53

1

A Have you heard the news?

B No … What?

A Apparently, Gabriel is leaving the company and moving to France.

B Surely not!

A Anna says that he bought a house and vineyard when he was on holiday there last month.

B Are you sure?

A Well, rumour has it he's planning to produce wine and he's been doing a wine-making course after work!

2

A You'll never guess what I heard?

B No … What?

A Well … You know that Dimitri went away on business last week and took one of the company's laptops with him?

B Yeah, but that's standard procedure.

A I know, but according to Sam, when Dimitri arrived back in Athens he was in such a hurry to get home, he forgot the laptop and left it in baggage reclaim at the airport!

B Oh, I don't believe it! Did he get it back?

A Not yet, no!

3

A Did you hear the latest about Sandra and Leroy?

B I heard they'd had some sort of argument.

A Yeah, a big one … Apparently, they were both named salesperson of the month and Leroy refused to share the prize.

B No! That's really childish.

A Well, I spoke to Robert and he told me that Leroy thinks he's better than everyone else since he got that award …

B That's nonsense!

A I know … but it's created bad feeling in the whole team!

B I'm not surprised.

54

1

John … but it wasn't really as good as we had expected. Anyway, Peter, what happened to you last week?

Peter Oh, sorry. Didn't Lisa explain?

John Explain what? I haven't seen her.

Peter Oh. Well, I'm sorry I missed the meeting – I did want to be there – but I was delayed at the airport … there was nothing I could do.

Anna Was that on Thursday? When there was a bomb scare?

Peter Yes … it was hopeless … the whole place was at a standstill … I didn't get home till after midnight.

Anna I saw it on TV – it looked chaotic.

Peter Yeah, it was …

2

John OK … Peter, have you got the October figures?

Peter Yes, … Starting with Europe … It looks good … overall monthly revenue has risen by 11% to 218,000.

Anna That's not bad.

Peter Well, October's often a good month …

John Is South America doing any better?

Peter A little, but sales are still down by 3% … The Venezuelan issue is still ongoing – supply chain problems are continuing, but we're working on it.

John OK – so a mixed picture … what about …

3

Anna … Peter, you haven't mentioned the US figures. Is there any reason for that? After all, it is the biggest market.

Peter Yes, you're quite right. There's a slight problem with the US figures – they aren't available yet … um … well, they haven't been finished.

John Mmm – that's not the first time.

Peter No … I have spoken to Paul about this … Anyway, I'll definitely circulate them as soon as they become available … that'll be tomorrow, or the day after at the latest …

4

John … Yeah, and I'm just wondering if there's anything else you'd like to bring up.

Anna Yes, there is actually. I need to know if there's any news on that fibre-optic order.

John The one you mentioned last week?

Anna Yes.

John Peter, any info on that? … I appreciate you weren't here last week.

Peter Yes … Marian mentioned it earlier … The order has been sent … It will come.

Anna I do need to know when it's coming because my team is having real problems – we've got customers calling all the time, complaining about the delay.

Peter OK. OK … As I said … the order has been sent. I've checked and it'll arrive either tomorrow or the day after.

Anna Fine … I hope you're right. Could you let me know as soon as it gets in …?

Unit 14

55

1

If you're working, or doing business, outside your home country, understanding the local culture is essential. You need to be informed about the culture you're working in and be prepared to be tolerant of different customs. And, you know, you can make some very expensive mistakes if you get it wrong.

I'll give you an example. My boss, Tony, … he used to sell mainframe computers, and a few years ago he was working in the Middle East. One of the big electricity companies said it was interested in buying a new system. Now Tony had been there a few years, he was familiar with the country and how things worked … so over a period of two or three months, he had a lot of meetings, making contacts, getting to know the right people … And then a competitor from the US came over – with a better product, and at a better price. Obviously he was used to doing things the American way – so he gave a few presentations, had a few quick meetings – and then he flew back to the States thinking he had a deal. But he didn't. In the end, it was Tony who got the contract, because even though his product wasn't as good, he understood the way business was done. The other guy was very, very good at his job back in the States, in a different context … but in this case, he was actually responsible for losing a multi-million-dollar deal because he'd completely failed to adapt to the culture, to a different way of doing things.

2

We run a training centre for employees of multinational companies who are going to be sent abroad for work … for sometimes up to three years … And they come from many different companies and industries – telecoms, engineering, computers, banking and so on.

Our aim is to help people be more aware of the culture they are going to. This involves all kinds of things. First of all, we give them a basic understanding of the country they are going to – its political system, the social structure, basic cultural norms. We talk about any issues that people are sensitive about – it's surprising how many countries have taboo subjects, often political, that you just don't talk about.

In the second part of the course, we look at the most significant cultural differences between the person's home country and the host country, and we focus particularly on aspects of the work culture – how meetings are conducted, how agreements are made, attitudes to time, the hierarchy in the workplace and how respectful of authority and seniority employees are, how important personal relationships are – all things which will help them adjust to working in the local culture.

And at the end – when they finally arrive at their destination – they will be far more sensitive to important local issues … And their colleagues and the people they meet through work will have much more respect for them.

56

1

Dieter There was one situation I remember while I was living in Korea. You know I went out there to help with an engineering project?

Tonya Yeah …

Dieter Well, I was responsible for a team of telecom engineers, great guys. We all got along very well and I was welcomed into the company as if I'd lived over there for years. As time went by, I noticed that things weren't being done that I'd requested them to do.

Tonya Oh?

Dieter Yes. If I asked someone to do something and they said 'yes', nine out of ten times it wasn't done. That was when I was aware we had a problem.

Tonya Go on …

Dieter At first I thought it might be a language problem.

Tonya Well, that's understandable.

Dieter Yeah. But it was actually nothing to do with language. And it wasn't until I talked to a Korean friend that I realized what was wrong.

Tonya What had you done?

Dieter Nothing. I told my friend what had happened and he explained that there were two problems … First, my team didn't want to refuse my request due to respect for my seniority … But also, they didn't want to give an argument why they couldn't do what I wanted. So their answer was 'yes'.

Tonya I see. So, you mean, they didn't want to admit they couldn't do what you'd asked them to do … or to show negativity towards you by saying 'no'?

Dieter Exactly. Luckily, I found this out before I confronted anyone about the jobs that hadn't been done.

Tonya And did you resolve it?

Dieter Yes. After that I was a lot more careful what I asked my team to do and how I phrased the request.

2

Gaby ... I was responsible for finalizing the new office building in Warsaw along with my manager in the Netherlands. While I was liaising with both the Polish employees and my manager I discovered our two cultures had quite different approaches.
Nico Go on ...
Gaby Well, for example, when we were finalizing the plans for the office space. My manager wanted glass partitions but the Polish employees hated the idea.
Nico Oh?
Gaby Yeah ... but then I realized they hadn't actually told him this – they told me and hoped I'd tell him on their behalf!
Nico So what did you do?
Gaby I told him! It seems that none of them wanted to question an authority figure. So that was the first problem solved.
Nico There were more?
Gaby Oh yes. Another situation occurred when I was mentoring a recent IT graduate, Magda. While we were developing a new database, I gave her the job of asking staff for their views on the database ... I even put together a few sample questions.
Nico What happened?
Gaby Well, she came back with very little information. I was extremely disappointed ... What's more, the information she had only related to the questions I'd written. She hadn't written any questions of her own to get useful information for us. I didn't know what to do. All in all it was a difficult situation.
Nico So what did you do?
Gaby Well, in the end I asked Anna, a Polish colleague.
Nico What was her view?
Gaby Well, despite Magda's qualifications, she was still the most junior person in the department, so apparently more senior people would be unwilling to answer her questions.
Nico Oh, a hierarchy thing?
Gaby Yes. It came about because of the lack of information about why we were questioning them. It seems that Magda also wasn't comfortable with the task, so she didn't add to the questions I suggested.
Nico So how did you solve the problem?
Gaby Well, I sent out a memo explaining what Magda would be doing and why. I also noted Magda's qualifications and wrote the memo in English. The reason being that Magda needed to be respected by her colleagues and English gave the note neutrality.
Nico And ...?
Gaby It really surprised me, but it worked.

57

1

A Have you read any good books recently?
B Well, I don't get much time to read, but I've just finished a novel called *Shadow of the Wind.*
C I read that – I really enjoyed it.
A What's it about?
B It's about a boy's quest to find the truth about an author who's mysteriously disappeared. It's set in Barcelona just after the Second World War. It's very atmospheric – I'd definitely recommend it.
C Absolutely. It's very well written and it's a real page-turner too. I took it on holiday with me and I couldn't put it down!

2

A ... and I must admit I'm completely hooked on it. I've watched this soap opera since it began ten years ago and I can't miss an episode!
B Sounds like you're addicted. I don't really have a favourite programme. But sometimes I just like to unwind in front of the TV, you know, after a bad day at work. The problem is I tend to channel-hop ... there are so many channels available.
C I don't have much time to watch TV. So much of it is just so bad. The live sport is good though.
A Yes ... When the World Cup was broadcast I recorded every match so I didn't miss any!
B Me too! What I really can't stand is all this reality TV. You know, like *Big Brother.*
A Oh ... I quite like that.

3

A ... It sounds great ... I mean, listen to this review ... 'A blockbuster of a movie which became a box office hit overnight. It's full of brilliant special effects with a star-studded cast and a gripping storyline that will have you on the edge of your seat from the beginning!'
B Well, I've seen it and it was really good. The whole thing is set in the future and it's about a group of historians who look back to the twenty-first century and analyse what we're doing and how we're behaving now.
C And were you 'on the edge of your seat'?
B I was, actually, yeah. I mean, OK, it's basically a science-fiction film, but it's very well done. It's very entertaining – there's quite a lot of humour in it. I don't want to spoil it for you, but there's a really surprising twist at the end – you must go and see it.

Unit 15

58

Interviewer Is it right that you've **moved on** from top-down staff appraisals to what you call 360° degree appraisals?
Manager No, we still have the more traditional top-down appraisals, but we're introducing 360° appraisals as well because they have different functions ...
Interviewer In what way?
Manager You have to think of 360° as a development tool basically ... a trigger for change ... rather than a way of deciding if anyone deserves a raise.
Interviewer So how does it work?
Manager Well, in 360°, instead of just your boss appraising you, you have several different people giving feedback ... So ... we **hand out** a feedback form to everyone you come into contact with – your manager, your colleagues, people on your team, your customers, contractors, suppliers – obviously it depends on the type of job and the organization, but we try to involve as many different people as possible ... and with this kind of peer rating, you **end up with** a more complete picture of how someone is doing in their job.
Interviewer And what do you ask them?
Manager We use a feedback form, with a scoring or value judgement system, asking them to comment on various different assessment criteria – job skills, abilities, attitudes, behaviour. Then you assess yourself using the same form to see how the two compare. ... There are two important considerations with 360° appraisal. First, it has to be completely confidential ... that way you get much more honest answers from people. And secondly, you need to make sure suitable counselling is available when you **go through** the feedback results.
Interviewer So, at the moment, you don't actually use it for appraising performance?
Manager No, it works better as a development tool. We use it as part of our overall performance management, a way of bringing about change, rather than assessing performance.
Interviewer Right. And does it really help change?
Manager Yes ... I had a new member on one of my teams recently ... I thought he was very communicative, very open, always said what he thought and I liked that. But when we did a 360° appraisal, the staff feedback was all negative, and he **came over** as domineering and forceful. As a result of this, he did change his behaviour ... and became more accepted by the team. And that's what I mean about it being different from top-down appraisals – in that example, a top-down appraisal from me would have told him to **carry on** speaking his mind ... but it was the 360° feedback that made us aware of the need for change.

59

Angelina ... I must say, we're very happy with your overall performance this year. What do you consider were your successes and failures?

Thomas Well … one success certainly was helping to produce the in-house magazine. I thought it was well produced with interesting content. I really enjoyed doing it, particularly interviewing colleagues from other countries for the staff profile column.

Angelina Yes, and I think you demonstrated great prioritizing skills, especially with the tight deadlines you had to meet.

Thomas How can I improve my chances of working more with international colleagues?

Angelina Well, you ought to sign up to one of our language courses. That'll put you in a better position for being selected when international projects come up. It's a pity we didn't think about this when you joined us. If you'd started a language course then, you'd be quite proficient now.

Thomas OK … Can I identify that as a personal goal for the coming year?

Angelina Of course.

Thomas Erm … What I didn't enjoy was when the magazine budget was cut … we had to lose a couple of staff on the editorial team and I ended up doing most of the work myself.

Angelina Hmm … You shouldn't have been expected to take on so much. I noticed your overtime hours were quite high at that time. Look, if this happens again, you need to let us know.

Thomas OK.

Angelina Are there any areas you feel you need to improve on?

Thomas Er, no … not really.

Angelina Hmm, all right. One area I'd like to mention is training. You turned down an office management course we offered you. Why was that?

Thomas I didn't think I really needed it. Besides, we were short-staffed. If Katy hadn't left, I probably would have done the course.

Angelina Mmm … You really should have done that course. I think it would have helped you deal with your workload better.

Thomas Yes … If I'd known that at the time, I might have done it.

Angelina I think you certainly need to focus on gaining some more qualifications. Let's put this course on your list of goals for the coming year, too. Now … were there any constraints that affected your performance?

Thomas Well, I mentioned that we're short-staffed and despite all this extra work, to be honest I've found it difficult to delegate. How should I do this?

Angelina You need to start by …

So that brings us on to the office environment and resources. You've managed to create a very positive atmosphere in the new office. The move went very smoothly thanks to your team's organization.

Thomas Thanks.

Angelina On a less positive note … You could have thought a bit more about the call centre rota. Feedback from that department has been poor.

Thomas I know. If we'd taken the old system to our new location, the rota would have been easier to organize … but no one likes the new scheduling program. What's the best way to solve this, do you think?

Angelina I'll need to look into it. Let's arrange a meeting to discuss it next week.

Thomas Thanks. We could do with some training on the new program – there are some functions we don't really understand.

Angelina I'll check the budget.

Thomas If there's enough money, I'd also like another software program. I've already spoken to IT about it.

Angelina OK. Put your request in an email and I'll consider it.

Thomas Thank you. Oh … and while we're talking about money, could we discuss …?

60

1

A Hello. Peter Li?
B Yes, that's right.
A Nice to meet you. I'm Jacqueline, Florence Talbot's PA.
B Ah, I think we've spoken on the phone.
A That's right. Please take a seat. Can I get you something to drink? Coffee or tea?
B A cup of tea would be nice.
A Certainly. Florence is just taking a phone call. She'll be out in a few minutes.

2

A Hello, Andrea … welcome to HGP Birgit. Let me take your coat.
B Thank you.
A You can leave your bag over there, if you like.
B Thanks.
A Did you have any trouble finding us?
B No, not at all, but the traffic was terrible.
A Yes, it's always like that on Fridays. I hope you managed to avoid the roadworks.
B Well, I went via the industrial zone …

3

A Hello. You must be our new technical adviser?
B Yes, that's right. Tom Schofield.
A Nice to meet you. Michel is in a meeting at the moment, but he'll be right with you.
B OK, no problem.
A So you've driven over from England today?
B Yes, I had quite a good journey. You have good roads in France.
A What was the weather like when you left? It's been raining all day here.
B Oh, it was much worse than this!
A Really?! … I can't imagine how it could possibly be …

Unit 16

61

Interviewer So you're quite happy with the idea of people in your organization taking a career break?

Employer Yes, although we prefer to use the term 'flexiwork', which is a better description.

Interviewer How did the idea come about? I mean, a lot of employers wouldn't like the idea of their staff disappearing for a year or so …

Employer We introduced flexiwork at a time when our industry was having a bit of a downturn … things were quiet … it meant we could cut the wage bill but also retain staff for when the situation improved again.

Interviewer So it was basically just a cost-cutting measure?

Employer No, it was more of an experiment … one that wouldn't be too expensive … and it's been very successful … in fact, it's now official company policy.

Interviewer Do you think this is something that other companies will take up?

Employer I'm not sure – I think we're lucky because we specialize in consultancy. A lot of our work is project-based, and our consultants do three months here, six months there … so it's quite easy for us to fit this kind of thing in.

Interviewer I think most people would see the advantages for the employee, but are there any other benefits for the company?

Employer Well, yes, apart from the cost savings that I mentioned before, it does a lot for our retention rate, so we don't get nearly so many resignations. If someone wants to broaden their horizons by having a long career break, they can have one, no problem. The other advantage is when we're recruiting, when we're looking for new talent. If we say we don't just allow career breaks, we actively encourage them – as part of your career development – that's very attractive to prospective employees.

Interviewer Presumably there are some people who go off for a few months and don't come back?

Employer For some people, yes, it acts as a catalyst for them to head off in a new direction … but for most people, it gives them a chance to recharge their batteries and they return with renewed enthusiasm. From the point of view of motivation, it's great, it's a win-win situation. And in terms of personal development, people come back having learned something new – maybe a new language – or they've developed a soft skill like leadership or whatever … but the bottom line is, those new skills are of value to the company as well.

62

Manager So what you're saying is you want to take an extended holiday?

Lena No, not really ... I'd see it as a sabbatical. A journalist friend has invited me to be her photographer on her next assignment. A team is heading out to the Antarctic to document the impact of global warming.

Manager And you'd like several months off to accompany her?

Lena Yes. It's been a long-term goal of mine to do something like this. I did photography before I moved into IT, but I never saw it as a career. The thing is, I've been inspired by the people I studied with who've become professional photographers.

Manager Hmm. So ... you take nine months off and we're left without a technical author and no team leader.

Lena I know, but it's a once-in-a-lifetime opportunity.

Manager But how do *we* benefit from this?

Lena Well, I think it's a win-win situation. I'd enjoy developing my creative side ... I'd fulfil a lifelong ambition ... so I'd come back to my job feeling more contented and satisfied with what I'd achieved in life ...

Manager Yes, and ...?

Lena And the experience I'd gain would be invaluable for managing the team.

Manager This isn't common practice, as far as I know. I'm not sure if ...

Lena I understand your misgivings – what if I don't come back, and so on – but the plus points are that I'd be working in extreme conditions with a team of strangers, and my leadership skills would be put to the test ...

Manager Mmm, I'm not convinced – go on.

Lena But there are also other benefits for you. I intend to put on an exhibition of my work after the trip and I'd like to do this with the support of the company. It would mean we'd get a lot of media exposure as well as great advertising opportunities.

Manager Yes, that sounds interesting; it's certainly worth thinking about.

Lena I really feel that this is a chance I can't afford to miss.

Manager Well, this would set a precedent. I'll have to discuss it with HR ... It's not going to be easy to persuade them. I'm afraid your arguments aren't very convincing from a business point of view.

Lena That's hardly fair. I've never refused to take on more work or to do overtime when it's been necessary. I've been extremely loyal when lots of employees went to the new competition and ... well ...

Manager OK. Fair point. I'll see what I can do.

Lena I'd really appreciate it if you could speak to HR and initiate a meeting for all of us.

Manager OK. I think I can manage that, Lena.

63

1

A Hi, Sami. Where were you yesterday? You missed the meeting.

B Didn't anyone tell you? I took the day off. I thought it was about time I used up some of my overtime.

A What did you do?

B Nothing much. I caught up on some DIY jobs I started in the summer!

A Not a very exciting way to spend your day off!

B I know. I didn't really enjoy it, but it needed doing.

2

A Are you back from your holiday already?

B Yes, we just had a long weekend away.

A How was it?

B It poured with rain the whole time!

A Oh, no.

B It didn't really matter. We were on a three-day spa break.

A Nice.

B Yeah, I wasn't particularly keen on going at first – I thought I'd be bored – but I must say it was great for relaxing, switching off.

A Oh, lovely ...

3

A Did you have a good weekend?

B Yes, we managed to get away for the day on Saturday.

A Anywhere nice?

B We visited my partner's family. It made a real change. They all love golf, so I was able to get a game in.

64

Interviewer Can you tell us something about your placement with SPARK?

Consultant Of course ... what would you like to know?

Interviewer Well, maybe you could start by telling us where you were based and what you did.

Consultant OK. Well, we were based in Manila, in a small office, working with a mixed-nationality team – some locals, but mainly British and Swedish expats. Our task was fundamentally to strengthen the SPARK organization, which involved working through a lot of business process documentation. Something I was already very familiar with.

Interviewer So what did you find most enjoyable during your placement?

Consultant Well, it was a very different experience for me and I liked the fact that there were immediate results. It was great to see real changes taking place in front of me.

Interviewer I can imagine ... You can actually see your work benefiting other people. So what did you feel you gained from this experience, personally?

Consultant Well ... I feel I've returned with new skills and ... I think I'm more confident than when I left ... and I know I can achieve things on my own, make good decisions. It was good just to spend some time in a developing country ... you get a real sense of how important developing countries are becoming for Western business generally. So I feel that the knowledge and cultural awareness that I've developed during my time with ADP ... erm ... has not only benefited SPARK and VSO now, but I'm sure they'll benefit Accenture in the future. Overall, it's been a fantastic experience. I'd recommend it to any of my colleagues.

OXFORD
UNIVERSITY PRESS

Great Clarendon Street, Oxford OX2 6DP

Oxford University Press is a department of the University of Oxford. It furthers the University's objective of excellence in research, scholarship, and education by publishing worldwide in

Oxford New York

Auckland Cape Town Dar es Salaam Hong Kong Karachi Kuala Lumpur Madrid Melbourne Mexico City Nairobi New Delhi Shanghai Taipei Toronto

With offices in

Argentina Austria Brazil Chile Czech Republic France Greece Guatemala Hungary Italy Japan Poland Portugal Singapore South Korea Switzerland Thailand Turkey Ukraine Vietnam

OXFORD and OXFORD ENGLISH are registered trade marks of Oxford University Press in the UK and in certain other countries

First published 2008

2012 2011 2010

10 9 8 7 6 5 4

ISBN: 978 0 19 476809 2 (pack)
ISBN: 978 0 19 476810 8 (book)

Printed in China

ACKNOWLEDGEMENTS

The authors and publisher are grateful to those who have given permission to reproduce the following extracts and adaptations of copyright material: p 36 Reproduced by kind permission of Patagonia (www.patagonia.com); p 55 Reproduced by kind permission of Ian Dickson, Tesco Europe; p 60 (James Murray Wells) Interview created by kind permission of Glasses Direct; p 60 (Jurga Zilinskiene) Interview adapted by kind permission of Jurga Zilinskiene, Today Translations Ltd.; p 71 Interview adapted by kind permission of Robert Turner, FWZ; p 90 © Crown copyright 2007. Reproduced under terms of the Click-Use licence

Although every effort has been made to trace and contact copyright holders before publication, this has not been possible in some cases. We apologize for any apparent infringement of copyright and if notified, the publisher will be pleased to rectify any errors or omissions at the earliest opportunity.

Illustrations by: Becky Halls/The Organisation p 87

The publishers would like to thank the following for permission to reproduce photographs: Alamy pp 53 (Russsian Babushka dolls/Carole Hewer), 67 (Africa phone/Alan Gignoux), 76 (Ablestock), 78 (display board/Mehdi Chebil), 78 (engine/Rob Bartee), 90 (sea anenome/David Boag), 95 (fruits/Terrance Klassen), 140 (Rob Walls); Courtesy of the Ashden Awards for Sustainable Energy www.ashdenawards.org, p 24 (*above*: increasing the efficiency of water mills in Nepal by replacing wooden runners with precision-made metal ones), (*below*: biogas plant under construction Kitarama prison, Rwanda); Axiom Photographic Agency p 12 (Luke White); Courtesy of Concrete Canvas Ltd. p 29; Courtesy of Cyclepods Ltd p 47; Corbis pp 13 (Claudia/Artiga Photo), 17 (Stephen Beaudet/zefa), 19 (construction site/Chris Sattlberger), 28 (camera/ Randy Faris), 30 (Don Mason), 35 (coffee/Benjamin Lowy), 38 (Ryan Pyle), 42 (Onne van der Wal), 48 (Bangalore/Jon Hicks), 80 (A. Inden/zefa), 101 (children/Rafiqur Rahman); Courtesy of Ian Dickson p 55; Eyevine p 84 (Geert Hofstede/Menno Boermans/HH); Getty Images pp 11 (meeting/Yellow Dog Productions), 13 (Peter/Ron Krisel), (Macie/David Lees), 18 (Peter Ginter), 20 (White Packert), 26 (Terry Vine), 36 (Alan Kearney), 44 (Photolibrary), 48 (shoe factory/Chung Sung-Jun), 49 (Paula Dale/Paul Taylor), (Christian Amiel/ Symphonie/Iconica), (Chitra Sampat/Ron Krisel), 54 (Tyler/Chabruken), 56 (William Edward King), 59 (relocation/Yoray Liberman), 68 (Peter Dazeley), 77 (medical equipment/Peter Ginter/Science Faction), 84 (Panoramic Images), 89 (Gavin Hellier/Robert Harding), 92 (Nuts/Iconica), 96 (Roberto/Ghislain & Marie David de Lossy/Iconica), (Jenny/Sami Sarkis/Photographer's Choice), 98 (Kim Heacox); Mercy Ships UK Ltd p 67; Bruce Osborn/Ozone Inc. p 65 (Miho Inagi/Maruichi Bagel); PA Photos p 60 (Taiwanese yew plants, anti-cancer drug production/Wally Santana/AP); Photolibrary.com p 90 (chefs/Anthony Blake); Punchstock pp 7 (Radius Images), 8 (Di [illegible] Girou/ PhotoAlto), 23 (John Wang/Didital Vision), 28 ([illegible] (laptop/Digital Vision), 31 (call centre/Blend Imag[illegible] 50 (Digital Vision), 54 (escalators/image100), (Fabia/Digital Vision), (Karl/ Digital Vision), 62 (Digital Vision), 71 (airport/Corbis), 73 (meeting/Digital Vision), 74 (Digital Vision), 78 (internet/Lawrence Manning), 83 (Stockbyte), 86 (Digital Vision), 96 (rock formations/Eastcott Momatiuk/Digital Vision), (Freya/Photodisc); Reuters p 6 (Victor Fraile); Rex Features pp 25 (Sipa Press), 66 (Mongolia tent/Jeremy Sutton Hibbert), 108; Science Photo Library pp 37 (turtle/Matthew Oldfield, Scubazoo), 72 (Peter Scoones), 78 (transistors/Ton Kinsbergen); Still Pictures p 41 (Antarctic/Mark Shenley); Courtesy of Robert Turner p 71; Courtesy of James Wells p 60; Courtesy of Jurga Zilinskiene p 60

Images sourced by: Pictureresearch.co.uk

Cover photo by: Chris King

Photos on p5 courtesy of Cranfield School of Management

The authors and publisher would also like to thank the following individuals for their advice and assistance in developing the material for this book: Lucy Adam, Peter Anderson, Kate Baade, Hannah Blanning, Jayne Chivers, Jo Cooke, Allison Dupuis, John Ferris, Joanne Fessler, Cindy Hauert, Christopher Holloway, John Hughes, Zsofia Kocsardi, Alastair Lane, David Massey, Penny McLarty, Yvonne O'Connor, Sylvia Renaudon, Margaret Ristagno, Paulina Scheenberg, John Sydes, Susan Tesar, Jonathan Villis.

The publisher would also like to thank the faculty, course participants, and alumni of Cranfield School of Management who contributed so much to the development of the course. Particular thanks are due to David Simmons, Director of International Development, whose enthusiasm, generosity, and persistence really have made all the difference.

Special thanks to Yvonne Harmer.